RENAISSANCE HUMANISM, 1300–1550

GARLAND REFERENCE LIBRARY
OF THE HUMANITIES
(VOL. 570)

RENAISSANCE HUMANISM, 1300–1550
A Bibliography of
Materials in English

Benjamin G. Kohl

GARLAND PUBLISHING INC. • NEW YORK & LONDON
1985

Library of Congress Cataloging in Publication Data

Kohl, Benjamin G.
  Renaissance humanism, 1300–1550.

  (Garland reference library of the humanities ; v. 570)
  Includes indexes.
  1. Humanism—Bibliography. 2. Renaissance—Biblio-
graphy. I. Title. II. Series.
Z7128.H9K64 1985 [B778]   016.9401'9   84-48760
ISBN 0-8240-8773-9 (alk. paper)

Printed on acid-free, 240-year-life paper
Manufactured in the United States of America

To the Memory of
Jonathan C. Clark
(1941–1983)
and
Mario Domandi
(1929–1979)

CONTENTS

PREFACE

More than any of my recent scholarly studies, this guide to materials in English in the field of Renaissance humanism has grown out of my teaching medieval and Renaissance history for nearly two decades at Vassar College in Poughkeepsie, New York. In my courses here I have always sought to provide students with full bibliographies on the Middle Ages and the Renaissance, and especially in my seminar on medieval and Renaissance humanism (History 325), I have developed an extensive reading list as a guide to students' papers and reports in the field of medieval and early modern cultural and intellectual history. Thus, this bibliography started as an aid to introducing advanced undergraduate students to the bibliographical riches (in English) on European humanism, but I should hope that in its present expanded form it will be useful to a variety of students of the early modern period, including undergraduates and beginning graduate students in such fields as art history, English, Romance languages, and classics as well as history and philosophy. I hope, too, that it will prove valuable to the general reader seeking orientation in the sometimes bewildering field of Renaissance cultural history and even to established academics in other fields who, for whatever reasons, wish to study some aspect of the intellectual history of the Renaissance.

My immediate inspiration for this bibliography has been the invaluable work of the late Roland H. Bainton of Yale University, *Bibliography of the Continental Reformation, Materials Available in English*, first published nearly a half-century ago and recently reissued in a revised edition coedited by Eric W. Gritsch (Hamden, Conn.: Archon Books, 1977). As Bainton's bibliography serves a sure and sound guide to the English-speaking student of the continental Reformation, so my bibliography is designed for the student of Renaissance humanism whose first (and often only) language is English. To be sure, any serious student of Renaissance humanism needs a good working knowledge of at least five languages: English, French, German, Italian, and Latin and many aspects of the subject require knowledge of Spanish, Dutch, and Greek, not to mention the languages of eastern Europe. But to require any putative American student of Renaissance humanism, even at the advanced level, to command all of these languages would be, I think, a counsel of perfection. This volume has grown out of my experience teaching able American undergraduates in the field, and I am convinced that a good start in the study of Renaissance humanism can be made using materials in English. The notable exception to only titles in English has been in the inclusion of bibliographies in foreign languages, such as the annual *Bibliographie internationale de l'Humanisme et de la Renaissance* and Margolin's bibliographies on Erasmus; these volumes include much of value in English as well as a complete guide to their subjects. My purpose here has been to provide a detailed and nearly complete guide to the journals, reference and general works, and for the period from 1300 to 1550 to the writings of humanists in English translation and studies in English on Renaissance humanism and individual humanists. The bibliography is nearly exhaustive for articles and books published through the end of 1982, and I have been able to list a few items published in 1983.

Helpers in this project have mainly been my student assistants at Vassar over the past few years: Susan Sherman of the Class of 1981, Tina Barbieri and Matthew Witten of the Class of 1983, and Dawn Gilpin of the Class of 1987. My son Benjamin G. Kohl, Jr., typed many of the cards for miscellanies and anthologies and a portion of the penultimate draft of the typescript. My greatest debt is to Jodi George of the Class of 1983 who spent the summer after her graduation typing most of the cards and hundreds of pages of the draft of the bibliography. Without her aid this project could never have been completed, and she is, in all but formal recognition, my coauthor.

I also wish to thank the staffs of Butler Library of Columbia University, the New York Public Library, and, most of all, the Vassar College Library, where the bulk of the research and checking has been done. I owe a special debt to David L. Paulus, currently the Head Librarian of Vassar, who during his years as Acquisitions Librarian helped to make Vassar's holdings a notable collection in Renaissance Studies. At Vassar, too, I have benefited from expert advice, especially for the works in the early chapters, from two reference librarians, Rebecca Mitchell and Joan E. Murphy. The Committee on Research at Vassar has generously met some of the costs of research and the preparation of the manuscript. I am deeply indebted to Eleanor Rogers, who typed the camera-ready copy with care, efficiency, and acumen, saving me from many errors. My colleague in the Department of History, Alison A. Smith, generously shared the exacting task of proofreading the several hundred pages of final copy, while the Department's Administrative Assistant Norma Torney coordinated the final stages of this project. At Garland Pamela Chergotis has been a vigilant and tactful editor. Finally, I owe much, as always, to my wife Judith C. Kohl, who has borne with affectionate and good-humored patience over these past years my efforts to become a bibliographer. To all these persons I express my gratitude, recognizing that the errors and omissions that remain are my sole responsibility.

In the dedication I seek to honor the memory of two close and cherished friends from the Vassar College faculty, each of whom was in his own way a distinguished humanist.

B.G.K.

INTRODUCTION

A DEFINITION OF RENAISSANCE HUMANISM

Since antiquity the term *humanitas* has had a double meaning: it expresses the idea of kindness and civility toward one's fellow human beings, a basic humaneness, and it also has the meaning of literary culture, an understanding and appreciation of literature, history, philosophy and aesthetics, and the ability to communicate that understanding through the appropriate rhetorical form. It was in this second sense of the "humanities" that Renaissance humanism developed in Italy in the course of the fourteenth century. It arose in the cities of Padua, Bologna, Milan and Verona at the time of Dante, fostered by the nascent professional classes of the Italian city-states—lawyers, notaries, school-masters and merchants. At its base was the study of the Latin literature and Roman antiquity, a study enhanced by a constantly improved knowledge of classical texts and a rigorous attempt to adapt the teaching of ancient literature and philosophy, especially of Roman Stoicism, to the needs of an urban, lay and literate society of the north and central Italian cities.

The key figure in the establishment of Renaissance humanism as an accepted and popular system of education and values was the Italian poet and man of letters, Francesco Petrarca (1304–1374), who showed to countless younger men the fame and good reputation a career in letters could bring. Other Italian rhetoricians had developed a sharp interest in ancient history and literature, but Petrarch's great personal charm, his capacity for trenchant social criticism, and his reputation as a great love-poet and student of human emotions made him a sort of culture hero, admired and emulated by the best minds of the next generation. Petrarch's many Latin works, especially his interior dialogue between St. Augustine and his own *persona* on the rival claims of glory and salvation (the *Secretum*) and his massive Stoic tract on the remedies for the apparent evils of adverse fortune and the beguiling hopes of good luck (*De remediis utriusque fortune*), gave definition and purpose to his program of classical study. By the later part of the fourteenth century, Coluccio Salutati in Florence had made Petrarchan humanism into a popular and established program of study, usually called the *studia humanitatis*.

At the turn of the fifteenth century, humanism received its programmatic definition in the treatise of Pier Paolo Vergerio *De ingenuis moribus* (*On liberal studies*). Vergerio's definition of humanism, or the liberal arts, became the dominant educational ideal of the Renaissance. For him the foundation of a humanistic education was the verbal arts of grammar and rhetoric, shaped by the power of reasoning provided by logic. To these methodological tools in communication were added the study of history as the empirical datum of all human action, moral philosophy as the guide to right action in this life, and poetry and poetics as the key to knowledge of the divine and inspired truth, the expression of the fundamental nature of God, man, and the world. For Vergerio and for later humanists, the core of the *studia humanitatis* lay in moral philosophy, eloquence, and history, from both pagan and Christian antiquity.

Hence, Renaissance humanism was always first and foremost a program of classical education, enriched in the early decades of the fifteenth century by the translation of many Greek classics (especially the works of Plato and Plutarch, Homer and the tragedians, and the Greek historians) into Latin, and by the beginning of instruction in ancient Greek by both Byzantine emigré scholars and native Italian Hellenists. Along with the addition of the Greek to the Roman classics, the corpus of Latin literature was itself enriched by such avid book-hunters as Poggio Bracciolini and Niccolò Niccoli so that by the end of the century virtually the whole of the surviving classical corpus known today had been recovered. And with the introduction of printing classical texts gained permanence, fixity, and widespread popularity. At the same time ancillary disciplines including archaeology and epigraphy were developed so that classical studies were put on something like the scholarly basis they now enjoy.

But the *studia humanitatis* remained the basic education for the rhetorician and public figure for the next few centuries. Renaissance humanists were often individuals who found their way to the top through obstacles that society put in the path of newcomers. They had to learn to live by their wits and persuade others by their rhetoric and style. Hence, humanists often served governments as chancellors and advisers, legates and ambassadors, since princes, prelates, and magistrates appreciated the value of their deep personal experience and convincing use of language. Yet despite their closeness to power, the humanists usually remained critical of the defects of their contemporary society and criticized corruption and evil from the viewpoint of the ethical standards of both ancient Stoicism and their Christian faith. They deeply believed in the importance of past traditions as a guide to present situations and hence examples from the history and literature of antiquity were constant features of their rhetoric. At the same time they appreciated that human beings were creators of their own past and thus had the power to mold the future.

The search for a richer and more varied heritage led in the second half of the fifteenth century to an affection for Plato and the adoption of his dialogues as a model for argumentation and discourse. Moreover, the conscious imitation of the thought and style of Plato was a stance against the Aristotelianism of the northern schools and contemporary scholasticism. This cosmopolitan spirit also prompted the search for a *philosophia perennia* (a system of belief that would be always and everywhere true). Making a syncretizing selection of the valid aspects of many ancient systems of thought, including the Jewish Cabala, Arab philosophy, and Hermeticism, such thinkers as Giovanni Pico della Mirandola proposed a new largely secular vision as the solution to questions of ethics and truth.

North of the Alps, the Christian humanism of Desiderius Erasmus combined a profound study of the Bible and Church Fathers with a search for the truths of ancient thought resulting in the moral essays of his *Adages* and a penchant for social criticism and satire best represented in his *Praise of Folly*. Erasmus became the prince of humanists in the early sixteenth century because he united deep moral concern with a compelling and flexible Latin style, two aspects at the base of the *studia human-itatis*. By the middle of the sixteenth century, Greek and Latin literature, ancient history and philosophy were firmly established in the schools and universities of Europe, from Sicily to Scotland and from Portugal to Sweden. In that sense, Renaissance humanism became one of the great success stories of the history of education. And the humanities were to remain the core of the education of statesmen, artists, thinkers, and rulers down to the present. At the same time, as European thinkers absorbed the history, mythology, and literature of antiquity, they developed a sense of anachronism and distance from this past. Thus, while Renaissance humanism promoted the study of antiquity and the classics, it also served to give classics a scholarly basis for understanding the past on its own terms. In the hands of the great figures of vernacular literature of the Renaissance, Cervantes in Spain, Rabelais and Montaigne in France, Shakespeare in England, the ancient world and its canons for civilized behavior, literary taste and compelling literary themes remained alive and indeed became an integral part of the popular imagination.

RENAISSANCE HUMANISM AND CURRENT HUMANISTIC SCHOLARSHIP

As the foregoing sketch suggests, the study of Renaissance humanism cuts across a number of traditional academic disciplines in the twentieth century. In its broadest sense Renaissance humanism has often been identified with the cultural and intellectual history of western Europe from the early fourteenth to the mid-sixteenth centuries. As a result, historians of the Renaissance have often made significant contributions to the study of Renaissance humanism. Hence, much of the work listed in this bibliography has been done by academic historians of the Renaissance, especially in Italy and England.

If the study of history forms the basis for most approaches to Renaissance humanism, so another closely allied field includes the national literatures of western Europe, especially England and France, Italy and Spain, because almost all vernacular authors of the Renaissance were trained in the classics to some extent, and the literary norms and canons of taste of antiquity informed both the themes and form of their works. Moreover, several of the most important literary figures of the Renaissance, including Petrarch, Boccaccio, and Poliziano in Italy, More in England, and Bodin in France, wrote in both Latin and the vernacular. Hence, any rounded view of their importance and achievements must take in account a study of their Latin works as well as their often more popular works in the vernacular. As a result of the use of both languages, notable contributions to the study of Neo-Latin literature have been made by students of French, English and Italian literature of the Renaissance.

A third modern field of scholarship that has made enormous contributions to the study of Renaissance humanism has been the history of philosophy. Although many contemporary teachers of philosophy hold that the Renaissance failed to produce a single thinker of enduring stature and hence in their courses jump from Anselm and Aquinas, or even from Aristotle, to Descartes and Leibnitz, still many major students of philosophical issues find Renaissance thought a fertile ground of inquiry. From Ernst Cassirer and Benedetto Croce down to Paul Oskar Kristeller and Eugenio Garin, many twentieth-century historians of philosophy have made the Renaissance a special object of study. For example, Kristeller had made major contributions to the study of Florentine Neoplatonism and other aspects of the Platonic tradition in his earlier works and lately contributed much to the study of Renaissance Aristotelianism. Students of ethics and political theory have found much of interest in Renaissance humanism, as have students of logic, theory of knowledge, and language-studies.

A fourth area of study depending on the scholarship of Renaissance humanism is classics. The very basic task of establishing critical editions of classical texts was first undertaken by the humanists, starting with Petrarch, and modern editors still must refer to their important, if relatively crude, efforts in any approach to establishing an ancient text. Crucial, too, to an understanding of the traditions of a classical author is the massive collaborative *Catalogue of Medieval and Renaissance Commentaries and Translations*, which eventually will list all translations of

Greek works into Latin and all commentaries in Latin on ancient texts made before 1600. Finally, the history of classical scholarship lies fully in the tradition of Renaissance humanism, beginning with the work of Sandys down to the studies of Pfeiffer, Highet, and Kenney.

The history of the fine arts, aesthetic theory, rhetoric and education have also gained much from the scholarship on Renaissance humanism. As rhetoric stood at the center of the program of the *studia humanitatis*, so the history of rhetoric is inextricably linked with current studies of humanists and humanistic education. Also major work on artistic theory by such great art historians as Panofsky and Meiss depend on the study of Renaissance humanism. And the basic fact that humanism was the educational program for the European elite for several centuries makes its study indispensable for students of the history of universities, schooling, and education generally.

CRITERIA FOR USING THIS BIBLIOGRAPHY

As stated in the preface, this bibliography grew out of reading lists and suggestions for papers prepared for students in history courses on medieval civilization, Renaissance Europe, and medieval and Renaissance humanism over nearly two decades. I have prepared it for Garland Publishing, Inc., with the needs of the undergraduate student in mind and hope that any student or scholar beginning with a bibliography of materials in English will soon see the need for a reading knowledge of other languages and work to acquire those skills. A bibliography of Renaissance humanism in all languages is indeed much desired, but it would be a lifetime endeavor for any scholar and should doubtless be a collaborative effort. Such a joint work is projected as the *Guide to Interdisciplinary Research in Renaissance Studies*, being created by the Institute for Renaissance Interdisciplinary Studies of the State University of New York under the direction of Professor Raymond Ortali. This work will undoubtedly go a long way in satisfying the need for a multi-language guide to Renaissance Studies as the recent volume of Everett U. Crosby, C. Julian Bishko, and Robert L. Kellogg, *Medieval Studies: A Bibli-*

ographical Guide (New York: Garland, 1983), has for medieval studies.

The volume presented here has the more modest purpose of providing a very full guide to Renaissance cultural and intellectual history for the beginning student whose native language is English. I have in mind as potential users of this book students in courses and seminars in Renaissance history, art history, and philosophy, and students of the Renaissance period of English, French, German and Italian literature who need a guide to the humanistic aspect of their subject. Certainly the guide will be useful to scholars in the intellectual history of other periods and areas who wish to gain some appreciation of the quality and scope of Renaissance humanist thought. Finally, the introductory paragraphs to each chapter are intended to lead the user to the most important works in the field and serve as guides to works for use in term papers and reports.

The *Bibliography* is divided into two halves. The first half (Chapters I–VIII) lists journals, reference tools, surveys and works in the several genres of Renaissance humanism. The second half (Chapters IX–XVIII) provides a section on the medieval background followed by a chronological and geographical survey of the sources and studies on Renaissance humanism from the dawn of the movement in Italy in the early fourteenth century to its spread to England, France, Iberia, Lowlands, Germany and Eastern Europe to ca. 1550. My aim has been for completeness for materials in English whenever this would seem feasible, as in reference works, anthologies, bibliographies and guides, and Festschriften. But the sixty journals listed in the first chapter only reflect the most likely source of articles in English on aspects of Renaissance humanism—obviously many other journals, including those cited in the *Bibliography* itself occasionally carry essays in the field. Similarly in the large Chapter VIII on Genres only the most important studies could be listed in such fields as fine arts, science, drama, and schools and universities. But the works listed there are those indispensable to any beginning study in their respective fields.

The second part attempts to provide the user with a complete list of Latin humanist writings available in English as of 1982 and of all significant books and articles in English in this field. Expressly omitted have been almost all review essays, book reviews and unpublished doctoral dissertations. This part of the bibliography is more sketchy for the medieval background than for later chapters where the aim has been to be as exhaustive as possible. Hence, the second part provides the most complete list extant of the English translations of the works by and studies in English on such figures as Petrarch, Boccaccio, Salutati, Bruni, Poliziano, More, Erasmus, and Vives. The two longest chapters treat Erasmus and More and provide lists of specialized guides and bibliographies as well as classified lists of the English translations of the works of these two humanists and a full bibliography of scholarly studies. The chapters on France and Iberia, Germany and the Lowlands, Byzantium and Eastern Europe are much shorter, reflecting the relative lack of studies in English on humanism in those areas.

The two indices completing this volume facilitate access to its contents in several ways. The first index—of authors, translators, editors, and of titles lacking the first three—will show at a glance what works of any Renaissance humanist are available in English translation and the studies in English of all scholars working on any aspect of Renaissance humanism in modern times. The subject index classifies material according to the individual humanist, geographic area, and genre or institution. Thus, at a glance, the user will be able to note the most important studies in English on, for example, Leonardo Bruni, humanism in Padua, Platonism, or historiography in England.

Perhaps after finishing this introduction the user should turn to the indices and test the bibliography for completeness on a favorite author or field. If the user is led to discover new fields and studies and thus begin research in the vital field of Renaissance humanism, I shall be very happy.

RENAISSANCE HUMANISM, 1300–1550

I. JOURNALS

In Renaissance humanism as in most fields of humanistic and social science scholarship, much of the work is published in the form of articles and essays in periodicals. While studies in English on one or another aspect of Renaissance humanism may be found in a great many journals, the bulk of the articles are to be found in the some sixty journals that I have read through and listed in this chapter. Of these sixty journals, those which contain numerous articles in the field are designated at the left by an abbreviation that will be used in the rest of this bibliography. Hence, any systematic search in the periodical literature on a topic of Renaissance humanism should begin with the journals listed here. All major essays in these sixty journals on any aspect of Renaissance humanism have been listed in the appropriate chapter later in the bibliography.

1   *American Historical Review.* New York: 1885-.

2 ARG   *Archiv für Reformationsgeschichte.* Gutersloh:
          1903.

3 BHR   *Bibliothèque d'Humanisme et de la Renaissance.*
          Geneva: 1939-.

4 BIHR *Bulletin of the Institute of Historical Research.*
          London: 1923-.

5 BJRL *Bulletin of the John Rylands Library.* Manchester:
          1903-.

6   *Catholic Historical Review.* Washington, D.C.:
          1915-.

7   *Church History.* Scottsdale, Pa.: 1932-.

8   *Classical Philology.* Chicago: 1906-.

9   *Classical Quarterly.* London: 1907-.

10 EHR   *English Historical Review.* London: 1885-.

11   *Erasmus in English.* Toronto: 1970-.

12   *Erasmus of Rotterdam Society Yearbook.* Oxon Hill,
          Maryland: 1981-.

13   *Greek, Roman and Byzantine Studies.* Durham, N.C.:
          1958-.

14   *Harvard Theological Review.* Cambridge, Mass.:
          1908-.

15   *Historical Journal.* Cambridge: 1958-.

16   *History.* London: 1916-.

17 *HL*   *Humanistica Lovaniensis.* Leuven: 1968-.

18   *Huntington Library Quarterly.* San Marino, Ca.:
            1937-.

19 *IMU*   *Italia Medioevale e Umanistica.* Padua: 1958-.

20   *Italian Studies.* Manchester: 1937-38, 1946-.

21   *Italica.* New York: 1924-.

22   *Journal of Ecclesiastical History.* London: 1950-.

23 *JMRS*   *Journal of Medieval and Renaissance Studies.*
            Durham, N.C.: 1971-.

24   *Journal of Modern History.* Chicago: 1930-.

25 *JHI*   *Journal of the History of Ideas.* Lancaster, Pa.:
            1940-.

26   *Journal of the History of Philosophy.* Claremont,
            Ca.: 1963-.

27 *JWCI*   *Journal of the Warburg and Courtauld Institutes.*
            London: 1940-, earlier known as

28 *JWI*   *Journal of the Warburg Institute.* London: 1937-
            40.

29   *The Library.* London: 1889-.

30   *Manuscripta.* St. Louis: 1957-.

31   *Mediaeval Studies.* Toronto: 1939-.

32   *Medievalia: A Journal of Medieval Studies.*
            Binghamton, N.Y.: 1976-.

33 *MH*   *Mediaevalia et Humanistica.* Boulder, Colorado:
            1943-66, n.s. Totowa, N.J.: 1971-.

34   *Medieval and Renaissance Studies.* London: 1941-.

35   *Modern Language Quarterly.* Seattle, Washington:
            1940-.

36   *Modern Language Review.* Cambridge: 1905-.

37   *Modern Philology.* Chicago: 1903-.

38   *Moreana.* Angers, France: 1963-.

39   *Past and Present.* Oxford: 1952-.

40   *Philological Quarterly.* Iowa City, Iowa: 1923-.

41   *Proceedings of the British Academy.* London:
            1903-.

42 PMLA   *Publications of the Modern Language Association.*
            New York: 1884-.

43   *Renaissance and Reformation.* Toronto: 1963-.

44 RQ   *Renaissance Quarterly.* New York: 1965-, formerly
            known as

45   *Renaissance News.* New York: 1948-64.

46   *Res Publica Litterarum: Studies in the Classical
            Tradition.* Lawrence, Kansas: 1978-.

47   *Rinascimento.* Florence: 1950-.

48   *Romanic Review.* New York: 1910-.

49   *Scriptorium.* Antwerp and Brussels: 1946-.

50   *Sixteenth-Century Journal.* St. Louis: 1970-.

51   *Speculum.* Cambridge, Mass.: 1925-.

52   *Studi Medievali.* Turin: 1906-.

53   *Studi Veneziani.* Florence: 1958-76, n.s. Pisa:
            1977-.

54 SMRH   *Studies in Medieval and Renaissance History.*
            Lincoln, Nebraska: 1964-73, n.s. Vancouver, Brit-
            ish Columbia: 1978-.

55   *Studies in Philology.* Chapel Hill, N.C.: 1906-.

56   *Studies in the Renaissance.* New York: 1954-74.

57   *Traditio: Studies in Ancient and Mediaeval History, Thought, and Religion.* New York: 1942-.

58   *TAPA*   *Transactions of the American Philological Association.* Boston: 1871-.

59   *TRHS*   *Transactions of the Royal Historical Society.* London: 1872-.

60   *Viator, Medieval and Renaissance Studies.* Los Angeles: 1970-.

II. BIBLIOGRAPHIES AND GUIDES

This chapter is divided into four sections: general guides
to Renaissance humanism; serial guides, both current and completed; bibliographies of sources available in translation; and
specialized studies. Of the first category, the most compre-
hensive is the guide by Louis B. Paetow to medieval history
to 1500, for publications to 1930, supplemented in five volumes by the massive bibliography of Gray Boyce for publications appearing from 1930 to 1975. For a more personal point
of view, see the bibliographical essays, by Kristeller and
Randall, covering studies from the nineteenth century to 1940,
by Kristeller for the period from 1940 to 1960, and by Charles
Trinkaus, for studies from about 1960 to 1975. For Neo-Latin
literature, from the Age of Petrarch to modern times, consult
the excellent companion by Jozef IJsewijn. Of serial bibliographies, see the annual listing in *Studies in Philology* to
1966, and after that date, the massive annual, compiled by a
team of scholars, and sponsored by the Renaissance Society of
America and other scholarly societies: *Bibliographie Internationale de l'Humanisme et de la Renaissance*. Of the specialized guides, noteworthy is P. Kristeller's *Iter Italicum*
which when completed in five volumes, will provide a world-
wide listing of all Renaissance manuscripts not already in
library or national catalogues.

A. GENERAL BIBLIOGRAPHIES

61 Bouwsma, William J. *The Culture of Renaissance Humanism.*
AHA Pamphlet 401. Washington, D.C.: American Historical Association, 1973. A revision of his earlier pamphlet, *The Interpretation of Renaissance Humanism.*

62 ———. *The Interpretation of Renaissance Humanism.*
2nd ed. Service Center for Teachers of History, Publication no.18. Washington, D.C.: American Historical
Association, 1966.

63 Boyce, Gray C. *Literature of Medieval History 1930-
1975. A Supplement to Louis Jacob Paetow's A Guide to
the Study of Medieval History.* 5 vols. Millwood,
N.Y.: Kraus, 1981. Especially valuable for humanism
are listings on Medieval Culture, 1100-1500, to be
found in vol.4.

64 Chabod, Federico. "Bibliography of the Renaissance."
Machiavelli and the Renaissance, introd. A.P.
D'Entrèves and trans. David Moore. London: Bowes and
Bowes, 1958, pp.201-247.

65 Chastel, André, et al. *The Renaissance: Essays in Interpretation.* London: Methuen, 1983. English version of
the Festschrift for Eugenio Garin with major inter-
pretive essays by P.O. Kristeller on humanism, Charles
Trinkaus on philosophy, Charles Schmitt on universities, and Walter Ullmann on political thought.

66 Corrigan, Beatrice M., and Bonner Mitchell. "Italian
Literature." *The Present State of Scholarship in Six-
teenth-Century Literature,* ed. William M. Jones.
Columbia: University of Missouri Press, 1978, pp.1-43.

67 Garin, Eugenio. "The Fifteenth Century in Italy," *Philosophy in Mid-Century,* vol.4, ed. Raymond Klibansky.
Florence: Nuova Italia, 1959, pp.95-106.

68   IJsewijn, Jozef. *Companion to Neo-Latin Studies.*
      Amsterdam: North-Holland, 1977.

69   Kohl, B.G. "The Classical Tradition in the Middle Ages
      and the Renaissance: the Past Quarter Century."
      Choice, 10 (1973); 911-19.

70   Krailsheimer, A.J., ed. *The Continental Renaissance,*
      1500-1600. Baltimore: Penguin, 1971; repr. Atlantic
      Highlands, N.J.: Humanities Press, 1978. Authoritative
      discussion of continental authors in both Latin and
      the vernaculars with full bibliographies.

71   Kristeller, Paul Oskar. "Studies on Renaissance Human-
      ism during the Last Twenty Years." *Studies in the*
      Renaissance, 9 (1962): 7-30. Continues the survey by
      Kristeller and Randall of 1941.

72   ————, and J.H. Randall. "The Study of the Philos-
      ophies of the Renaissance." *JHI,* 2 (1941): 449-96.

73   Ladner, Gerhard B. "Some Recent Publications on the
      Classical Tradition in the Middle Ages and Renaissance
      and on Byzantium." *Traditio,* 19 (1954): 578-594.

74   McGuire, Martin R.P., and Hermigild Dressler. *Intro-*
      duction to Medieval Latin Studies: A Syllabus and
      Bibliographical Guide. Washington, D.C.: The Catholic
      University of America Press, 1977.

75   Nichols, Fred J. "Latin Literature." *The Present State*
      of Scholarship in Fourteenth-Century Literature, ed.
      Thomas D. Cooke. Columbia: University of Missouri
      Press, 1982, pp.195-257. Admirable survey of human-
      ist literature in the fourteenth century.

76   Paetow, Louis John. *Guide to the Study of Medieval*
      History. New York: Crofts, 1931, rev. and corrected
      by G.C. Boyce. Millbrook, N.Y.: Kraus, 1980.

77   Ryan, Lawrence V. "Neo-Latin Literature." *The Present*
      State of Scholarship in Sixteenth-Century Literature,
      ed. William M. Jones. Columbia: University of Missouri
      Press, 1978, pp.197-257.

78   Tobey, Jeremy L. *The History of Ideas: A Bibliographi-*
      cal Introduction, vol.2, Medieval and Early Modern
      Europe. Santa Barbara, California: ABC-Clio, 1977.

79   Trinkaus, Charles. "Humanism." *Encyclopedia of World Art,* 7 (1963), cols.702-43, with bibliography on 734-43.

80   ————. "Humanism, Religion, Society: Concepts and Motivations of Some Recent Studies." *RQ,* 29 (1976): 676-713. Perceptive and thoughtful review of past decade's work in Renaissance humanism. Continues Kristeller's survey of 1962 (item 71).

81   Warburg Institute. *A Bibliography on the Survival of the Classics,* trans. from the German with an English introd., 2 vols. London: Cassell, 1934-38. Divided by topics with summaries of books and articles.

B.   SERIAL BIBLIOGRAPHIES

82   *L'Année Philologique: Bibliographie Critique et Analytique de l'Antiquité Gréco-Latine,* publ. sous la direction de J.Marouzeau, et al. 1924-26. Paris: Soc. d'Editions les Belles-Lettres, 1928. Annual. Dedicated principally to ancient history and authors, but contains much on the later "Fortuna" of authors, especially in the Renaissance.

83   *Bibliographie de la Philosophie....* 1937-52/53. Paris: J. Vrin, 1937-58. Annual. An international bibliography of books, articles, and dissertations. Suspended publication from July 1939 to December 1945. Superseded by:

84   *Bibliographie de la Philosophie, Bulletin Trimestrial.* Bibliography of Philosophy, a Quarterly Bulletin. Paris: Vrin, 1954-. Quarterly. Contains abstracts of books only.

85   *Bibliographie Internationale de l'Humanisme et de la Renaissance.* Geneva: Droz, 1966-. Great annual bibliography of Renaissance history and humanism in all languages, beginning for the year 1965. Vols.1-6 list by author with subject index; vol.7 (1971) onward has part 1 for personages, and part 2 classified by subject with index by authors. Now several years behind with the volume for 1977 appearing only in 1983.

86   *Humanistica Lovaniensis.* Leuven: University Press, 1968-.
     Since 1974 this journal has published a bibliography
     on current work in Neo-Latin studies entitled "Instru-
     mentum Bibliographicum."

87   "Literature of the Renaissance." *Studies in Philology,*
     vols.14-66. Chapel Hill: University of North Carolina
     Press, 1917-1966. Annual. The single most valuable
     serial bibliography on Italian Renaissance humanism
     before the *Bibliographie Internationale de l'Humanisme
     et de la Renaissance* (item 85), which supersedes it.

88   Modern Language Association of America. *MLA Inter-
     national Bibliography of Books and Articles on the
     Modern Languages and Literatures.* 1921-. Annual.
     Includes valuable section on medieval and Neo-Latin
     material.

89   "Neo-Latin News." *Seventeenth-Century News.* Univer-
     sity Park, Pa.: 1954-. Provides an annotated list of
     studies on and editions of Latin literature written
     after the thirteenth century.

90   *Progress of Medieval and Renaissance Studies in the
     United States and Canada,* vols.1-25. Boulder,
     Colorado: 1923-1960. Renaissance studies added with
     no.15. Each issue contains lists of papers, publi-
     cations, projects, and doctoral dissertations.

91   *Quarterly Check-List of Renaissance Studies.* Darien,
     Connecticut: American Bibliographical Service, 1959-74.
     Lists books, brochures and separates, but no journal
     articles.

92   *Renaissance Quarterly,* formerly *Renaissance News, 1948-.*
     Includes a list of books published on Renaissance art,
     history, literature, philosophy, and science, which
     was discontinued in 1980.

93   *Scriptorium. Revue International des Etudes Relatives
     aux Manuscrits.* Brussels: 1947-. Includes current
     bibliography on manuscript studies.

94   *Year's Work in Modern Language Studies.* London: Oxford
     University Press, 1931-. Includes material on medieval
     Latin and Neo-Latin literature since 1970.

C. *SOURCES IN ENGLISH TRANSLATION*

95   Farrar, Clarissa Palmer, and Austin P. Evans. *Bibliog-
      raphy of English Translations from Medieval Sources*.
      Records of Civilization, sources and studies, vol.39.
      New York: Columbia University Press, 1946. Includes
      English translations of literary sources to 1500 made
      until 1942. More than 4,000 entries with some annota-
      tions on context, editions, reprints and adequacy of
      the translation. Index of authors, translations,
      editions, titles, and subjects.

96   Ferguson, Mary Anne Heyward. *Bibliography of English
      Translations from Medieval Sources, 1943-1967*.
      Records of Civilization, sources and studies, vol.88.
      New York: Columbia University Press, 1974. Designed
      as a supplement to Farrar and Evans (item 95), with
      greater attention to non-literary sources. Nearly
      2,000 items. Index.

97   *Index Translationum. Repertoire International des Tra-
      ductions. International Bibliography of Translations*.
      Paris: International Institute of Intellectual Co-
      operation, 1932-40, no.1-31; n.s. Paris: UNESCO, 1949-.

98   Parks, George B., and Ruth Z. Temple, eds. *The Greek
      and Latin Literatures*. Literatures of the World in
      English Translation, vol.1. New York: Ungar, 1968.
      Separate sections for Greek and Latin literature,
      each arranged chronologically with good coverage of
      translations from Renaissance Latin literature. Pub-
      lications through 1965 are included; index of authors
      and titles of anonymous works, but not of translators.

99   Pugliese, Olga Zorzi. "English Translations from the
      Italian Humanists: An Interpretive Survey and Bibliog-
      raphy." *Italica,* 50 (1973): 408-34.

100   *Repertorium Fontium Historiae Medii Aevi*. 4 vols. to
      date. Rome: Istituto Storico Italiano per il Medio
      Evo, 1962-1976. Vol.1, Series Collectionum; Vols.
      2-4, Fontes, A-Gez. Lists all major medieval narra-
      tive sources to the year A.D.1500, and gives editions
      of English translations under heading: Translatio,
      anglice.

101   Scott, Mary Augusta. *Elizabethan Translations from the*
      Italian. Vassar Semi-Centennial Series. Boston and
      New York: Houghton Mifflin Company, 1916. Includes
      translations from Latin works of Italian humanists.

                            D. SPECIAL TOPICS

102   Baron, Hans. "Burckhardt's *Civilisation of the Renais-*
      sance a Century after Its Publication." *Renaissance*
      News, 13 (1960) : 207-22.

103   Braswell, Laurel Nichols. *Western Manuscripts from*
      Classical Antiquity to the Renaissance, A Handbook.
      New York: Garland, 1981.

104   Buck, August. "Hans Baron's Contribution to the Lite-
      rary History of the Renaissance." *Renaissance Studies*
      in Honor of Hans Baron (item 296), pp.xxxi-lviii.

105   Burke, Peter. "Renaissance Studies." *Historical*
      Journal, 22 (1979) : 974-84. Review essay on books
      mainly on Florence and Rome.

106   Church, Frederic C. "The Literature of the Italian
      Reformation." *Journal of Modern History,* 3 (1931):
      457-73.

107   Della Terza, Dante. "Italian Renaissance and American
      Scholars." *Italian Quarterly,* 3, no.9 (1959) : 34-39.
      Mainly on Baron and Kristeller.

108   Gilbert, Felix. "Political Thought of the Renaissance
      and Reformation." *Huntington Library Quarterly,* 4
      (1941): 443-68. A review essay.

109   Grant, Leonard. "Neo-Latin Studies." *Renaissance News,*
      16 (1963): 102-06.

110   Hay, Denys. "The Place of Hans Baron in Renaissance
      Historiography." *Renaissance Studies in Honor of*
      Hans Baron (item 296), pp.xi-xxx.

111   Horowitz, Maryanne C. "Kristeller's Impact on Renais-
      sance Studies." *JHI,* 39 (1978): 677-83.

112   Kristeller, Paul Oskar. "Medieval and Renaissance
      Studies: Reflections of a Scholar." *Speculum*, 52
      (1977): 1-4.

113   ————. "Changing Views of the Intellectual History of
      the Renaissance since Jacob Burckhardt." *The Renais-
      sance, A Reconsideration of the Theories and Inter-
      pretations of the Age*, ed. Tinsley Helton. Madison:
      University of Wisconsin Press, 1961, pp.27-52.

114   ————. *Iter Italicum. A Finding List of Uncatalogued
      or Incompletely Catalogued Humanistic Manuscripts of
      the Renaissance in Italian and other Libraries.*
      3 vols. Leiden: Brill, 1963-83.

115   ————. *Latin Manuscript Books before 1600.* 3rd ed.
      New York: Fordham University Press, 1965. Supplement-
      ed by:

116   Lohr, C.H. "Further Additions to Kristeller's Reper-
      torium." *Scriptorium*, 26 (1972): 343-48.

117   Mahoney, Edward P. "Paul Oskar Kristeller and His Con-
      tribution to Scholarship." *Philosophy and Humanism*
      (item 293), pp.1-18.

118   Murphy, James J. *Renaissance Rhetoric, A Short-Title
      Catalogue of Works on Rhetorical Theory from the
      Beginning of Print to A.D. 1700.... with a Select
      Basic Bibliography of Secondary Works on Renaissance
      Rhetoric.* New York: Garland, 1981.

119   "Renaissance Books of 1953, a Bibliographical Supple-
      ment." *Studies in the Renaissance,* 1 (1954): 157-79.

120   Taylor, Archer. *Renaissance Guides to Books: An Inven-
      tory and Some Conclusions.* Berkeley: University of
      California Press, 1945.

121   Tedeschi, John A., and Andrew W. Lewis. "Bibliography
      of the Writings of Hans Baron." *Renaissance Studies
      in Honor of Hans Baron* (item 296), pp.lxxi-lxxxvii.

122   Tracy, James D. "Humanism and the Reformation." *Ref-
      ormation Europe: A Guide to Research,* ed. Steven
      Ozment. St. Louis: Center for Reformation Research,
      1982.

123   Weinstein, Donald. "In Whose Image and Likeness? In-
       terpretations of Renaissance Humanism." *JHI*, 33
       (1972): 165-76.

124   Williams, Harry Franklin. *An Index of Mediaeval Stud-
       ies Published in Festschriften, 1865-1945, with
       Special Reference to Romanic Material*. Berkeley:
       University of California Press, 1951. More than
       5,000 essays selected from 500 homage volumes, with
       a list of reviews of some 170 *Festschriften*. Indexes
       of authors and some subject matter.

See also items 388, 400, 752, 756, 758, 776, 1439, 1495.

III. REFERENCE WORKS

In addition to standard general encyclopedias, such as the *Britannica* and *Americana,* there are several specialized reference works useful to the study of Renaissance humanism. Of these, the most valuable is the work of Mario Cosenza, a printed catalogue in six volumes of a mammoth card-file listing biographical data and bibliographical references for all known Italian Renaissance humanists. This work is best approached through the typewritten summaries contained in Vol.5. On church figures and questions of doctrine, consult the *New Catholic Encyclopedia,* on important concepts, the *Dictionary of the History of Ideas,* and for Italian literary figures, the Bondanellas' handy *Dictionary of Italian Literature.* The most valuable and authoritative single volume encyclopedia is that edited recently by J.R. Hale, which is, however, stronger on political than cultural history.

125   Avery, Catherine B., ed. *The New Century Italian Renaissance Encyclopedia*. New York: Appleton-Century-Crofts, 1972. Biographies only.

126   Bondanella, Peter E., and Julia Conaway Bondanella, eds. *Dictionary of Italian Literature*. Westport, Ct.: Greenwood, 1979. Authoritative short articles on Italian humanists and philosophers of the Renaissance.

127   Cosenza, Mario Emilio. *Biographical and Bibliographical Dictionary of the Italian Humanists and of the World of Classical Scholarship in Italy, 1300-1800*. 2nd ed., 6 vols. Boston: G.K.Hall, 1962-67.

128   ————. *Checklist of Non-Italian Humanists*. Boston: G.K.Hall, 1969.

129   *Dictionary of the History of Ideas*. 5 vols. New York: Scribner's, 1973-74. Organized by pivotal ideas treated in authoritative articles.

130   *Dictionary of the Middle Ages*. New York: Scribner's, 1982-. In progress.

131   *The Encyclopedia of Philosophy*. 8 vols. New York: Macmillan and the Free Press, 1967.

132   *Encyclopedia of World Art*. 15 vols. New York: McGraw-Hill, 1959-68.

133   Hale, J.R., ed. *A Concise Encyclopaedia of the Italian Renaissance*. New York: Oxford University Press, 1981.

134   *New Catholic Encyclopedia*. 15 vols. New York: McGraw-Hill, 1967.

135   Rachum, Ilan. *The Renaissance: An Illustrated Encyclopedia*. London: Octopus Books, 1979. Popular, with short bibliographies.

136   Riedl, John. *Catalogue of Renaissance Philosophers
       (1350-1650)*. Milwaukee: Marquette University Press,
       1940. Arranged by schools with alphabetic author
       index. Gives biographical notes and bibliographies
       of writings.

See also item 3081.

IV. GENERAL WORKS ON HUMANISM AND THE RENAISSANCE

This chapter aims at providing a listing of major historical texts on the Renaissance, more specialized studies of
Renaissance humanism, and interpretation and definitions of
humanism that are broad in scope and often controversial. In
the first category, the works by Ferguson, Gilmore,and Hay
are most useful; in the second the most important studies
are by Garin, Kristeller, and Trinkaus; and in the third
seminal studies are by Baron, Bouwsma, Gray, Kessler,
Kristeller, and Oberman.

Any serious student of Renaissance humanism will find the
consultation of many of the works listed here indispensable
for a fundamental understanding of the field.

A. WORKS ON THE RENAISSANCE PERIOD

137   Aston, Margaret. *The Fifteenth Century: The Prospect of Europe*. New York: Harcourt, Brace and World, 1968.

138   Allen, John William. *A History of Political Thought in the Sixteenth Century*. 3rd ed. London: Methuen, 1951.

139   Breisach, Ernst. *Renaissance Europe, 1300-1517*. New York: Macmillan, 1973.

140   Burke, Peter. *Culture and Society in Renaissance Italy, 1420-1540*. London: Batsford, 1972.

141   Burckhardt, Jacob. *The Civilization of the Renaissance in Italy*, trans. S.G.C. Middlemore. London: Kegan Paul & Co., 1878; repr. 2 vols. New York: Harper and Row, 1958.

142   *Cambridge Medieval History*, vols.7-8. Cambridge: At the University Press, 1932-34. Excellent chapters on the fourteenth and fifteenth centuries.

143   Chastel, André. *The Age of Humanism, 1480-1530*. New York: McGraw-Hill, 1963. Well-illustrated survey of the art and culture of the Renaissance.

144   Coates, William Havelock, et al. *The Emergence of Liberal Humanism: An Intellectual History of Western Europe*, vol.1. New York: McGraw-Hill, 1966.

145   Duby, Georges. *Foundations of a New Humanism*, trans. Peter Price. Geneva: Skira, 1966. Profusely illustrated interpretation of the culture of late-medieval Europe.

146   Ferguson, Wallace K. *Europe in Transition, 1300-1520*.
       Boston: Houghton Mifflin, 1962. The classic intro-
       duction to the history of Renaissance Europe.

147   ————. *The Renaissance in Historical Thought*.
       Cambridge, Mass.: Houghton Mifflin, 1948.

148   ————, et al. *The Renaissance: Six Essays*. New York:
       Harper and Row, 1962.

149   Gilmore, Myron P. *The World of Humanism, 1453-1517*.
       New York: Harper and Row, 1952. A balanced, penetrat-
       ing survey of the political and cultural history of
       Europe in the High Renaissance.

150   Hale, J.R. *Renaissance Europe, The Individual and
       Society, 1480-1520*. New York: Harper and Row, 1971.
       Strong on the new social history approach.

151   Hays, Denys. *Europe in the Fourteenth and Fifteenth
       Centuries*. New York: Holt, Rinehart and Winston,
       1966.

152   ————. *The Italian Renaissance in Its Historical
       Background*. 2nd ed. Cambridge: Cambridge University
       Press, 1977.

153   ————, ed. *The Age of the Renaissance*. London: Thames
       and Hudson, 1967. Profusely illustrated introduction
       to Renaissance thought, art and culture by several
       eminent specialists.

154   Haydn, Hiram. *The Counter Renaissance*. New York:
       Scribner's, 1950.

155   Heller, Agnes. *Renaissance Man*, trans. from Hungarian
       by Richard E. Allen. London: Routledge and Kegan Paul,
       1978. Sophisticated Marxist interpretation of Renais-
       sance as blending of Stoic-Epicurean antiquity and the
       Christian tradition seen through the vernacular
       authors.

156   Hyma, Albert. *Renaissance to Reformation*. Grand
       Rapids: Eerdmans, 1951.

157   Johnson, Jeran, and William Percy. *The Age of Recovery,
       The Fifteenth Century*. Ithaca: Cornell University
       Press, 1970. Political and cultural survey.

158   Larner, John. *Culture and Society in Italy, 1290-1420.*
      New York: Scribner's, 1971.

159   ———. *Italy in the Age of Dante and Petrarch, 1216-
      1380.* London: Longmans, 1980.

160   Laven, Peter. *Renaissance Italy, 1464-1535.* London:
      Batsford, 1965.

161   Lopez, Robert S. *The Three Ages of the Italian Renais-
      sance.* Charlottesville: The University Press of
      Virginia, 1970.

162   Lucki, Emil. *History of the Renaissance.* 5 vols.
      Salt Lake City: University of Utah Press, 1963-64.
      Especially useful for humanism is vol.3 on Educa-
      tion, Learning and Thought.

163   Martines, Lauro. *Power and Imagination, City-States in
      Renaissance Italy.* New York: Knopf, 1979.

164   *New Cambridge Modern History,* vol.1, The Renaissance,
      1493-1520. Cambridge: Cambridge University Press,
      1957.

165   *New Cambridge Modern History,* vol.2, The Reformation,
      1520-1559. Cambridge: Cambridge University Press,
      1958.

166   Pullan, Brian. *A History of Early Renaissance Italy
      from the Mid-Thirteenth to the Mid-Fifteenth Century.*
      New York: St. Martin's, 1973.

167   Rice, Eugene F., Jr. *The Foundations of Early Modern
      Europe, 1460-1559.* New York: W.W.Norton and Co.,
      1970.

168   Sellery, George Clarke. *The Renaissance, Its Nature
      and Origins.* Madison: University of Wisconsin Press,
      1950.

169   Schaff, Philip. *The Renaissance, The Revival of Learn-
      ing and Art in the Fourteenth and Fifteenth Century.*
      New York: G.P.Putnam's Sons, 1891.

170   Skinner, Quentin. *The Foundations of Modern Political
      Thought.* 2 vols. Cambridge: Cambridge University
      Press, 1978. The best study of the contribution of
      the humanists in early political thought.

171   Wilcox, Donald J. *In Search of God and Self, Renais-*
       sance and Reformation Thought. Boston: Houghton
       Mifflin, 1975.

    B. *GENERAL WORKS ON RENAISSANCE HUMANISM AND THOUGHT*

172   Allen, Don Cameron. *Mysteriously Meant: the Redis-*
       covery of Pagan Symbolism and Allegorical Interpre-
       tation in the Renaissance. Baltimore and London:
       Johns Hopkins Press, 1970.

173   Baker, Herschel. *The Image of Man.* Cambridge, Mass.:
       Harvard University Press, 1947.

174   Bouwsma, William J. "The Two Faces of Humanism.
       Stoicism and Augustinianism in Renaissance Thought."
       Itinerarium Italicum (item 298), pp.3-60.

175   Brehier, Emile. *The History of Philosophy, The*
       Middle Ages and the Renaissance, trans. W. Baskin.
       Chicago: University of Chicago Press, 1965.

176   Cassirer, Ernst. *The Individual and the Cosmos in*
       Renaissance Philosophy, trans. Mario Domandi. New
       York: Barnes and Noble, 1964.

177   Copleston, Frederick. S.J. *A History of Philosophy,*
       vols.2-3. London: Burns Oates, 1950,1953. On
       medieval and Renaissance periods.

178   Dresden, Sem. *Humanism in the Renaissance,* trans.
       Margaret King. New York: McGraw-Hill, 1968.

179   Ferguson, Wallace K. *Renaissance Essays.* New York:
       Harper and Row, 1963.

180   Garin, Eugenio. *Italian Humanism, Philosophy and*
       Civic Life in the Renaissance, trans. Peter Munz.
       New York: Harper and Row, 1966.

181   Gilbert, Neal W. *Renaissance Concepts of Method.* New
       York: Columbia University Press, 1960.

182   Gordon, D.J. *The Renaissance Imagination, Essays and*
       Lectures, ed. S.Orgel. Berkeley and Los Angeles:
       University of California Press, 1975.

183   Harbison, E.H. *The Christian Scholar in the Age of the
      Reformation.* New York: Scribner, 1956.

184   Kristeller, Paul Oskar. *Eight Philosophers of the
      Italian Renaissance.* Stanford: Stanford University
      Press, 1964.

185   ————. "Humanism and Scholasticism in the Italian
      Renaissance." *Byzantion,* 17 (1944-45): 346-64; repr.
      in *Studies in Renaissance Thought and Letters* (item
      194): chap. 25, in *Renaissance Thought* (item 192),
      pp.92-119, and in *Renaissance Thought and Its Sources*
      (item 191), pp.85-115.

186   ————. "The Impact of Early Italian Humanism on
      Thought and Learning." *Developments in the Early
      Renaissance,* ed. Bernard S. Levy. Albany: State Uni-
      versity of New York Press, 1972.

187   ————. *Medieval Aspects of Renaissance Learning, Three
      Essays,* ed. by and trans. Edward P. Mahoney. Duke
      Monographs in Medieval and Renaissance Studies, no.1.
      Durham, N.C.: Duke University Press, 1974.

188   ————. "Philosophy and Humanism in Renaissance Per-
      spective." *The Renaissance Image of Man and the
      World,* ed. Bernard O'Kelly. Columbus, Ohio: Ohio
      State University Press, 1968, pp.29-51.

189   ————. *Renaissance Concepts of Man and Other Essays.*
      New York: Harper and Row, 1972. Contains item 190.

190   ————. *Renaissance Philosophy and the Medieval Tradi-
      tion.* Wimmer Lecture, 15. Latrobe: The Archabbey
      Press, 1966; repr. in *Renaissance Concepts of Man*
      (item 189), pp.110-155, and *Renaissance Thought and
      Its Sources* (item 191), pp.106-33.

191   ————. *Renaissance Thought and Its Sources,* ed.
      Michael Mooney. New York: Columbia University Press,
      1979. Contains items 185, 190.

192   ————. *Renaissance Thought: The Classic, Scholastic,
      and Humanist Strains.* Cambridge, Mass.: Harvard Uni-
      versity Press, 1955; rev. ed. New York: Harper, 1961.
      Contains items 185, 1763.

193   Kristeller, Paul Oskar. *Renaissance Thought II: Papers
       on Humanism and the Arts.* New York: Harper and Row,
       1965. Contains items 807, 808, 1751, 1765.

194   ————. *Studies in Renaissance Thought and Letters.*
       Rome: Storia e Letteratura, 1956. Contains items 185,
       246, 1753, 1756, 1766, 1770.

195   Randall, John H., Jr. *The Career of Philosophy,* vol.1.
       From the Middle Ages to the Enlightenment. New York:
       Columbia University Press, 1962. Especially valuable
       for its treatment of humanism and science in the
       opening chapters.

196   Rice, E.F., Jr. *The Renaissance Idea of Wisdom.*
       Cambridge, Mass.: Harvard University Press, 1957;
       repr. Westport, Ct.: Greenwood, 1973.

197   Seigel, Jerrold E. *Rhetoric and Philosophy in Renais-
       sance Humanism.* Princeton: Princeton University
       Press, 1968.

198   Seung, Thomas K. *Cultural Thematics.* New Haven: Yale
       University Press, 1976.

199   Taylor, Henry Osborn. *Thought and Expression in the
       Sixteenth Century.* 2 vols. 2nd ed. New York:
       Macmillan, 1930.

200   Toffanin, Giuseppe. *History of Humanism,* trans. Elio
       Gianturco. New York: Las Americas, 1954.

201   Trinkaus, Charles E. *Adversity's Noblemen. The
       Italian Humanists on Happiness.* Studies in History,
       Economics and Public Law, no.475. New York:
       Columbia University Press, 1940; repr. New York:
       Octagon, 1965.

202   ————. *In Our Image and Likeness: Humanity and Divin-
       ity in Italian Humanist Thought.* 2 vols. Chicago:
       University of Chicago Press, 1970.

203   Ullman, B.L. *Studies in the Italian Renaissance.* 2nd
       ed. Rome: Storia e Letteratura, 1973. Contains
       items 424, 466, 1068-9, 1238, 1369, 1370.

204   Ullmann, Walter. *Medieval Foundations of Renaissance
       Humanism.* London: Paul Elek, 1977.

205   Weinberg, Bernard. *History of Italian Literary Criticism in the Renaissance.* 2 vols. Chicago: University of Chicago Press, 1961.

206   Weiss, Roberto. *Medieval and Humanist Greek, Collected Essays.* Padua: Antenore, 1977.

207   ————. *The Renaissance Discovery of Classical Antiquity.* Oxford: Blackwell, 1969.

208   ————. *The Spread of Italian Humanism.* New York: Hillary House, 1964.

See also items 705, 717.

C.   STUDIES ON THE DEFINITION AND ASPECTS
     OF RENAISSANCE HUMANISM

209   Abbagnano, Nicola. "Italian Renaissance Humanism." *Cahiers d'Histoire Mondiale,* 7 (1962-63): 267-82. On humanism as new vision of the place of man in the world.

210   Allen, Don Cameron. "Latin Literature." *Modern Language Quarterly,* 2 (1941): 403-20. Survey of Neo-Latin literature.

211   Baron, Hans. "Moot Problems of Renaissance Interpretation: An Answer to Wallace K. Ferguson." *JHI,* 19 (1958): 26-34.

212   ————. "Secularization of Wisdom and Political Humanism in the Renaissance (review of Eugene F. Rice, Jr.'s *The Renaissance Idea of Wisdom).*" *JHI,* 21 (1961): 131-50.

213   ————. "Towards a More Positive Evaluation of the Fifteenth-Century Renaissance." *JHI,* 4 (1943): 21-49.

214   Bennett, Josephine Waters. "On the Causes of the Renaissance." *Renaissance News,* 2 (1949): 5-6.

215   Bouwsma, William J. "Renaissance and Reformation: An Essay in Their Affinities and Connections." *Luther and the Dawn of the Modern Era,* ed. H.A. Oberman.

Leiden: Brill, 1971, pp.124-47. Argues that the
Reformation accepted certain ideas of early humanists, such as Petrarch and Valla.

216   Bouwsma, William J.   "The Renaissance and the Drama of
       Western History."   *American Historical Review*, 84
       (1979) : 1-16.

217   Bradner, L.   "The Renaissance."   *MH*, 5 (1947) : 62-72.

218   Breen, Quirinus. *Christianity and Humanism*. Grand
       Rapids: Eerdmans, 1968. Contains items 614, 1659,
       1660.

219   Brown, Peter.   "A Significant Sixteenth-Century Use of
       the Word 'Umanista.'"   *Modern Language Review*, 64
       (1969) : 565-75.

220   Campana, A.   "The Origin of the Word 'Humanist.'"
       JWCI, 9 (1946) : 60-73.

221   Cassirer, Ernst.   "Some Remarks on the Question of the
       Originality of the Renaissance."   *JHI*, 4 (1943) :
       49-56.

222   Craig, Hardin.   "Problems in Renaissance Scholarship."
       Philological Quarterly, 1 (1922) : 81-99.

223   Ferguson, Wallace K.   "Humanist Views of the Renaissance."
       American Historical Review, 45 (1939-40) : 1-28.

224   ————.   "The Interpretation of Italian Humanism: The
       Contribution of Hans Baron."   *JHI*, 14 (1953) : 14-25.

225   ————.   "The Interpretation of the Renaissance: Sug-
       gestions for a Synthesis."   *JHI*, 13 (1952) : 483-95;
       repr. *Renaissance Essays*   (item 290), pp.61-73.

226   Gilmore, Myron Piper. *The Argument from Roman Law,
       1200-1600*. Cambridge, Mass.: Harvard University
       Press, 1941.

227   ————. *Humanists and Jurists: Six Studies in the
       Renaissance*. Cambridge, Mass.: Harvard University
       Press, 1963. Contains item 694.

228   Gombrich, E.H.   "Renaissance and Golden Age."   *JWCI*, 24
       (1961) : 306-09.

229   Grant, W. Leonard. "European Vernacular Works in
      Latin Translation." *Studies in the Renaissance,*
      1 (1954): 120-56.

230   Grassi, Ernesto. "Italian Humanism and Heidegger's
      Thesis of the End of Philosophy." *Philosophy and
      Rhetoric,* 13 (1980): 79-98.

231   Gray, Hanna H. "Renaissance Humanism: The Pursuit of
      Eloquence." *JHI,* 24 (1963): 497-514; repr. *Renais-
      sance Essays* (item 290), pp.199-216.

232   Grendler, Paul F. "Five Italian Occurrences of 'Uman-
      ista,' 1540-1574." *RQ,* 20 (1967): 317-25.

233   Hägglund, Bengt. "Renaissance and Reformation." *Luther
      and the Dawn of the Modern Era,* ed. H.A. Oberman.
      Leiden: Brill, 1971, pp.150-57.

234   Hay, Denys. "'Europe' and 'Christendom': A Problem in
      Renaissance Terminology and Historical Semantics."
      Diogenes, 17 (Spring 1957): 45-55.

235   ————. "Humanists, Scholars and Religion in the Later
      Middle Ages." *Religion and Humanism* (item 301),
      pp.1-18.

236   ————. "The Italian View of Renaissance Italy."
      *Florilegium Historiale. Essays Presented to Wallace
      K. Ferguson* (item 302), p.4-17.

237   ————. "Italy and Barbarian Europe." *Italian Renais-
      sance Studies* (item 289), pp.48-68.

238   Jacob, E.F. "An Approach to the Renaissance." *Italian
      Renaissance Studies* (item 289), pp.15-47.

239   Kamen, Henry. "Golden Age, Iron Age: A Conflict of
      Concepts in the Renaissance." *JMRS,* 4 (1974): 135-56.

240   ————. *The Rise of Toleration.* New York: McGraw-Hill,
      1967.

241   Kelley, Donald R. "Civil Science in the Renaissance:
      Jurisprudence Italian Style." *Historical Journal,*
      22 (1979): 777-94.

242   Kelly-Gadol, Joan. "The Unity of the Renaissance:
      Humanism, Natural Science, and Art." *From Renais-
      sance to Counter Reformation* (item 279), pp.29-55.

243   Kelso, Ruth. *Doctrine for the Lady of the Renaissance*.
      Urbana, Ill.: University of Illinois Press, 1956.

244   Kessler, Eckhart. "Humanist Thought: A Response to
      Scholastic Philosophy." *Res Publica Litterarum*, 2
      (1979) : 149-66.

245   Kisch, Guido. "Humanistic Jurisprudence." *Studies in
      the Renaissance,* 8 (1961) : 71-87.

246   Kristeller, Paul Oskar. "Augustine and the Early
      Renaissance." *Review of Religion*, 8 (1943-44) : 339-58;
      repr. *Studies in Renaissance Thought and Letters*
      (item 194), chap.17.

247   ――――. "The Place of Classical Humanism in Renais-
      sance Thought." *JHI*, 4 (1943) : 59-63.

248   ――――. "The Role of Religion in Renaissance Humanism
      and Platonism." *Pursuit of Holiness* (item 304),
      pp.367-70.

249   Kuznetsov, Boris. "The Tragedy of Knowledge at the
      Time of the Renaissance." *Diogenes*, 10 (1978): 66-92.

250   Levin, Harry. *The Myth of the Golden Age in the
      Renaissance*. Bloomington, Ind.: Indiana University
      Press, 1969.

251   Logan, George M. "Substance and Form in Renaissance
      Humanism." *JMRS*, 7 (1977): 1-34.

252   McKeon, Richard. "Renaissance and Method in Philosophy."
      Studies in the History of Ideas, 3 (1935): 37-114.

253   Martin, Alfred von. *Sociology of the Renaissance,*
      introd. W.K. Ferguson. New York: Harper and Row, 1963.

254   Mazzeo, Joseph Anthony. "Universal Analogy and the
      Culture of the Renaissance." *JHI*, 15 (1954): 299-304.

255   Montano, Rocco. "From Italian Humanism to Shakespeare,
      Humanistic Positions." *Italian Quarterly*, 13, no.50
      (1969) : 3-31.

256   Nauert, Charles. "Renaissance Humanism: An Emergent
      Consensus and Its Critics." *Indiana Social Studies
      Quarterly,* 33 (1980): 5-20.

257   Nelson, N. "Individualism as a Criterion of the
      Renaissance." *Journal of English and German Phil-
      ology,* 32 (1933): 316-34.

258   Oberman, Heiko A. "The Shape of Late Medieval Thought:
      The Birthpangs of the Modern Era." *ARG,* 64 (1972):
      13-33.

259   ————. "Some Notes on the Theology of Nominalism
      with Attention to Its Relation to the Renaissance."
      Harvard Theological Review, 53 (1960): 47-76.

260   Ong, Walter J. "Renaissance Ideas and the American
      Catholic Mind." *Thought,* 29 (1954): 327-56.

261   ————. "System, Space and Intellect in Renaissance
      Symbolism." *BHR,* 18 (1956): 222-39.

262   Perella, Nicholas J. "Humanism and the Spirit of the
      Renaissance." *Italica,* 40 (1963): 132-44.

263   Romualdez, Antonio V. "Towards a History of the
      Renaissance Idea of Wisdom." *Studies in the Renais-
      sance,* 11 (1964): 133-50.

264   Starnes, D.T. "The Figure Genius in the Renaissance."
      Studies in the Renaissance, 11 (1964): 234-44.

265   Struever, Nancy. "Humanities and Humanists." *Humani-
      ties in Society,* 1 (1978): 25-34.

266   Thorndike, Lynn. "Renaissance or Prenaissance?" *JHI,*
      4 (1943): 65-74.

267   Trinkaus, Charles. "Italian Humanism and the Problem
      of 'Structures of Conscience.'" *JMRS,* 2 (1972): 19-
      34.

268   ————. "The Problem of Free Will in the Renaissance
      and the Reformation." *JHI,* 10 (1949): 51-62; repr.
      Renaissance Essays (item 290), pp.187-98.

269   Trinkaus, Charles.   "The Religious Thought of the
       Italian Humanists, and the Reformers: Anticipation or
       Autonomy?" *Pursuit of Holiness* (item 304), pp. 339-
       66.

270   Weisinger, Herbert.   "The Attack on the Renaissance in
       Theology Today." *Studies in the Renaissance,* 2 (1955):
       176-89.

271   ————.   "Renaissance Accounts of the Revival of Learn-
       ing." *Studies in Philology,* 45 (1948): 105-18.

272   ————.   "The Renaissance Theory of the Reaction Against
       the Middle Ages as a Cause of the Renaissance."
       Speculum, 20 (1949): 461-67.

273   Weiss, Roberto.   "Italian Humanism in Western Europe."
       Italian Renaissance Studies (item 289), pp.69-93.

274   Wilkins, Ernest H.   "On the Nature of the Italian
       Renaissance." *Italica,* 27 (1950): 67-76.

V. MISCELLANIES AND FESTSCHRIFTEN

Many of the most significant essays on Renaissance humanism
are to be found in proceedings of conferences, volumes in
honor of eminent scholars, and other types of miscellaneous
volumes. Fine examples of the first type are the volumes con-
taining proceedings of conferences on the classical influences held at King's College, Cambridge, edited by R.R. Bolgar;
of the second, the Festschriften for Hans Baron, Myron Piper
Gilmore, and Paul Oskar Kristeller, and of the third, the
selection of important studies from the *Journal of the History
of Ideas*, entitled *Renaissance Essays*. Many of the volumes in
this chapter have been analysed and individual essays are
listed at the appropriate place in the bibliography with
cross-reference to the volumes listed below.

275 Bertelli, Sergio and Gloria Ramakus, eds. *Essays Presented to Myron P. Gilmore*. 2 vols. Florence: La Nuova Italia, 1978. Contains items 793, 1226, 1556, 1805, 1866, 1867, 1908, 2675.

276 ————, et al.,eds. *Florence and Venice: Comparison and Relations*. 2 vols. Florence: La Nuova Italia, 1979. Contains items 1276, 1334, 1385, 1455.

277 Bolgar, R.R., ed. *Classical Influences on European Culture A.D. 500-1500*. Proceedings of an International Conference Held at King's College, Cambridge, April 1969. Cambridge: Cambridge University Press, 1971. Contains items 404, 539, 800, 1200, 1896, 2071, 2115.

278 ————. *Classical Influences on European Culture A.D. 1500-1700*. Cambridge: Cambridge University Press, 1976. Contains items 568, 611, 623, 2137, 2858, 2868, 2896.

279 Carter, Charles H., ed. *From Renaissance to Counter Reformation: Essays in Honor of Garrett Mattingly*. New York: Random House, 1965. Contains items 1759, 2493.

280 Clough, Cecil H., ed. *Cultural Aspects of the Italian Renaissance*. Manchester: Manchester University Press, 1976. Contains items 344, 355, 551, 671, 1048, 1195, 1477, 1513, 1544, 1646, 1674, 1696, 1785, 1837, 1907.

281 Dannenfeldt, Karl H. *The Renaissance, Basic Interpretations*. 2nd ed. Lexington, Mass.: D.C. Heath, 1974.

282 Gabel, Leona, et al. *The Renaissance Reconsidered, A Symposium*. Smith College Studies in History, 45. Northampton, Mass.: Department of History of Smith College, 1964.

283   Gordon, D.J., ed. *Fritz Saxl, 1890-1948. A Volume of
       Memorial Essays from His Friends in England.* London:
       Nelson, 1957. Contains items 838, 990, 1061.

284   Hale, J.R., ed. *Renaissance Venice.* London: Faber and
       Faber, 1973. Contains items 817, 1430, 1431, 1557.

285   ――――, J.R.L. Highfield, and B. Smalley, eds. *Europe
       in the late Middle Ages.* Evanston: Northwestern Uni-
       versity Press, 1965.

286   Hearnshaw, F.J.C., ed. *The Social and Political Ideas
       of Some Great Thinkers of the Renaissance and the
       Reformation. A Series of Lectures Delivered at King's
       College, University of London.* New York: Barnes and
       Noble, 1949.

287   Henderson, Charles, ed. *Classical, Mediaeval and Re-
       naissance Studies in Honor of Berthold Louis Ullman.*
       2 vols. Rome: Storia e Letteratura, 1964.

288   IJsewijn, Jozef, and E. Kessler, eds. *Acta Conventus
       Neo-Latini Lovaniensis. Proceedings of the First
       International Congress of Neo-latin Studies, Louvain,
       23-28 August 1971.* Munich: Wilhelm Fink; Leuven:
       University Press, 1973. Contains items 554, 750,
       1441, 1678, 2024, 3011, 3069, 3071.

289   Jacob, E.F., ed. *Italian Renaissance Studies.* London:
       Faber and Faber, 1960. Contains items 237, 238, 273,
       802, 2361.

290   Kristeller, Paul O. and Philip P. Weiner, eds. *Renais-
       sance Essays.* New York: Harper and Row, 1968.
       Reprints an important selection of articles from the
       Journal of the History of Ideas. Contains items 231,
       268, 339, 704, 708, 729, 810, 2348, 2790.

291   Labalme, Patricia H., ed. *Beyond Their Sex. Learned
       Women of the European Past.* New York: New York Uni-
       versity Press, 1980.

292   Lewis, Archibald R., ed. *Aspects of the Renaissance.
       A Symposium. Papers Presented at a Conference on the
       Meaning of the Renaissance.* Austin: University of
       Texas Press, 1967.

293   Mahoney, Edward P., ed. *Philosophy and Humanism: Re-*
       naissance Essays in Honor of Paul Oskar Kristeller.
       New York: Columbia University Press, 1976. Contains
       items 117, 533, 728, 730, 1363, 1448, 1482, 1503,
       1512, 1518, 1523, 1746, 1779, 1850, 1898, 2488, 2629,
       2829, 2860.

294   *Medioevo e Rinascimento. Studi in Onore di Bruno Nardi.*
       2 vols. Florence: Sansoni, 1955.

295   *Miscellanea Giovanni Mercati. Vol.4. Letteratura*
       Classica e Umanistica. Studi e Testi, 124. Vatican
       City: Biblioteca Apostolica Vaticana, 1946. Contains
       twenty essays by leading students of manuscript stud-
       ies and humanism at mid-century.

296   Molho, Anthony, and John A. Tedeschi, eds. *Renaissance*
       Studies in Honor of Hans Baron. Florence: Sansoni,
       1971. Contains items 121, 1316, 1333, 1383, 1466,
       1567, 1712, 1899, 2812, 2822, 2828, 2830, 2863, 2997,
       3019, 3026.

297   Murdoch, John Emery, and Edith Dudley Sylla, eds. *The*
       Cultural Context of Medieval Learning. Proceedings
       of the First International Colloquium on Philosophy,
       Science, and Theology in the Middle Ages--September
       1973. Boston Studies in the Philosophy of Science,
       26. Boston: D. Reidell, 1975. Contains items 981,
       988.

298   Oberman, Heiko A., and Thomas A. Brady, Jr., eds.
       Itinerarium Italicum. The Profile of the Italian
       Renaissance in the Mirror of Its European Transfor-
       mations. Dedicated to Paul Oskar Kristeller on the
       Occasion of His 70th Birthday. Leiden: Brill, 1975.
       Contains items 174, 2079, 2174, 2492, 2804, 3018.

299   Rabb, Theodore K., and Jerrold E. Seigel, eds. *Action*
       and Conviction in Early Modern Europe. Essays in
       Memory of E.H. Harbison. Princeton: Princeton Uni-
       versity Press, 1969. Contains items 1322, 1454,
       1857, 2078, 2146, 2286, 2507, 2967.

300   Ramsey, P.A., ed. *Rome in the Renaissance: The City and*
       the Myth. Papers of the Thirteenth Annual Conference
       of the Center for Medieval and Early Renaissance
       Studies. Binghamton, N.Y.: Center for Medieval and

Early Renaissance Studies, 1982. Contains items
790, 1668, 1728, 1789, 1868, 1903, 1909.

301   Robbins, Keith, ed. *Religion and Humanism.* Studies
in Church History, vol.17. Oxford: Blackwell, 1981.
Contains items 235, 1327, 2729, 3048.

302   Rowe, J.G., and W.H. Stockdale, eds. *Florilegium Historiale. Essays Presented to Wallace K. Ferguson.*
Toronto: University of Toronto Press, 1971. Contains
items 236, 1134, 1313, 2077, 2132, 2862.

303   Schwoebel, Robert, ed. *Renaissance Man and Ideas.* New
York: St. Martin's Press, 1971. Short original essays
by J.E. Seigel on Petrarch and Valla, and Schwoebel
on Pius II.

304   Trinkaus, Charles E., and Heiko A. Oberman, eds. *The
Pursuit of Holiness in Late Medieval and Renaissance
Religion.* Leiden: Brill, 1974. Contains items 248,
269, 810, 2140.

305   Tuynman, P., G.C. Kuiper, and E. Kessler, eds. *Acta
Conventus Neo-Latini Amstelodamensis. Proceedings of
the Second International Congress of Neo-Latin Studies, Amsterdam, 19-24 August, 1973.* Munich: Wilhelm
Fink Verlag, 1979. Contains items 529, 662, 1330,
1493, 1527, 1649, 2197, 2344, 2352, 2574, 2838, 2881,
3072.

306   Wallach, Luitpold, ed. *The Classical Tradition. Literary and Historical Studies in Honor of Harry Caplan.*
Ithaca: Cornell University Press, 1966. Contains
items 765, 1499.

307   Werkmeister, William H., ed. *Facets of the Renaissance.* Los Angeles: University of Southern California
Press, 1959; repr. New York: Harper Torchbooks, 1963.

VI. ANTHOLOGIES OF SOURCES IN ENGLISH TRANSLATION

Perhaps the bulk of the writings of Renaissance humanists
available in English are to be found in anthologies of sources
published over the past century. Each generation of scholars
has produced at least one notable anthology of English translations, beginning with the volume of writings on educational
theory edited by W.H. Woodward at the end of the last century,
followed by Emerton's book on humanism and tyranny of the
Interwar period, and by the distinguished collection of Renaissance philosophical texts conceived by Ernst Cassirer
and brought to fruition by P.O. Kristeller and John H. Randall,
Jr. in 1948. In recent years have appeared three major anthologies: works from Florentine humanism, edited by Renée
Watkins; treatises by Italian humanists on questions of politics and social theory, by B.G. Kohl and R.G. Witt; and works
by and about women humanists, by Margaret King and Albert
Rabil. Almost all of the anthologies listed in this chapter
have been analysed, and individual works of humanists are
given at the appropriate chapter elsewhere in the bibliography.

308   Aldington, Richard, ed. *Latin Poems of the Renaissance.*
      2 vols. London: The Egoist Press, 1919.

309   Blanchard, Harold Hooper, ed. *Prose and Poetry of the
      Continental Renaissance in Translation.* New York:
      Longmans, Green and Co., 1949. Mainly translations
      from vernacular works in short selections, rich in
      poetry of Petrarch, Ronsard, Tasso.

310   Burke, Peter, ed. *The Renaissance.* New York: Barnes
      and Noble, 1964. Short selections of sources organ-
      ized by topic.

311   Cassirer, Ernst, P.O. Kristeller, and John H. Randall,
      Jr., eds. *The Renaissance Philosophy of Man, Selec-
      tions in Translation.* Chicago: University of Chicago
      Press, 1948. Contains items 1126, 1127, 1409, 1596,
      1617, 2778.

312   Clements, Robert J., and Lorna Levant, eds. *Renaissance
      Letters, Revelations of a World Born.* New York: New
      York University Press, 1976. Letters mainly from
      sixteenth-century figures, including Erasmus, Machia-
      velli, and Elizabeth I.

313   Conklin, George N., ed. *Aspects of Renaissance Culture.*
      Middletown, Ct.: Wesleyan University Press, 1953.
      Mainly plays and poetry from the sixteenth century.

314   Davies, Stevie, ed. *Renaissance Views of Man.* New
      York: Barnes and Noble, 1979. Short selections from
      Ficino, Erasmus, Luther and others.

315   Emerton, Ephraim. *Humanism and Tyranny, Studies in the
      Italian Trecento.* Cambridge, Mass.: Harvard Univer-
      sity Press, 1925. Contains items 1298, 1302.

316   Fallico, Arturo B., and Herman Shapiro, eds. *Renais-
      sance Philosophy, Vol.1, The Italian Philosophers.*
      New York: Random House, 1967. Contains items 1408,
      1572, 1594, 1607, 1612, 1618, 1633.

317   Greswell, W. Parr, trans. *Memoirs of Angelus Politianus,*
       Joannes Picus of Mirandola, Actius Sincerus Sanna-
       zarius, Petrus Bembus, Hieronymus Fracastorius, Marcus
       Antonius Flaminius, and the Amalthei. London: Cadel
       and Davies, 1805.

318   Gundersheimer, Werner L., ed. *The Italian Renaissance.*
       Englewood Cliffs, N.J.: Prentice-Hall, 1965. Short
       selections.

319   Haydn, Hiram, and J.C. Nelson, eds. *A Renaissance*
       Treasury. A Collection of Representative Writings of
       the Renaissance on the Continent of Europe. Garden
       City, N.Y.: Doubleday, 1953. Mainly translations from
       vernacular works.

320   Kennedy, Leonard A., ed. *Renaissance Philosophy. New*
       Translations. The Hague and Paris: Mouton, 1973.
       Contains items 1387, 1587, 1591, 1632.

321   King, Margaret L., and Albert Rabil, Jr., eds. *Her*
       Immaculate Hand: Selected Works by and about Women
       Humanists of Quattrocento Italy. Binghamton, N.Y.:
       Center for Medieval and Early Renaissance Studies,
       1983.

322   Kohl, Benjamin G., and Ronald G. Witt, eds. *The*
       Earthly Republic, Italian Humanists on Government and
       Society. Philadelphia: University of Pennsylvania
       Press, 1978. Contains items 1123, 1293, 1300, 1301,
       1391, 1580, 1626.

323   Lind, L.R., ed. *Latin Poetry in Verse Tradition from*
       the Beginnings to the Renaissance. Boston: Houghton
       Mifflin, 1957.

324   McFarlane, I.D., ed. *Renaissance Latin Poetry.* New
       York: Barnes and Noble, 1980. Latin texts with fac-
       ing English translation of poets from Poliziano to
       Buchanan.

325   Nichols, Fred J., ed. and trans. *An Anthology of Neo-*
       Latin Poetry. New Haven: Yale University Press,
       1979. Superb selection with Latin text and English
       prose translation, enhanced by bio-bibliography of
       authors.

326   Nugent, Elizabeth M., ed. *The Thought and Culture of the English Renaissance. An Anthology of Early Tudor Prose (1481-1555)*. Cambridge: At the University Press, 1956.

327   Oberman, Heiko A., ed. *Forerunners of the Reformation: The Shape of Late Medieval Thought*, trans. P.L. Nyhus. New York: Holt, Rinehart and Winston, 1966.

328   Ross, J.B., and M.M. McLaughlin, eds. *The Portable Medieval Reader*. New York: Viking, 1949. Important selections from Petrarch and other early humanists.

329   ————. *The Portable Renaissance Reader*. New York: Viking, 1953. Short selections from major authors, including Petrarch, Alberti, Poggio, and Pius II.

330   Schevill, Ferdinand. *The First Century of Italian Humanism*. New York: Crofts, 1928.

331   Speroni, Charles, ed. and trans. *Wit and Wisdom in the Italian Renaissance*. Berkeley: University of California Press, 1964.

332   Spinka, Matthew, ed. and trans. *Advocates of Reform from Wycliff to Erasmus*. The Library of Christian Classics, 14. Philadelphia: Westminster Press, 1953.

333   Strauss, Gerald, ed. *Manifestations of Discontent in Germany on the Eve of the Reformation*. Bloomington: Indiana University Press, 1971. Selections include pieces by Pope Pius II and Ulrich von Hutten.

334   Thompson, David, and A.F. Nagel, ed. and trans. *The Three Crowns of Florence: Humanist Assessments of Dante, Petrarca, and Boccaccio*. New York: Harper and Row, 1972. Contains items 1291, 1299.

335   Thorndike, Lynn. *University Records and Life in the Middle Ages*. New York: Columbia University Press, 1944. Contains much on fifteenth-century university life and curriculum.

336   Watkins, Renée Neu, ed. *Humanism and Liberty, Writings on Freedom from Fifteenth-Century Florence*. Columbia: University of South Carolina Press, 1978. Contains items 1294, 1568, 1569, 1579, 1627, 1628.

337   Whitcomb, Merrick, ed. *A Literary Source-Book of the
       Renaissance*. Philadelphia: Department of History of
       the University of Pennsylvania, 1903.

338   Woodward, William Harrison. *Vittorino da Feltre and
       Other Humanist Educators*. Cambridge: University
       Press, 1897; repr. with introd. by E.F. Rice, Jr.
       New York: Columbia Teachers' College, 1963. Contains
       items 1290, 1414.

See also item 865.

VII. THE CLASSICAL TRADITION

In a real sense, Renaissance humanism was based on the
reading, study, editing, and explication of classical authors.
Hence, the history of the classical tradition is central to
understanding Renaissance humanism, and indeed, many of the
best studies of this tradition are themselves major contributions to the history of humanism in the early modern period.
Of these especially recommended are the works of Bolgar,
Highet, Pfeiffer, and Wilson and Reynolds. Still useful for
names, dates, and works is the massive three-volume survey by
Sir John Sandys. Of a different sort is the ongoing *Catalogue
of Medieval and Renaissance Translations and Commentaries,*
which aims at listing all commentaries on ancient authors,
Latin and Greek, and all Greek authors made available in Latin
translation to about A.D. 1600. This monument of learning
also provides complete bibliographies of each ancient author
treated as well as a brief discussion of the author's *Fortuna*
in the Middle Ages and the Renaissance. In Part B are listed
alphabetically by ancient author major studies in English on
each author's *Fortuna,* manuscript tradition, and influence in
the Middle Ages and the Renaissance.

A. GENERAL STUDIES

339   Baron, Hans. "The 'Querelle' of the Ancients and the
      Moderns as a Problem for Renaissance Scholarship."
      JHI, 20 (1959): 3-22; repr. in *Renaissance Essays*
      (item 290), pp.95-114.

340   Beddie, Rex. "The Ancient Classics in Medieval Librar-
      ies." *Speculum*, 5 (1930): 3-20.

341   Bolgar, R.R. *The Classical Heritage and Its Benefi-
      ciaries*. Cambridge: Cambridge University Press,
      1955; repr. New York: Harper and Row, 1964.

342   ————. "The Classical Curriculum and Its Link with
      the Renaissance." *Didaskalos*, 4 (1972): 18-24.

343   Botfield, Beriah. *Prefaces to the First Editions of
      the Greek and Roman Classics and of the Second Scrip-
      tures*. London: H.G. Bohn, 1861.

344   Clough, Cecil H. "The Cult of Antiquity: Letters and
      Letter Collections." *Cultural Aspects of the Italian
      Renaissance* (item 280), pp.33-67.

345   Dannenfeldt, Karl H. "Egypt and Egyptian Antiquities
      in the Renaissance." *Studies in the Renaissance*, 6
      (1959): 7-27.

346   ————. "The Renaissance Humanists and the Knowledge
      of Arabic." *Studies in the Renaissance*, 2 (1955): 96-
      117.

347   Hall, F.W. *A Companion to Classical Texts*. Oxford:
      Clarendon Press, 1913. Especially valuable for
      nomenclature and MSS authorities of major ancient
      authors; brief discussion of the history of the texts.

348   Highet, G. *The Classical Tradition.* Oxford: Oxford
       University Press, 1949.

349   Hunt, R.W. "The Deposit of Latin Classics in the
       Twelfth-Century Renaissance." *Classical Influences
       on European Culture, A.D. 500-1500* (item 277), pp.51-
       55.

350   Kenney, E.J. "The Character of Humanist Philology."
       *Classical Influences on European Culture, A.D. 500-
       1500* (item 277), pp.119-28.

351   ————. *The Classical Text. Aspects of Editing in
       the Age of the Printed Book.* Berkeley: University of
       California Press, 1974.

352   Kristeller, Paul Oskar, and F. Edward Cranz, eds.
       *Catalogus Translationum et Commentariorum, Medieval
       and Renaissance Latin Translations and Commentaries.*
       4 vols. to date. Washington, D.C.: Catholic Univer-
       sity of America Press, 1960-80. Lists Latin transla-
       tions of Greek works and Latin commentaries on all
       authors to 1600 with discussion of the *Fortuna* of
       individual authors in the Renaissance. Important
       treatments of individual ancient authors are given
       below.

353   Law, Helen Hull. "Croesus: From Herodotus to Boccaccio."
       Classical Journal, 43 (1947-48): 456-62.

354   Lockwood, D.P., and R.H. Bainton. "Classical and Bib-
       lical Scholarship in the Age of the Renaissance and
       Reformation." *Church History,* 10 (1941): 3-21.

355   McDonald, A.H. "Study of the Renaissance Manuscripts
       of Classical Authors." *Cultural Aspects of the Ital-
       ian Renaissance* (item 280), pp.1-8.

356   Mulryan, J. "Venus, Cupid, and the Italian Mythog-
       raphers." *HL,* 23 (1974): 31-41.

357   Palmer, Henrietta R. *List of English Editions and
       Translations of Greek and Latin Classics Printed
       before 1641.* London: Blades, East and Blades, 1911.

358   Panofsky, Erwin, and Fritz Saxl. "Classical Mythology
       in Mediaeval Art." *Metropolitan Museum Studies,* 4
       (1933): 228-80.

359   Pfeiffer, Rudolf. *History of Classical Scholarship
      from 1300-1850.* London: Oxford University Press,
      1976.

360   Prete, Sesto. "The Contribution of the Humanists to
      Classical Philology." *Thought,* 40 (1965): 41-55.

361   Quain, E.A. "The Medieval *Accessus ad auctores.*"
      Traditio, 3 (1945): 215-64.

362   Rawson, Elizabeth. *The Spartan Tradition in European
      Thought.* Oxford: Oxford University Press, 1969.

363   Reynolds, L.D., ed. *Texts and Transmission. A Survey
      of the Latin Classics.* Oxford: Clarendon Press, 1983.

364   Rouse, R.H. "*Florilegia* and Latin Classical Authors
      in Twelfth and Thirteenth-Century Orleans." *Viator,*
      10 (1979): 131-60.

365   Sandys, John Edwin. *Harvard Lectures on the Revival of
      Learning.* Cambridge: Cambridge University Press,
      1905.

366   ————. *A History of Classical Scholarship.* 3 vols.
      3rd ed. Cambridge: At the University Press, 1921;
      repr. New York: Hafner, 1958.

367   ————. *A Short History of Classical Scholarship.*
      Cambridge: Cambridge University Press, 1915.

368   Sanford, E.M. "The Use of Classical Latin Authors in
      the *Libri Manuales.*" *TAPA,* 55 (1924): 190-248.

369   Starnes, De Witt Talmage, and Ernest Talbert. *Classi-
      cal Myth and Legend in Renaissance Dictionaries: A
      Study of Renaissance Dictionaries in Their Relation
      to the Classical Learning of Contemporary English
      Writers.* Chapel Hill: University of North Carolina
      Press, 1955.

370   Ullman, B.L. "Classical Authors in Certain Mediaeval
      Florilegia." *Classical Philology,* 27 (1932): 1-42.

371   Walzer, R. "Arabic Transmission of Greek Thought in
      Medieval Europe." *BJRL,* 29 (1945): 160-83.

372   Wilson, Nigel G., and L.D. Reynolds. *Scribes and
       Scholars: A Guide to the Transmission of Greek and
       Latin Literature*. 2nd ed. Oxford: Clarendon Press,
       1974.

373   Wright, Frederick Adam, and T.A. Sinclair. *History of
       Later Latin Literature from the Middle of the Fourth
       to the End of the Seventeenth Century*. New York:
       Macmillan, 1931.

See also items 822, 990, 1675.

           B. THE FORTUNA *OF ANCIENT AUTHORS
       FROM HOMER TO BOETHIUS (LISTED ALPHABETICALLY)*

                    Aeschylus

374   Hirsch, R. "The Printing Tradition of Aeschylus, Euri-
       pides, Sophocles, and Aristophanes." *Gutenberg-
       Jahrbuch*, 1964, pp.138-46.

375   Lachmann, Vera R., and F. Edward Cranz. "Aeschylus."
       Catalogus Translationum et Commentariorum (item 352),
       vol.2, pp.5-26.

               Alexander of Aphrodisias

376   Cranz, F. Edward. "Alexander Aphrodisiensis." *Cata-
       logus Translationum et Commentariorum* (item 352),
       vol.1, pp.77-135.

377   ————. "The Prefaces to the Greek Editions and Latin
       Translations of Alexander of Aphrodisias, 1450-1575."
       Proceedings of the American Philosophical Society,
       102 (1958): 510-46.

                    Apuleius

378   Haight, Elizabeth H. "Apuleius and Boccaccio." *More
       Essays on Greek Romances*. New York: Longmans, Green
       and Co., 1945, pp.113-41.

379   ————. *Apuleius and His Influence*. New York: Long-
       mans, Green and Co., 1927.

380 ————. "Introducing Apuleius: On Certain Uses of
Apuleius' Story of Cupid and Psyche in English Literature." *Poet Lore,* 26.6 (1915): 694-706, 744-62.

381 ————. "The Myth of Cupid and Psyche in Renaissance
Art: The Vassar College Psyche Tapestries." *Art and
Archaeology,* 15 (1923): 107-16.

382 Robertson, D.S. "The Manuscripts of the *Metamorphoses*
of Apuleius." *Classical Quarterly,* 18 (1924): 27-47,
85-99.

383 Scobie, A. "The Influence of Apuleius' *Metamorphoses*
in Renaissance Italy and Spain." *Aspects of Apuleius'
Golden Ass.* Ed. B.L. Hijmans, Jr., and R.Th. van der
Paardt. Groningen: Bouma's Boekhuis, 1978, pp.211-25.
Survey of influence, mainly on vernacular literature
from Petrarch to Cervantes.

384 Vetova, Luisa. "The Tale of Cupid and Psyche in
Renaissance Painting before Raphael." *JWCI,* 42
(1979): 104-21.

Aristophanes

385 Lord, Louis Eleazer. *Aristophanes, His Plays and His
Influence.* Boston: Marshall Jones Co., 1925.

386 Wilson, N.G. "The Triclinian Edition of Aristophanes."
Classical Quarterly, 56 (1962): 32-47.

Aristotle

387 Cerreta, Florindo V. "Alessandro Piccolomini's Commentary on the *Poetics* of Aristotle." *Studies in the
Renaissance,* 4 (1957): 139-68.

388 Cranz, F. Edward. *A Bibliography of Aristotle Editions
1501-1600 with an Introduction and Indexes.* Bibliotheca Bibliographica Aureliana 38. Baden-Baden:
Aureliana, 1971.

389 Gilbert, A.H. "Notes on the Influence of the *Secretum
Secretorum.*" *Speculum,* 3 (1928): 84-98.

390 Herrick, Marvin T. "The Early History of Aristotle's
Rhetoric in England." *Philological Quarterly,* 5
(1926): 242-57.

391   Kristeller, P.O. "Renaissance Aristotelianism." *Greek,*
       Roman and Byzantine Studies, 6 (1965): 157-74.

392   Lohr, Charles H. "Mediaeval Latin Aristotle Commenta-
       ries." *Traditio,* 23 (1967): 313-413; 24 (1968): 149-
       245; 26 (1970): 135-216; 27 (1971): 251-351; 28 (1972):
       281-396; 29 (1973): 93-197; 30 (1974): 119-44.

393   ————. "Renaissance Latin Aristotle Commentaries."
       Studies in the Renaissance, 24 (1974): 228-89; *RQ* 28
       (1975): 689-741; *RQ* 29 (1976): 714-45; *RQ* 30 (1977):
       681-741; *RQ* 31 (1978): 532-603; *RQ* 32 (1979): 529-80;
       RQ 33 (1980): 623-734; *RQ* 35 (1982): 164-256. Exhaus-
       tive and invaluable guides to western scholars com-
       menting on Aristotle's works to A.D. 1600.

394   Menut, Albert D. "Castiglione and the *Nicomachean*
       Ethics." *PMLA,* 58 (1943): 309-21.

395   Muckle, J.T. "Greek Works Translated Directly into
       Latin before 1350." *Mediaeval Studies,* 4 (1942):
       33-42; 5 (1943): 102-14. Especially valuable for
       translations of Aristotle's works.

396   Murphy, James J. "Aristotle's Rhetoric in the Middle
       Ages." *Quarterly Journal of Speech,* 52 (1966): 109-
       15.

397   Rose, Paul Lawrence, and Stillman Drake. "The Pseudo-
       Aristotelian 'Questions in Mechanics' in Renaissance
       Culture." *Studies in the Renaissance,* 18 (1971):
       65-104.

398   Schmitt, Charles B. *Aristotle and the Renaissance.*
       Cambridge, Mass.: Harvard University Press, 1983.

399   ————. "Aristotle as a Cuttlefish: the Origin and
       Development of a Renaissance Image." *Studies in the*
       Renaissance, 12 (1965): 60-72.

400   ————. *A Critical Survey and Bibliography of Studies*
       on Renaissance Aristotelianism, 1958-1969. Padua:
       Antenore, 1971.

401   Tigerstedt, E.N. "Observations on the Reception of the
       Aristotelian 'Poetics' in the Latin West." *Studies in*
       the Renaissance, 15 (1968): 7-24.

402 Van Steenberghen, F. *Aristotle in the West: The Origins of Latin Aristotelianism.* Trans. Leonard Johnston. Louvain: E. Nauwelaerts, 1955.

See also items 730, 1363, 1365, 1549, 2561, 2750.

Ausonius

403 Felber, Howard, and Sesto Prete. "Ausonius." *Catalogus Translationum et Commentariorum* (item 352), vol.4, pp.193-222.

404 Weiss, R. "Ausonius in the Fourteenth Century." *Classical Influences on European Culture A.D. 500-1500* (item 277), pp.67-72.

Boethius

405 Dean, Ruth J. "The Dedication of Nicholas Trevet's Commentary on Boethius." *Studies in Philology,* 63 (1966): 593-603. Includes edition of Latin text of dedication.

406 Fontaine, William Thomas. *Fortune, Matter, and Providence: A Study of Ancius Severincus, Boethius and Giordano Bruno.* Scotlandville, La.: Privately Printed, 1939.

407 Gibson, M.T., ed. *Boethius: His Life, Thought, and Influence.* Oxford: Blackwell, 1981.

408 Patch, Howard Rollin. *The Tradition of Boethius: A Study of His Importance in Medieval Culture.* New York: Oxford University Press, 1935.

409 Wilkins, E.H. "Lorenzo de' Medici and Boethius." *Modern Philology,* 15 (1917-1918): 255-56.

Caesar

410 Brown, Virginia. "Caesar." *Catalogus Translationum et Commentariorum* (item 352), vol.3, pp.87-140.

411 ————. "Portraits of Julius Caesar in Latin Manuscripts of the *Commentaries.*" *Viator,* 12 (1981): 319-54.

412   ————. *The Textual Transmission of Caesar's Civil
       War*. Leiden: Brill, 1972.

413   Gordon, D.J. "Giannotti, Michelangelo and the Cult of
       Brutus." *Fritz Saxl. 1890-1948* (item 283), pp.281-96.

414   Gundolf, Friedrich. *The Mantle of Caesar*, trans. Jacob
       Wittmer Hartmann. New York: Vanguard Press, 1928.
       Julius Caesar's history and legend into the Renais-
       sance and modern times. Especially good for Petrarch
       and the Middle Ages.

415   Webb, H.J. "English Translations of Caesar's *Com-
       mentaries* in the Sixteenth Century." *Philological
       Quarterly,* 28 (1949): 490-95.

Cato

416   Brown, Virginia. "Cato the Censor." *Catalogus Trans-
       lationum et Commentariorum* (item 352), vol.4, pp. 223-
       48.

Cato's Distichs

417   Chase, Wayland Johnson, trans. *The Distichs of Cato.
       A Famous Medieval Textbook*. Madison: University of
       Wisconsin Press, 1922.

418   Hazelton, R. "The Christianization of 'Cato': The
       Disticha Catonis in the Light of Late Mediaeval Com-
       mentaries." *Mediaeval Studies,* 19 (1957): 157-73.

Catullus

419   Ellis, Robinson. *Catullus in the XIVth Century*. Lon-
       don: Henry Frowde, 1905.

420   Gaisser, Judith Haig. "Catullus and His First Inter-
       preters: Antonius Parthenius and Angelo Poliziano."
       TAPA, 112 (1982): 83-106.

421   Harrington, K.P. *Catullus and His Influence*. New
       York: Cooper Square Publishers, 1963.

422   Morrison, Mary. "Catullus and the Poetry of the Renais-
       sance." *BHR,* 25 (1963): 25-56.

423   —————. "Catullus in the Neo-Latin Poetry of France
       before 1550." *BHR*, 17 (1955): 365-94.

424   Ullman, B.L. "Hieremias de Montagnone and His Citations
       from Catullus." *Classical Philology*, 5 (1910): 66-
       82; repr. in *Studies in the Italian Renaissance* (item
       203), pp.79-112.

See also item 1128.

       Cicero

425   Baron, Hans. "Cicero and the Roman Civic Spirit in the
       Middle Ages and the Early Renaissance." *BJRL*, 22
       (1938): 72-97; repr. in *Lordship and Community in
       Medieval Europe,* ed. F.L. Cheyette. New York: Holt,
       Rinehart, and Winston, 1968, pp.292-314.

426   Breen, Quirinus. "The 'Antiparadoxon' of Marcantonius
       Majoragius, or, A Humanist Becomes a Critic of Cicero
       as a Philosopher." *Studies in the Renaissance,* 5
       (1958): 37-48.

427   —————. "The 'Observationes in M.T. Ciceronem' of Marius
       Nizolius." *Studies in the Renaissance,* 1 (1954): 49-
       58.

428   Clarke, M.L. "Non Hominis Nomen, Sed Eloquentiae."
       Cicero, ed. T.A. Dorey. London: Routledge & Kegan
       Paul, 1964, pp.81-107. On Cicero's fortune as a
       model for Latin prose style from the Middle Ages
       into the modern era.

429   Colish, Marcia L. "Cicero's *De Officiis* and Machia-
       velli's *Prince*." *The Sixteenth-Century Journal,* 9
       (1978): 81-94.

430   Fahy, Conor. "The Composition of Ortensio Lando's Dia-
       logue 'Cicero Relegatus et Cicero Revocatus.'" *Italian
       Studies,* 30 (1975): 30-41.

431   Leighton, Robert F. "The Medicean MSS of Cicero's
       Letters." *TAPA*, 21 (1890): 59-87.

432   Martin, R.H. "A Twelfth-Century Manuscript of Cicero's
       De Officiis." *Classical Quarterly,* 45 (1951): 35-38.

433   Meador, Prentice A. "Rhetoric and Humanism in Cicero."
       Philosophy and Rhetoric, 3 (1970): 1-12.

434   Rolfe, John C. *Cicero and His Influence.* Boston:
       Marshall Jones Co., 1923.

435   Schmitt, Charles B. *Cicero Scepticus: A Study of the
       Influence of the 'Academica' in the Renaissance.* The
       Hague: Nijhoff, 1972.

436   Scott, Izora. *Controversies over the Imitation of
       Cicero.* New York: Teachers' College, Columbia Uni-
       versity, 1911.

437   Ward, J.O. "The Date of the Commentary on Cicero's
       De Inventione by Thierry of Chartres (ca. 1095-1190?)
       and the Cornifician Attack on the Liberal Arts."
       Viator, 3 (1972): 210-73.

438   Wertis, Sandra Karaus. "The Commentary of Bartolinus
       de Benincasa de Canulo on the *Rhetorica ad Herennium.*"
       Viator, 10 (1979): 283-310. Treats early fourteenth
       century Bolognese commentator including manuscripts
       with edition of the accessus.

See also items 1531, 2896.

        Epicurus

439   Allen, Don Cameron. "The Rehabilitation of Epicurus
       and His Theory of Pleasure in the Early Renaissance."
       Studies in Philology, 41 (1944): 1-15.

        Frontinus

440   Wood, Neal. "Frontinus as a Possible Source for
       Machiavelli's Method." *JHI,* 28 (1967): 243-48.

        Galen

441   Durling, Richard J. "A Chronological Census of Renais-
       sance Editions and Translations of Galen." *JWCI,* 24
       (1961): 230-305.

Gellius, Aulus

442 Baron, Hans. "Aulus Gellius in the Renaissance and a
Manuscript from the School of Guarino." *Studies in
Philology,* 68 (1951): 107-25; 69 (1952): 248-50; rev.
ed. in Hans Baron, *From Petrarch to Leonardo Bruni*
(item 1133), pp.196-215.

443 De la Mare, A.C., P.K. Marshall, and R.H. Rouse.
"Pietro da Montagnana and the Text of Aulus Gellius
in Paris B.N. lat. 13038." *Scriptorium,* 30 (1976):
219-24.

444 Martin, Janet. "Uses of Tradition: Gellius, Petronius,
and John of Salisbury." *Viator,* 10 (1979): 57-76.

Greek Anthology

445 Hutton, James. *The Greek Anthology in France and in
the Latin Writers of the Netherlands to the Year 1800.*
Ithaca: Cornell University Press, 1946.

446 ———. *The Greek Anthology in Italy to the Year 1800.*
Ithaca: Cornell University Press, 1935.

447 Saunders, Alison. "Alciati and the Greek Anthology."
JMRS, 12 (1982): 1-18.

Hesiod

448 West, M.L. "The Medieval Manuscript of the *Works and
Days.*" *Classical Quarterly,* n.s. 24 (1974): 161-85.

449 ———. "The Medieval and Renaissance Manuscripts of
Hesiod's *Theogony.*" *Classical Quarterly,* n.s. 14
(1964): 165-89.

Homer

450 Coulter, Cornelia C. "Boccaccio's Acquaintance with
Homer." *Philological Quarterly,* 5 (1926): 44-53.

451 Myres, Sir John L. *Homer and His Critics.* London:
Routledge & Kegan Paul, 1958.

452 Ross, James Bruce. "On the Early History of Leontius'
Translation of Homer." *Classical Philology,* 22
(1927): 341-55.

453   Rubinstein, Alice Levine. "Imitation and Style in
       Angelo Poliziano's *Iliad* Translation." *RQ,* 36 (1983):
       48-70.

454   Shepard, S. "Scaliger on Homer and Virgil: A Study of
       Literary Prejudice." *Emerita,* 29 (1961): 313-40.

See also item 1242.

Horace

455   Rand, E.K. "Horace and the Spirit of Comedy." *Rice
       Institute Pamphlet,* 24 (1937): 39-117. On Horace and
       Erasmus.

456   Saintonge, P.F., et al. *Horace: Three Phases of His
       Influence.* Chicago: University of Chicago Press, 1936.

Hyginus

457   Holzworth, Jean. "Light from a Medieval Commentary on
       the Text of *Fabulae* and *Astronomica* of Hyginus."
       Classical Philology, 38 (1943): 126-31.

Justinus

458   Ross, D.J.A. "An Illustrated Humanistic Manuscript of
       Justin's Epitome of the 'Historiae Philippicae' of
       Trogus Pompeius." *Scriptorium,* 10 (1956): 261-67.

Juvenal

459   Bühler, Curt F. "The Earliest Editions of Juvenal."
       Studies in the Renaissance, 2 (1955): 84-95.

460   Sanford, Eva M. "Giovanni Tortelli's Commentary on
       Juvenal." *TAPA,* 82 (1951): 207-18.

461   ————. "Juvenal." *Catalogus Translationum et Com-
       mentariorum* (item 352), vol.1, pp.175-238.

462   ————. "Renaissance Commentaries on Juvenal." *TAPA,*
       79 (1948): 92-112.

See also item 1644.

Laus Pisonis

463   Ullman, B.L. "The Text Tradition and Authorship of the
       Laus Pisonis." *Classical Philology,* 24 (1929):
       109-32.

Livy

464   Dean, Ruth J. "The Earliest Medieval Commentary on
       Livy--by Nicholas Trevet." *MH,* 3 (1945): 86-98;
       4 (1946): 110.

465   McDonald, A.H. "Livius." *Catalogus Translationum et
       Commentariorum* (item 352), vol.2, pp.331-48.

466   Ullman, B.L. "Poggio's Manuscripts of Livy." *Scrip-
       torium,* 19 (1965): 71-76; repr. in his *Studies in the
       Italian Renaissance* (item 203), pp.483-90.

467   ————. "Poggio's Manuscripts of Livy--Alleged and
       Actual." *Classical Philology,* 28 (1933): 282-88.

468   ————. "The Post Mortem Adventures of Livy." *Studies
       in the Italian Renaissance* (item 203), pp.53-77.

Lucan

469   Crosland, Jessie. "Lucan in the Middle Ages, with Some
       Special Reference to the Old French Epic." *Modern
       Language Review,* 25 (1930): 32-51.

Lucian

470   Allison, Francis G. *Lucian: Satirist and Artist.*
       Boston: Marshall Jones Co., 1926. See Chapter 8 on
       Lucian's legatées.

471   Duncan, Douglas. *Ben Jonson and the Lucianic Tradition.*
       Cambridge: Cambridge University Press, 1979.

472   Goldschmidt, E.Ph. "Lucian's 'Calumnia.'" *Fritz Saxl
       1890-1948* (item 283), pp.228-44.

473   Stevens, L.C. "The Reputation of Lucian in Sixteenth-
       Century France." *Studi francesi,* 33 (1967): 401-06.

474   Thompson, Craig R. *The Translations of Lucian by Erasmus*
      and St. Thomas More. Ithaca: Privately Printed, 1940.

See also items 2259, 2434, 2758.

Lucretius

475   Bloomfield, Morton. "The Source of Boccaccio's Filo-
      strato 3, 74-79 and Its Bearing on the MS Tradition
      of Lucretius' 'De Rerum Natura.'" *Classical Philology,*
      47 (1952): 162-65.

476   Fleischmann, Wolfgang B. "Lucretius." *Catalogus Trans-*
      lationum et Commentariorum (item 352), vol.2, pp.349-66.

477   Hadzsits, G.D. *Lucretius and His Influence.* New York:
      Longmans, Green & Co., 1935.

478   Lind, L.R. "Lucretius and the Modern World." *Res*
      Publica Litterarum, 3 (1980): 73-86.

479   Mustard, W.P. "Humanistic Imitations of Lucretius."
      Classical Weekly, 12 (1918-1919): 7-48.

480   Reeve, Michael. "The Italian Tradition of Lucretius."
      IMU, 23 (1980): 27-48.

Martial

481   Hausmann, F.R. "Martialis." *Catalogus Translationum et*
      Commentariorum (item 352), vol.4, pp.249-96.

482   Nixon, Paul. *Martial and the Modern Epigram.* New York:
      Longmans, Green & Co., 1927.

Martianus Capella

483   Lutz, Cora E. "Aesticampianus' Commentary on the *De*
      Grammatica of Martianus Capella." *RQ,* 26 (1973):
      157-66.

484   ————. *Essays on Manuscripts and Rare Books.* Hamden,
      Ct.: Archon, 1975. Collected important essays on
      Martianus Capella.

485   Quinn, Betty Nye. "Martianus Capella." *Catalogus*
      Translationum et Commentariorum (item 352), vol.2,
      pp.367-82.

486   Stahl, W.H., et al. *Martianus Capella and the Seven
       Liberal Arts.* Vol.1, *The Quadrivium of Martianus
       Capella.* New York: Columbia University Press, 1971.
       Important discussion of the use of *The Marriage of
       Philology and Mercury* in the Middle Ages.

       Ovid

487   Binns, J.W., ed. *Ovid.* London and Boston: Routledge
       and Kegan Paul, 1973. Essays by C. Jameson and D.M.
       Robathan.

488   Javitch, Daniel. "The Influences of the *Orlando Furi-
       oso* on Ovid's *Metamorphoses* in Italian." *JMRS,* 11
       (1981): 1-21.

489   Rand, Edward Kennard. *Ovid and His Influence.* New
       York: Longmans, 1928.

490   Robathan, D.M. "Introduction to the Pseudo-Ovidian
       De Vetula." *TAPA,* 88 (1957): 197-207. On MSS from
       the 13th-15th centuries.

491   Steiner, Grundy. "Source-Editions of Ovid's *Meta-
       morphoses* (1471-1500)." *TAPA,* 82 (1951): 219-31.

See also item 1649.

       Persius

492   Elder, J.P. "A Mediaeval Cornutus on Persius." *Spec-
       ulum,* 22 (1947): 240-48.

493   Robathan, D.M., and F. Edward Cranz. "Persius."
       Catalogus Translationum et Commentariorum (item 352),
       vol.3, pp.201-312.

       Petronius

494   De la Mare, A.C. "The Return of Petronius to Italy."
       *Medieval Learning and Literature. Essays Presented
       to R.W. Hunt,* ed. J.J.G. Alexander and M.T. Gibson.
       Oxford: Clarendon Press, 1976, pp.220-54.

495   Rini, Anthony. *Petronius in Italy.* New York: Cappa-
       bianca Press, 1937. From the thirteenth century to
       the present time.

496   Sage, Evan T. "Petronius, Poggio, and John of Salis-
       bury." *Classical Philology*, 11 (1916): 11-24.

497   Sochatoff, A. Fred. "Petronius." *Catalogus Transla-
       tionum et Commentariorum* (item 352), vol.3, pp.313-40.

498   Ullman, B.L. "Petronius in the Mediaeval *Florilegia*."
       Classical Philology, 25 (1930): 11-21.

499   ————. "The Text of Petronius in the Sixteenth
       Century." *Classical Philology*, 25 (1930): 128-54.

Plato

500   Bernard, Robert W. "Platonism--Myth or Reality in the
       Heptameron?" *The Sixteenth-Century Journal*, 5 (1974):
       3-14.

501   Cassirer, Ernst. *The Platonic Renaissance in England*,
       trans. J.P. Pettegrove. London: Nelson, 1953.

502   Dronke, Peter. *Fabula. Explorations into the Uses of
       Myth in Medieval Platonism*. Leiden: Brill, 1974.

503   Gersh, Stephen. "Platonism-Neoplatonism-Aristotelian-
       ism: A Twelfth-Century Metaphysical System and Its
       Sources." *Renaissance and Renewal in the Twelfth
       Century* (item 935), pp.512-34.

504   Klibansky, Raymond. *The Continuity of the Platonic
       Tradition during the Middle Ages: With a New Preface
       and Four Supplementary Chapters; together with Plato's
       Parmenides*. London: 1939; repr. Millwood, N.Y.:
       Kraus, 1982.

505   Kristeller, P.O. "Renaissance Platonism." *Facets of
       the Renaissance* (item 307), pp.87-107.

506   Novotny, F. *The Posthumous Life of Plato*. The Hague:
       Nijhoff, 1977.

507   Shorey, Paul. *Platonism, Ancient and Modern*. Berkeley:
       University of California Press, 1938.

508   Walker, Daniel Pickering. *The Ancient Theology: Stud-
       ies in Christian Platonism from the Fifteenth to the
       Eighteenth Century*. Ithaca: Cornell University Press,
       1972.

509 ———. "Orpheus the Theologian and the Renaissance
Platonists." *JWCI,* 16 (1953): 100-20.

See also items 1012, 1353, 1598-1599, 1610, 1656, 1752, 1754-
1756, 1764-1765, 1834, 2593-2594, 2787, 2965.

Plautus

510 Costa, C.D.N. "The Amphitryo Theme." *Roman Drama.*
Ed. T.A. Dorey and Donald R. Dudley. London: Routledge and Kegan Paul, 1965, pp.87-122. Plautus'
influence on later comedy.

511 Hough, John N. "Plautus, Student of Cicero, and
Walter Burley." *MH,* 11 (1957): 58-68.

512 Paster, Gail Stern. "The City in Plautus and Middle-
ton." *Renaissance Drama,* n.s. 6 (1973): 29-44.

513 Small, Jocelyn Penny. "Platus and the Three Princes of
Serendip." *RQ,* 29 (1976): 183-94.

514 Smith, Bruce R. "Sir Amorous Knight and the Indecorous
Romans; or, Plautus and Terence Play Court in the
Renaissance." *Renaissance Drama,* n.s. 6 (1973): 3-27.

Pliny the Elder

515 Campbell, D.J. "A Mediaeval Excerptor of the Elder
Pliny." *Classical Quarterly,* 26 (1932): 116-19.

516 Castiglioni, C. "The School of Ferrara and the Controversy on Pliny." *Science, Medicine and History.*
Essays on the Evolution of Scientific Thought and
Medical Practice Written in Honour of Charles Singer,
ed. E. Underwood. Oxford: Oxford University Press,
1953. Vol.2, pp.269-79.

517 Guder, E.W. "Pliny's *Historia Naturalis,* the Most Popular Natural History Ever Published." *Isis,* 6 (1924):
269-81.

518 Nauert, Charles G. "Humanists, Scientists, and Pliny:
Changing Approaches to a Classical Author." *American*
Historical Review, 84 (1979): 72-86.

519 ———. "Plinius Secundus." *Catalogus Translationum et*
Commentariorum (item 352), vol.4, pp.297-422.

Pliny the Younger

520   Boyer, Blanche B., and A.P. Dorjahn. "On the 1508
       Aldine Pliny." *Classical Philology*, 20 (1925): 50-61.

521   Merrill, Elmer Truesdell. "The Morgan Fragment of
       Pliny's Letters." *Classical Philology*, 18 (1923):
       97-119.

522   ————. "On the Early Editions of Pliny's Correspond-
       ence with Trajan." *Classical Philology*, 5 (1910):
       451-87.

523   ————. "On the Eight-Book Tradition of Pliny's *Letters*
       in Verona." *Classical Philology*, 5 (1910): 175-88.

524   Ullman, B.L. "Another 1508 Aldine Pliny." *Classical
       Philology*, 23 (1928): 138-74.

525   Winship, G.P. "The Aldine Pliny of 1508." *The Library*,
       ser.4, 6 (1925): 358-69.

       Plutarch

526   Russell, D.A. *Plutarch*. New York: Scribner's, 1973.
       See Chapter 9 on Plutarch's influence.

See also item 1385.

       Polybius

527   Momigliano, Arnaldo. "Polybius' Reappearance in Western
       Europe." *Polybe, Entretiens sur l'Antiquité Classique
       20*. Geneva: Vandoeuvre, 1973, pp. 347-72.

528   Moore, J.M. *The Manuscript Tradition of Polybius*.
       Cambridge: Cambridge University Press, 1965.

       Pomponius Mela

529   Milham, Mary Ella. "An Introduction to the Renaissance
       Tradition of Pomponius Mela." *Acta Conventus Neo-
       latini Amstelodamensis* (item 305), pp. 786-93.

Priscian

530   Gibson, M. "The Collected Works of Priscian: The Printed
         Editions 1470-1859." *Studi Medievali*, ser.3, 18.1
         (1977): 249-60.

531   Hunt, R.W. "Studies on Priscian in the Twelfth Century--
         II: The School of Ralph of Beauvais." *Mediaeval and
         Renaissance Studies,* 2 (1950): 1-56; repr. in Hunt,
         Grammar in the Middle Ages (item 598), pp.39-94.

532   ————. "Studies on Priscian in the Eleventh and
         Twelfth Centuries." *Mediaeval and Renaissance Studies,*
         1 (1943): 194-231; repr. in Hunt, *Grammar in the
         Middle Ages* (item 598), pp.1-38.

Protagoras

533   Trinkaus, Charles. "Protagoras in the Renaissance: An
         Exploration." *Philosophy and Humanism* (item 293),
         pp.190-213.

Prudentius

534   Gaston, Robert W. "Prudentius and Sixteenth-Century
         Antiquarian Scholarship." *MH,* n.s.4 (1973): 161-76.

Quintilian

535   Boskoff, Priscilla S. "Quintilian in the Late Middle
         Ages." *Speculum,* 27 (1952): 71-78.

536   Winterbottom, Michael. "Fifteenth-Century Manuscripts of
         Quintilian." *Classical Quarterly,* n.s.17 (1967):
         339-69.

See also item 1168.

Sallust

537   Archambault, P. "Sallust in France. Thomas Basin's
         Idea of History and of the Human Condition." *Papers
         on Language and Literature,* 4 (1968): 227-57.

538   McCuaig, W. "Bernard Rucellai and Sallust." *Rinasci-
         mento,* 2nd ser.22 (1982): 75-98.

539   Smalley, B. "Sallust in the Middle Ages." *Classical
       Influences on European Culture A.D. 500-1500* (item
       277), pp.165-75.

              Seneca: Tragedian and Philosopher, the Younger

540   Belsey, Catherine. "Senecan Vacillation and Eliza-
       bethan Deliberation: Influence or Confluence?"
       Renaissance Drama, n.s. 6 (1973): 65-88.

541   Binns, J.W. "Seneca and Neo-Latin Tragedy in England."
       Seneca, ed. C.D.N. Costa. London and Boston:
       Routledge and Kegan Paul, 1975, pp.205-34.

542   Cunliffe, John W. *The Influence of Seneca on Eliza-
       bethan Tragedy.* Hamden, Ct.: Archon, 1965.

543   Davis, Harold H. "An Unknown and Early Translation of
       Seneca's *De beneficiis.*" *The Huntington Library
       Quarterly,* 24 (1960/61): 137-44.

544   Gummere, Richard Mott. *Seneca the Philosopher and His
       Modern Message.* Boston: Marshall Jones Co., 1922.

545   Palmer, Ralph Graham. *Seneca's De remediis fortuitorum
       and the Elizabethans.* Chicago: Institute of Eliza-
       bethan Research, 1953. Includes Latin text and
       English translation of 1547.

546   Reynolds, L.D. "The Medieval Tradition of Seneca's
       Dialogues." *Classical Quarterly,* 18 (1968): 355-72.

547   ————. *The Medieval Tradition of Seneca's Letters.*
       Oxford: Clarendon Press, 1965.

548   Smith, Bruce R. "Toward the Rediscovery of Tragedy:
       Productions of Seneca's Plays on the English Renais-
       sance Stage." *Renaissance Drama,* n.s. 9 (1978): 3-37.

See also items 1525, 2038, 2421, 2440, 2768.

                          Seneca the Elder

549   Sussman, Lewis A. *The Elder Seneca.* Leiden: Brill,
       1978. See Chapter 6: "The Elder Seneca, Afterwards."

550   Wood, Neal. "Some Common Aspects of the Thought of
       Seneca and Machiavelli." *RQ,* 21 (1968): 11-23.

Sextus Empiricus

551 Schmitt, Charles B. "An Unstudied Fifteenth-Century
Latin Translation of Sextus Empiricus by Giovanni
Lorenzi (Vat. lat. 2990)." *Cultural Aspects of the
Italian Renaissance* (item 280), pp.244-61.

Silius Italicus

552 Bassett, Edward L., et al. "Silius Italicus." *Catalogus Translationum et Commentariorum* (item 352),
vol.3, pp.341-98.

Sophocles

553 Turyn, A. *Studies in the Manuscript-Tradition of the
Tragedies of Sophocles.* Illinois Studies in Language
and Literature, 36. Urbana: 1952.

Statius

554 Clogan, Paul. "The Latin Commentaries to Statius: A
Bibliographic Project." *Acta Conventus Neo-latini
Lovaniensis* (item 288), pp.149-57.

555 ――――. "The Manuscripts of Lactantius Placidus' Commentary on the 'Thebaid.'" *Scriptorium,* 22 (1968):
87-91.

556 Postgate, J.P. "The Manuscript Problem in the *Silvae*
of Statius." *Classical Review,* 17 (1903): 344-51.

557 Reeve, Michael. "Statius' *Silvae* in the Fifteenth
Century." *Classical Quarterly,* 27 (1977): 202-25.

See also item 1883.

Strabo

558 Diller, Aubrey, and P.O. Kristeller. "Strabo." *Catalogus Translationum et Commentariorum* (item 352),
vol.2, pp.225-34.

Suetonius

559 McGrath, Geraldine. "An Unknown Fourteenth-Century Commentary on Suetonius and Caesar." *Classical Philology,*
65 (1970): 182-85.

560   Ullman, B.L. "Pontano's Handwriting and the Leiden Manu-
      script of Tacitus and Suetonius." *IMU*, 2 (1959): 309-
      36.

      Tacitus

561   Allen, Walter, Jr. "Beatus Rhenanus, Editor of Tacitus
      and Livy." *Speculum*, 12 (1937): 382-85.

562   Burke, Peter. "Tacitism." *Tacitus*, ed. T.A. Dorey.
      New York: Basic Books, 1969, pp.149-71.

563   Coulter, C.C. "The Manuscripts of Tacitus and Livy in
      the Parva Libreria." *IMU*, 3 (1960): 281-86.

564   Haverfield, F. "Tacitus During the Late Roman Period."
      Journal of Roman Studies, 6 (1916): 196-201.

565   Momigliano, Arnaldo. "The First Political Commentary
      on Tacitus." *Journal of Roman Studies*, 37 (1947):
      91-101.

566   Oliver, R.P. "The First Medicean MS of Tacitus and the
      Titulature of Ancient Books." *TAPA*, 82 (1961): 232-61.

567   Schellhase, Kenneth C. *Tacitus in Renaissance Politi-
      cal Thought*. Chicago: University of Chicago Press,
      1977.

568   Whitfield, J.H. "Livy--Tacitus." *Classical Influences
      on European Culture A.D. 1500-1700* (item 278), pp.
      281-93.

      Terence

569   Beck, Ervin. "Terence Improved: The Paradigm of the
      Prodigal Son in English Renaissance Comedy." *Renais-
      sance Drama*, n.s. 6 (1973): 107-22.

570   Rand, E.K. "Early Mediaeval Commentaries on Terence."
      Classical Philology, 4 (1909): 359-89.

      Theophrastus

571   Boyce, B. *The Theophrastan Character in England to 1642*.
      Cambridge, Mass.: Harvard University Press, 1947.

572   Schmitt, Charles B.   "Theophrastus." *Catalogus Trans-
      lationum et Commentariorum* (item 352), vol.2, pp.239-
      322.

573   ———. "Theophrastus in the Middle Ages." *Viator*, 2
      (1971): 251-70.

      Thucydides

574   Powell, J.U. "The Papyri of Thucydides and the Trans-
      lation of Laurentius Valla." *Classical Quarterly*,
      23 (1929): 11-14.

      Tibullus

575   Ullman, B.L. "Achilles Statius' Manuscripts of Tibullus."
      Didascaliae: Studies in Honor of Anselm M. Albareda,
      ed. Sesto Prete. New York: Bernard M. Rosenthal,
      1961, pp.451-68.

576   ———. "Tibullus in the Mediaeval *Florilegia*."
      Classical Philology, 23 (1928): 128-74.

      Valerius Flaccus

577   Ullman, B.L. "Valerius Flaccus in the Mediaeval *Flor-
      ilegia*."   *Classical Philology*, 26 (1931): 21-30.

      Valerius Maximus

578   Belincourt, Marjorie A.   "The Relationship of Some
      Fourteenth-Century Commentaries on Valerius Maximus."
      Mediaeval Studies, 34 (1972): 361-87.

579   Schullian, D.M. "A Revised List of Manuscripts of
      Valerius Maximus." *Miscellanea Augusto Campana*.
      Padua: Antenore, 1980, pp.695-728.

      Varro

580   Weiss, R. "The Study of Varro at Montecassino in the
      Middle Ages." *Medium Aevum*, 16 (1947): 27-30.

      Virgil

581   Bruère, Richard T. "Virgil and Vida." *Classical
      Philology*, 61 (1966): 21-43.

582   Comparetti, Domenico. *Vergil in the Middle Ages,* trans.
       E.F.M. Benecke. London: Swan Sonnenschein & Co.,
       1895.

583   Crosland, Jessie. "Virgil and the Old French Epic."
       Modern Language Review, 23 (1928): 164-73.

584   Field, Arthur. "A Manuscript of Cristoforo Landino's
       First Lectures on Virgil, 1462-63. (Codex 1368,
       Biblioteca Casanatense, Rome)." *RQ,* 31(1978): 17-20.

585   Gardner, Edmund G. "Virgil in Italian Poetry." *Pro-
       ceedings of the British Academy,* 17 (1931): 75-101.

586   Harrison, I.E.L. "Virgil, Sebastian Brant, and Maxi-
       milian." *Modern Language Review,* 76 (1981): 99-115.

587   Nitchie, Elizabeth. *Vergil and the English Poets.* New
       York: Columbia University Press, 1919.

588   Spargo, John W. *Virgil the Necromancer: Studies in
       Virgilian Legends.* Cambridge, Mass.: Harvard Univer-
       sity Press, 1934.

589   Storer, W.H. *Virgil and Ronsard.* Paris: E. Champion,
       1923.

590   Ullman, B.L. "Virgil in Certain Mediaeval *Florilegia.*"
       Studi Medievali, 5 (1937): 59-66.

591   Upson, Hollis Ritchie. "Medieval Lives of Virgil."
       Classical Philology, 38 (1943): 103-11.

See also items 974, 1229.

Vitruvius

592   Ciapponi, Lucia A. "Vitruvius." *Catalogus Transla-
       tionum et Commentariorum* (item 352), vol.3, pp.399-
       410.

593   Krinsky, Carol H. "Seventy-Eight Vitruvius Manuscripts."
       JWCI, 30 (1967): 36-70.

VIII. GENRES, MOVEMENTS, AND INSTITUTIONS OF RENAISSANCE HUMANISM

This chapter is one of the longest, and certainly the most complicated, in this volume. An attempt has been made to cover the bibliography of Renaissance humanism as a program of learning, a field contributing to literature, music and the visual arts, and to its institutional context. Since the *studia humanitatis* both grew out of and transformed the older medieval system of the arts, this section begins with important studies in the Trivium of the seven liberal arts and then treats works in those fields comprising Renaissance humanism as an educational program: poetry, history, science, drama, and aesthetic theory. Finally, major works in those fields central to humanism are given: manuscript studies and handwriting, the birth and growth of printing, and the history of schools and universities. In this chapter no pretense can be made to complete coverage, though it is hoped that the major works in each area and standard guides and texts will be found. The objective has always been to list only those works which make a direct contribution to understanding humanism in its intellectual and institutional context.

A. THE VERBAL ARTS: THE TRIVIUM

1. GRAMMAR

594   Bursill-Hall, G.L. *Speculative Grammars of the Middle Ages: The Doctrine of "Partes orationis" of the Modistae.* The Hague: Mouton, 1971.

595   Clark, A.C. *The Cursus in Medieval and Vulgar Latin.* Oxford: Clarendon Press, 1910.

596   Clark, Victor Seldan. *Studies in the Latin of the Middle Ages and the Renaissance.* Lancaster, Pa.: New Era Printing Co., 1900.

597   Constable, Giles. *Letters and Letter-Collections, Typologie des sources du moyen age occidental, fasc.17.* Turnhout, Belgium: Brepols, 1976. Analyses medieval Latin epistolography.

598   Hunt, R.W. *Collected Papers on the History of Grammar in the Middle Ages,* ed. with introd. G.L. Bursill-Hall. Amsterdam: Benjamins, 1980.

599   Percival, W. Keith. "The *Artis Grammaticae Opusculum* of Bartolomeo Sulmonese: A Newly Discovered Latin Grammar of the Quattrocento." *RQ,* 31 (1978): 39-47.

600   ————. "The Grammatical Tradition and Rise of the Vernacular." *Current Trends in Linguistics 13, Historiography of Linguistics.* The Hague and Paris: Mouton, 1975, pp.321-75. Survey of humanist theories of grammar with full bibliography of sources and studies.

601   Plimpton, George Arthur. "Grammatical Manuscripts and Early Printed Grammars in the Plimpton Library." *TAPA,* 64 (1933): 150-78. Useful list from Donatus to sixteenth century.

602   Robins, Robert H. *Ancient and Mediaeval Grammatical*
      Theory in Europe with Particular Reference to
      Modern Linguistic Doctrine. London: Bell, 1951.

603   ————. *A Short History of Linguistics.* Bloomington:
      Indiana University Press, 1968.

604   Rothwell, William. "Lexical Borrowing in a Medieval
      Context." *BJRL,* 63 (1980-1981): 118-43.

605   Scaglione, Aldo D. *Ars Grammatica.* The Hague: Mouton,
      1970.

606   ————. *The Classical Theory of Composition from Its*
      Origins to the Present: A Historical Survey. Univer-
      sity of North Carolina Studies in Comparative Litera-
      ture, 53. Chapel Hill: University of North Carolina
      Press, 1972.

See also items 530-32, 897, 910, 914, 979, 1529.

2. LOGIC

607   Ashworth, E.J. "Agostino Nifo's Reinterpretation of
      Medieval Logic." *Rivista critica di storia della*
      filosofia, 31 (1976): 355-74.

608   ————. *Language and Logic in the Post-Medieval Period.*
      Synthèse Historical Library 12. Dordrecht and Boston:
      D. Reidel, 1974.

609   ————. *The Tradition of Medieval Logic and Specula-*
      tive Grammar. Subsidia Mediaevalia 9. Toronto:
      Pontifical Institute of Mediaeval Studies, 1978.

610   Henry, Desmond Paul. *Medieval Logic and Metaphysics: A*
      Modern Introduction. London: Hutchinson, 1972.

611   Jardine, L. "Humanism and Dialectic in Sixteenth-
      Century Cambridge: A Preliminary Investigation."
      Classical Influences on European Culture A.D. 1500-
      1700 (item 278), pp.141-54.

See also items 1976, 2519.

3. RHETORIC

612   Baldwin, Charles Sears. *Medieval Rhetoric and Poetic (to 1400) Interpreted from Representative Works.* New York: Macmillan, 1928; repr. Gloucester, Mass.: Peter Smith, 1959.

613   ————. *Renaissance Literary Theory and Practice.* New York: Columbia University Press, 1939.

614   Breen, Quirinus. "Three Renaissance Humanists on the Relation of Philosophy and Rhetoric." *Christianity and Humanism* (item 218), pp.1-68. On Pico, Ermolao Barbaro, and Melanchthon.

615   Cantimori, Delio. "Rhetoric and Politics in Italian Humanism." *JWI,* 1 (1937): 83-102.

616   Caplan, Harry. *Of Eloquence, Studies in Ancient and Mediaeval Rhetoric,* ed. with introd. Anne King and Helen North. Ithaca: Cornell University Press, 1970.

617   Clark, Donald Lemen. "Rhetoric and the Literature of the English Middle Ages." *Quarterly Journal of Speech,* 45 (1959): 19-28.

618   Faulhaber, Charles. *Latin Rhetorical Theory in Thirteenth and Fourteenth Century Castile.* Berkeley: University of California Press, 1972.

619   Grassi, Ernesto. "Can Rhetoric Provide a New Basis for Philosophy? The Humanist Tradition." *Philosophy and Rhetoric,* 11 (1978): 1-17, 75-97.

620   Grayson, Cecil. "Lorenzo, Machiavelli and the Italian Language." *Italian Renaissance Studies* (item 289), pp.410-32.

621   ————. *A Renaissance Controversy: Latin or Italian?* Oxford: Inaugural Lecture, 1960.

622   Hardison, O.B., Jr. "The Orator and the Poet: The Dilemma of Humanist Literature." *JMRS,* 1 (1971): 33-44.

623   Howell, W.S. "Poetics, Rhetoric, and Logic in Renaissance Criticism." *Classical Influences on European Culture A.D. 1500-1700* (item 278), pp.155-62.

624   ———. *Logic and Rhetoric in England, 1500-1700.*
       Princeton: Princeton University Press, 1965.

625   Kennedy, George A. *Classical Rhetoric and Its Christian
       and Secular Tradition from Ancient to Modern Times.*
       Chapel Hill: University of North Carolina Press, 1980.

626   Klein, Robert. "The Figurative Thought of the Renais-
       sance." *Diogenes,* 32 (Winter 1960): 107-23.

627   Lanham, Richard A. *The Motives of Eloquence, Literary
       Rhetoric in the Renaissance.* New Haven: Yale Univer-
       sity Press, 1976.

628   McKeon, Richard. "The Methods of Rhetoric and Philos-
       ophy: Invention and Judgment." *The Classical Tradi-
       tion* (item 306), pp.365-73.

629   ———. "Rhetoric in the Middle Ages." *Speculum,* 17
       (1942): 1-32.

630   Murphy, James J. "The Arts of Discourse, 1050-1400."
       Mediaeval Studies, 23 (1961): 194-205.

631   ———. *Medieval Eloquence: Studies in the Theory and
       Practice of Medieval Rhetoric.* Berkeley: University
       of California Press, 1978.

632   ———. *Rhetoric in the Middle Ages: A History of
       Rhetorical Theory from St. Augustine to the Renais-
       sance.* Berkeley: University of California Press,
       1974.

633   ———, ed. *Renaissance Eloquence: Studies in the
       Theory and Practice of Renaissance Rhetoric.*
       Berkeley and Los Angeles: University of California
       Press, 1983.

634   Ong, Walter J. *Ramus, Method, and the Decay of Dia-
       logue.* Cambridge, Mass.: Harvard University Press,
       1958.

635   Sloan, Thomas O. "Rhetoric and Meditation: Three Case
       Studies." *JMRS,* 1 (1971): 45-58.

636   Spencer, John R. "Ut rhetorica pictura." *JWCI,* 20
       (1957): 26-44.

637   Vickers, Brian. "Rhetorical and Anti-rhetorical
      Tropes: On Writing the History of *elocutio.*" *Com-
      parative Criticism, A Yearbook,* 3 (1981): 105-32.
      On Renaissance rhetorical theory.

638   Webb, Diana. "Eloquence and Education: A Humanist
      Approach to Hagiography." *Journal of Ecclesiastical
      History,* 31 (1980): 19-39.

See also items 118, 231, 390, 396, 1020-21, 1079, 1081, 1509.

              B. POETRY, POETICS AND LITERARY CRITICISM

639   Binns, J.W. "Alberico Gentili in Defense of Poetry and
      Acting." *Studies in the Renaissance,* 19 (1972):
      224-72.

640   Clements, Robert John. *Picta Poesis: Literary and
      Humanistic Theory in Renaissance Emblem Books.* Rome:
      Storia e Letteratura, 1960.

641   Deneef, A. Leigh. "Epideictic Rhetoric and the Renais-
      sance Lyric." *JMRS,* 3 (1973): 203-32.

642   Durling, Robert M. *The Figure of the Poet in the Renais-
      sance Epic.* Cambridge, Mass.: Harvard University
      Press, 1965.

643   Fucilla, Joseph G. "A Rhetorical Pattern in Renaissance
      and Baroque Poetry." *Studies in the Renaissance,* 3
      (1956): 23-48.

644   Giovanni, G. "Agnolo Segni and a Renaissance Defini-
      tion of Poetry." *Modern Language Quarterly,* 6 (1945):
      167-73.

645   ————. "Historical Realism and the Tragic Emotions in
      Renaissance Criticism." *Philological Quarterly,* 32
      (1953): 304-20.

646   Grant, W. Leonard. "The Neo-Latin 'Lusus Pastoralis' in
      Italy." *MH,* 11 (1957): 94-98.

647   ———. "Neo-Latin Biblical Pastorals." *Studies in
       Philology*, 58 (1961): 25-43. Includes bibliography
       from fourteenth to seventeenth century of studies,
       anthologies and texts.

648   ———. "Neo-Latin Verse-Traditions of the Bible."
       Harvard Theological Review, 52 (1959): 205-11.

649   ———. *Neo-Latin Literature and the Pastoral*. Chapel
       Hill: University of North Carolina Press, 1965.

650   ———. "New Forms of Neo-Latin Pastoral." *Studies in
       the Renaissance*, 4 (1957): 71-100.

651   Gravelle, Sarah Stever. "Humanist Attitudes to Conven-
       tion and Innovation in the Fifteenth Century." *JMRS*,
       11 (1981): 193-209.

652   Greene, Thomas M. *The Light in Troy, Imitation and
       Discovery in Renaissance Poetry*. New Haven: Yale
       University Press, 1982.

653   Greenfield, C.G. *Humanist and Scholastic Poetics,
       1250-1500*. Lewisburg, Pa.: Bucknell University Press,
       1981.

654   Hall, Vernon, Jr. "Decorum in Italian Renaissance Lit-
       erary Criticism." *Modern Language Quarterly*, 4 (1943):
       177-83.

655   ———. *Renaissance Literary Criticism: A Study of Its
       Social Content*. New York: Columbia University Press,
       1945.

656   Heninger, S.K., Jr. *Touches of Sweet Harmony: Pythagor-
       ean Cosmology and Renaissance Poetics*. San Marino,
       Ca.: Huntington Library, 1974.

657   Hudson, H.H. *The Epigram in the English Renaissance*.
       Princeton: Princeton University Press, 1947.

658   Hutton, James. *Essays on Renaissance Poetry*, ed. Rita
       Guerlac. Ithaca: Cornell University Press, 1980.

659   Kaiser, Leo M. "The Earliest Verse of the New World."
       RQ, 25 (Winter 1972): 429-40.

660   McFarlane, I.D. "Neo-Latin Literature and the Pastoral."
       Forum for Modern Language Studies, 3 (1967): 67-76.

661   Mustard, W.P. "Later Echoes of the Greek Bucolic Poets."
       American Journal of Philology, 30 (1909): 245-83.

662   Nichols, Fred J. "Conventions of Punctuation in Renais-
       sance Latin Poetry." *Acta Conventus Neo-Latini
       Amstelodamensis* (item 305), pp.835-50.

663   ————. "The Development of Neo-Latin Theory of the
       Pastoral in the Sixteenth Century." *HL,* 18 (1969):
       95-114.

664   Nichols, Stephen G., Jr. "A Poetics of Historicism?
       Recent Trends in Medieval Literary Study." *MH,* n.s.
       8 (1977): 77-101.

665   Patterson, Annabel M. *Hermogenes and the Renaissance.
       Seven Ideas of Style.* Princeton: Princeton University
       Press, 1970.

666   Pigman, G.W., III. "Versions of Imitation in the
       Renaissance." *RQ,* 33 (1980): 1-33.

667   Prete, Sesto. "Some Observations on Epigram in the
       Quattrocento." *Res Publica Litterarum,* 2 (1979):
       263-72.

668   Salman, Phillips. "Instruction and Delight in Medieval
       and Renaissance Criticism." *RQ,* 32 (1979): 303-32.

669   Scollen, Christine. *The Birth of the Elegy in France,
       1500-1550.* Geneva: Droz, 1967.

670   Smith, A.J. "Theory and Practice in Renaissance Poetry:
       Two Kinds of Imitation." *BJRL,* 47 (1964-65): 212-43.

671   Sparrow, John. "Renaissance Latin Poetry: Some Six-
       teenth-Century Latin Anthologies." *Cultural Aspects
       of the Italian Renaissance* (item 280), pp.386-405.

672   ————. "Latin Verses of the High Renaissance." *Italian
       Renaissance Studies* (item 289), pp.354-409.

673   Spitzer, Leo. "The Problem of Latin Renaissance Poetry."
       Studies in the Renaissance, 2 (1955): 118-38.

674   Thomson, D.F.S. "The Latin Epigram in Scotland: The
       Sixteenth Century." *Phoenix,* 11 (1957): 63-78.

675   Trapp, J.B. "The Owl's Ivy and the Poet's Bays."
       JWCI, 21 (1958): 227-55.

676   Trimpi, Wesley. "The Ancient Hypothesis of Fiction: An
       Essay on the Origins of Literary Theory." *Traditio,*
       27 (1971): 1-78.

677   ————. "The Meaning of Horace's 'Ut Pictura Poesis.'"
       JWCI, 36 (1972): 1-34.

678   ————. "The Quality of Fiction: The Rhetorical Trans-
       mission of Literary Theory." *Traditio,* 30 (1974):
       1-119.

679   Weinberg, Bernard. *A History of Literary Criticism in
       the Italian Renaissance.* Chicago: University of
       Chicago Press, 1961.

680   ————. "The Problem of Literary Aesthetics in Italy
       and France in the Renaissance." *Modern Language
       Quarterly,* 14 (1953): 448-56.

681   Williams, Ralph C. "Epic Unity as Discussed by Six-
       teenth-Century Critics in Italy." *Modern Philology,*
       18 (1920-1921): 383-400.

682   Williamson, Edward. "Form and Content in the Develop-
       ment of the Italian Renaissance Ode." *PMLA,* 65[1]
       (1950): 55-67.

683   Wilson, Harold. "Some Meanings of 'Nature' in Renais-
       sance Literary Theory." *JHI,* 2 (1491): 430-48.

See also items 401, 612-13, 925-26, 929, 995-96, 1098, 1345,
       1376, 1412, 1473, 2453, 2475, 2516, 2584.

C. HISTORY AND HISTORIOGRAPHY

684   Burke, Peter. *The Renaissance Sense of the Past.* New
       York: St. Martin's Press, 1970. An anthology of
       historical writings in translation.

685   ————. "The Sense of Historical Perspective in
       Renaissance Italy." *Cahiers d'histoire mondiale,* 11
       (1968-1969): 615-31.

686   ————. "A Survey of Popularity of Ancient Historians,
       1450-1700." *History and Theory,* 5 (1966): 135-52.

687   Cochrane, Eric. *Historians and Historiography in the
       Italian Renaissance.* Chicago: University of Chicago
       Press, 1981. A very useful compendium with some
       questionable judgments on the value of individual
       historians.

688   Dannenfeldt, Karl H. "The Renaissance and Pre-Classical
       Civilizations." *JHI,* 13 (1952): 435-49.

689   Erasmus, Hendrik J. *The Origins of Rome in Historiog-
       raphy from Petrarch to Perizonius.* Assen: Von Gorcum,
       1962.

690   Fryde, Edmund B. *Humanism and Renaissance Historiography.*
       London: Hambledon Press, 1983.

691   ————. *The Revival of 'Scientific' and Erudite His-
       toriography in the Earlier Renaissance.* Inaugural
       Lecture. Cardiff: University of Wales Press, 1974.

692   Gilbert, Felix. "The Renaissance Interest in History."
       Art, Science, and History in the Renaissance, ed.
       Charles S. Singleton. Baltimore: The Johns Hopkins
       Press, 1967, pp.373-87.

693   ————. *History: Choice and Commitment.* Cambridge,
       Mass.: Harvard University Press, 1977.

694   Gilmore, Myron P. "Freedom and Determinism in Renais-
       sance Historians." *Studies in the Renaissance,* 3
       (1956): 49-60; repr. *Humanists and Jurists* (item
       227).

695   Grafton, Anthony T.   "Joseph Scaliger and Historical
       Chronology." History and Theory, 14 (1975): 156-85.

696   Green, Louis. "Historical Interpretation in Fourteenth-
       Century Florentine Chronicles." JHI, 28 (1967):
       161-78.

697   Grendler, Paul F. "Francesco Sansovino and Italian
       Popular History 1560-1600." Studies in the Renais-
       sance, 16 (1969): 139-80.

698   Hay, Denys. Annalists and Historians: Western His-
       toriography from the Eighth to the Eighteenth
       Centuries. New York: Barnes and Noble, 1977.

699   ————. "History and Historians in France and England
       during the Fifteenth Century." BIHR, 35 (1962):
       111-27.

700   IJsewijn, J. "Humanistic Autobiography." Studia
       Humanitatis Ernesto Grassi zum 70. Geburtstag, ed.
       E. Hora and E. Kessler. Munich: Wilhelm Fink, 1973,
       pp.209-19.

701   Kelley, Donald R. "Legal Humanism and the Sense of
       History." Studies in the Renaissance, 13 (1966):
       184-99.

702   ————. "The Rise of Legal History in the Renaissance."
       History and Theory, 9 (1970): 174-94.

703   Reynolds, Beatrice R. "Latin Historiography: A Survey
       1400-1600." Studies in the Renaissance, 2 (1955):
       7-66.

704   ————. "Shifting Currents in Historical Criticism."
       JHI, 14 (1953): 471-92; repr. Renaissance Essays
       (item 290), pp.115-36.

705   Struever, Nancy S. The Language of History in the
       Renaissance: Rhetoric and Historical Consciousness
       in Florentine Humanism. Princeton: Princeton Univer-
       sity Press, 1970.

706   Sypher, G. Wylie. "Similarities between the Scientific
       and the Historical Revolutions at the End of the
       Renaissance." JHI, 26 (1965): 353-68.

707   Von Leyden, W. "Antiquity and Authority: A Paradox in
       the Renaissance Theory of History." *JHI,* 19 (1958):
       473-92.

708   Weisinger, Herbert. "Ideas of History during the
       Renaissance." *JHI,* 6 (1945): 415-35; repr. *Renais-
       sance Essays* (item 290), pp.74-94.

709   Wilcox, Donald J. *The Development of Florentine Human-
       ist Historiography in the Fifteenth Century.* Cam-
       bridge, Mass.: Harvard University Press, 1969.

See also items 227, 1019, 1035, 1058, 1123, 1192, 1316, 1329,
       1369, 1421, 2453, 2484, 2496, 2551, 2765, 2823, 2827-28,
       2885, 3027, 3074-75.

D. SCIENCE

710   Arber, Agnes R. *Herbals, Their Origin and Evolution, A
       Chapter in the History of Botany, 1470-1670.* Rev. ed.
       Cambridge: Cambridge University Press, 1938.

711   Brown, Harcourt. "The Renaissance and Historians of
       Science." *Studies in the Renaissance,* 7 (1960): 27-42.

712   Campbell, Anna M. *The Black Death and Men of Learning.*
       New York: Columbia University Press, 1935; repr. New
       York: AMS Press, 1966.

713   Cochrane, Eric. "Science and Humanism in the Italian
       Renaissance." *American Historical Review,* 81 (1976):
       139-57.

714   Crombie, A.C. *Medieval and Early Modern Science.* Rev.
       2nd ed. Garden City, N.Y.: Doubleday, 1959.

715   Edelstein, Ludwig. "Andreas Vesalius, the Humanist."
       Bulletin of the History of Medicine, 14 (1943): 547-
       61.

716   Garin, Eugenio. *Astrology in the Renaissance, The
       Zodiac of Life,* trans. Carolyn Jackson and June Allen.
       London and Boston: Routledge and Kegan Paul, 1983.

717   ———. *Science and Civic Life in the Italian Renais-
       sance (Scienza e vita civile nel Rinascimento ital-
       iano)*, trans. Peter Munz. Garden City, N.Y.: Double-
       day, 1969.

718   Hall, Marie Boas. *The Scientific Renaissance 1450-1630*.
       London: Fontana, 1962.

719   Heninger, S.K. *A Handbook of Renaissance Meteorology*.
       New York: Greenwood Press, 1968.

720   Keller, A.C. "Zilsel, the Artisans, and the Idea of
       Progress in the Renaissance." *JHI*, 11 (1950): 235-40.

721   Lemay, Richard. "The Teaching of Astronomy in Medieval
       Universities, Principally at Paris in the Fourteenth
       Century." *Manuscripta*, 20 (1976): 197-217.

722   McKeon, Richard. "Philosophy and the Development of
       Scientific Methods." *JHI*, 27 (1966): 3-22.

723   Molland, A.G. "Medieval Ideas of Scientific Progress."
       JHI, 39 (1978): 561-77. On Zilsel's thesis on
       scientific progress.

724   Oakeshott, Walter. "Some Classical and Medieval Ideas
       in Renaissance Cosmography." *Fritz Saxl, 1890-1948*
       (item 283), pp.245-60.

725   O'Malley, Charles D. *Andreas Vesalius of Brussels,
       1514-1564*. Berkeley: University of California Press,
       1964.

726   Patrides, C.A. "Renaissance Ideas on Man's Upright
       Form." *JHI*, 19 (1958): 256-58.

727   ———. "Renaissance Thought on the Celestial Hier-
       archy: The Decline of a Tradition." *JHI*, 20 (1959):
       155-66.

728   Popkin, Richard H. "The Pre-Adamite Theory in the
       Renaissance." *Philosophy and Humanism* (item 293),
       pp.50-69.

729   Randall, John Herman, Jr. "The Development of Scien-
       tific Method in the School of Padua." *JHI*, 1 (1940):
       177-206; repr. *Renaissance Essays* (item 290), pp.217-
       51.

730 ———. "Paduan Aristotelianism Reconsidered." *Philosophy and Humanism* (item 293), pp.275-82.

731 ———. *The School of Padua and the Emergence of Modern Science*. Padua: Antenore, 1961.

732 Reeds, K.M. "Renaissance Humanism and Botany." *Annals of Science*, 33 (1976): 519-42.

733 Rose, Paul Lawrence. "Humanist Culture and Renaissance Mathematics: The Italian Libraries of the 'Quattrocento.'" *Studies in the Renaissance*, 20 (1973): 46-105.

734 ———. *The Italian Renaissance of Mathematics: Studies on Humanists and Mathematicians from Petrarch to Galileo*. Geneva: Droz, 1975.

735 Rosen, Edward. "Maurolico's Attitude Toward Copernicus." *Proceedings of the American Philosophical Society*, 101 (1975): 177-94.

736 Sarton, George. *The Appreciation of Ancient and Medieval Science during the Renaissance (1450-1600)*. Philadelphia: University of Pennsylvania Press, 1950.

737 ———. *Six Wings: Men of Science during the Renaissance*. Bloomington: Indiana University Press, 1957.

738 Singer, Charles. "The Confluence of Humanism, Anatomy and Art." *Fritz Saxl, 1890-1948* (item 283), pp.261-69.

739 Siraisi, Nancy G. "The *Libri Morales* in the Faculty of Arts and Medicine at Bologna: Bartolomeo da Varignana and the Pseudo-Aristotelian Economics." *Manuscripta*, 20 (1976): 105-18.

740 ———. "The Music of Pulse in the Writings of Italian Academic Physicians (Fourteenth and Fifteenth Centuries)." *Speculum*, 50 (1975): 689-710.

741 ———. *Taddeo Alderotti and His Pupils, Two Generations of Italian Medical Learning*. Princeton: Princeton University Press, 1981.

742 Stillwell, Margaret B. *The Awakening Interest in Science during the First Century of Printing, 1450-1550*. New York: Bibliographical Society of America, 1970.

743   Thorndike, Lynn. *History of Magic and Experimental
       Science.* 8 vols. New York: Columbia University
       Press, 1923-58.

744   ———. *Science and Thought in the Fifteenth Century.*
       New York: Columbia University Press, 1929.

745   Vasoli, Cesare. "The Contribution of Humanism to the
       Birth of Modern Science." *Renaissance and Reforma-
       tion,* 15 (1979): 1-15.

746   Voise, Waldeman. "The Renaissance and the Sources of
       the Modern Social Sciences." *Diogenes,* 23 (Fall
       1958): 41-63.

747   Wightman, William Persehous Delisle. *Science and the
       Renaissance.* 2 vols. Aberdeen University Studies,
       143-144. Edinburgh: Oliver & Boyd, 1962.

748   Zilsel, Edgar. "The Genesis of the Concept of Scien-
       tific Progress." *JHI,* 6 (1945): 325-49.

See also items 397, 441, 516-18, 706, 894, 902, 1400-1, 2566.

                            E. DRAMA

749   Bergel, Lienhard. "The Horatians and the Curiatians in
       the Dramatic and Political-Moralistic Literature
       before Corneille." *Renaissance Drama,* n.s. 3 (1970):
       205-38.

750   Berrigan, Joseph R. "Early Neo-Latin Tragedy in Italy."
       Acta Conventus Neo-latini Lovaniensis (item 288),
       pp.85-93.

751   ———. "Latin Tragedy of the Quattrocento." *HL,* 22
       (1973): 1-9.

752   Bradner, Leicester. "A Check-list of Original Neo-
       Latin Dramas by Continental Writers Printed before
       1650." *PMLA,* 582 (1943): 621-33.

753   ———. "Desiderata for the Study of Neo-Latin Drama."
       Research Opportunities in Renaissance Drama, 6 (1963):
       17-20.

754   ————. "The Latin Drama of the Renaissance (1314-
       1650)." *Studies in the Renaissance,* 4 (1957): 31-70.

755   ————. "The Rise of Secular Drama in the Renaissance."
       Studies in the Renaissance, 3 (1956): 7-22.

756   Clubb, Louis George. *Italian Plays (1500-1700) in the
       Folger Library: A Bibliography with Introduction.*
       Florence: Olschki, 1968.

757   Cole, Howard C. "Bernardo Accolti's Virginia: The
       Uniqueness of Unico Aretino." *Renaissance Drama,*
       n.s. 10 (1979): 3-32.

758   Corrigan, Beatrice. *Catalogue of Italian Plays, 1500-
       1700, in the Library of the University of Toronto.*
       Toronto: University of Toronto Press, 1961.

759   ————. "Italian Renaissance Plays." *Renaissance
       News,* 16 (1963): 298-307.

760   ————. "Tasso's Erminia in the Italian Theater of the
       Seicento." *Renaissance Drama,* 7 (1964): 127-50.

761   Gilbert, Allan H. "Fortune in the Tragedies of
       Giraldi Cintio." *Philological Quarterly,* 20 (1941):
       224-35.

762   Greenwood, David. "The Staging of Neo-Latin Plays in
       Sixteenth-Century England." *Educational Theatre
       Journal,* 16 (1964): 311-23.

763   Harbage, A. "A Census of Anglo-Latin Plays." *PMLA,*
       53 (1938): 624-29.

764   Hardison, O.B., Jr. *Christian Rite and Christian Drama
       in the Middle Ages, Essay in the Origin and Early
       History of Modern Drama.* Baltimore: Johns Hopkins
       Press, 1965.

765   Herrick, Marvin T. "Hyrcanian Tigers in Renaissance
       Tragedy." *The Classical Tradition* (item 306),
       pp.559-71.

766   ————. *Italian Comedy in the Renaissance.* Urbana:
       University of Illinois Press, 1965.

767   ————. *Italian Plays, 1500-1700, in the University of Illinois Library.* Urbana: University of Illinois Press, 1966.

768   ————. "Opportunities for Research in the Italian Drama of the Renaissance." *Research Opportunities in Renaissance Drama,* 6 (1963): 21-23.

769   ————. *Tragicomedy: Its Origin and Development in Italy, France, and England.* Urbana: University of Illinois Press, 1955.

770   Priest, Harold M. "Marino, Leonardo, Francini, and the Revolving Stage." *RQ,* 35 (1982): 36-61.

771   Radcliff-Umstead, Douglas. *The Birth of Modern Comedy in Renaissance Italy.* Chicago: University of Chicago Press, 1969.

772   Schuster, Louis A. "Pioneering in Neo-Latin Drama." *Research Opportunities in Renaissance Drama,* 6 (1963): 14-17.

773   Steadman, John M. "Iconography and Renaissance Drama: Ethical and Mythological Themes." *Research Opportunities in Renaissance Drama,* 13 (1970): 73-122.

774   Sticca, Sandro. *The Latin Passion Play: Its Origin and Development.* Albany: State University of New York Press, 1970.

775   ————, ed. *The Medieval Drama. Papers of the Third Annual Conference of the Center for Medieval and Early Renaissance Studies, State University of New York at Binghamton,* 1969. Albany: State University of New York Press, 1972.

776   Stratman, Carl Joseph. *Bibliography of Medieval Drama.* New York: Frederick Ungar, 1972.

777   Tydeman, William. *The Theatre in the Middle Ages: Western European Stage Conditions, c.800-1576.* Cambridge: Cambridge University Press, 1978.

778   Young, Karl. *The Drama of the Medieval Church.* Oxford: Clarendon Press, 1933.

See also items 511-14, 540-42, 548, 569, 1016, 2407.

F. THE FINE ARTS

779   Alpatov, Mikhail Vladmirovich. "Allegory and Symbol-
      ism in Italian Renaissance Painting." *Diogenes*, 76
      (Winter 1971): 1-25.

780   Argan, Giulio Carlo. "The Architecture of Brunelleschi
      and the Origins of Perspective Theory in the Fifteenth
      Century." *JWCI*, 9 (1946): 96-121.

781   Barasch, Meshe. "Character and Physiognomy: Bucchi on
      Donatello's St. George, A Renaissance Text on Expres-
      sion in Art." *JHI*, 36 (1975): 413-30.

782   Baxandall, Michael. "Bartholomaeus Facius on Painting."
      JWCI, 27 (1964): 90-107.

783   ────────. *Painting and Experience in Fifteenth-Century
      Italy: A Primer in the Social History of Pictorial
      Style*. Oxford: Clarendon Press, 1972.

784   Blunt, Anthony. *Artistic Theory in Italy, 1450-1600*.
      Oxford: Clarendon Press, 1940.

785   Brown, Howard M. *Music in the Renaissance*. Englewood
      Cliffs, N.J.: Prentice-Hall, 1970.

786   Carpenter, Nan Cooke. *Music in the Medieval and
      Renaissance Universities*. Norman: University of
      Oklahoma Press, 1972.

787   Cast, David. "Liberty: Virtue: Honor: A Comment on the
      Position of the Visual Arts in the Renaissance." *Yale
      Italian Studies*, 1 (1977): 371-97. On humanist inter-
      pretations of the arts. See also Baxandall (item 783).

788   Close, A.J. "Commonplace Theories of Art and Nature in
      Classical Antiquity and in the Renaissance." *JHI*,
      30 (1969): 467-86.

789   Comito, Terry. "Renaissance Gardens and the Discovery
      of Paradise." *JHI*, 32 (1971): 483-506.

790   Dempsey, Charles. "Mythic Inventions in Counter-
      Reformation Painting." *Rome in the Renaissance* (item
      300), pp.55-75.

791   Dent, Edward J. "Music of the Renaissance in Italy."
      Proceedings of the British Academy, 19 (1933): 293-
      317.

792   Drake, Stillman. "Renaissance Music and Experimental
      Science." *JHI,* 31 (1970): 483-500.

793   Edgerton, Samuel. "The Art of Renaissance Picture-
      making and the Great Western Age of Discovery."
      Essays Presented to Myron P. Gilmore (item 275),
      vol. II, pp.133-54.

794   ————. *The Renaissance Rediscovery of Linear Perspec-
      tive.* New York: Basic Books, 1975.

795   Fenlon, Iain, ed. *Music in Medieval and Early Modern
      Europe: Patronage, Sources, and Texts.* Cambridge:
      Cambridge University Press, 1980.

796   Gombrich, E.H. *The Heritage of Apelles.* Ithaca:
      Cornell University Press, 1971.

797   ————. *"Icones symbolicae*: The Visual Image in Neo-
      Platonic Thought." *JWCI,* 11 (1948): 163-92.

798   ————. *Ideals and Idols.* Oxford: Phaidon, 1979.

799   ————. *Norm and Form, Studies in the Art of the
      Renaissance.* London: Phaidon, 1966.

800   ————. "Personification." *Classical Influences on
      European Culture, A.D. 500-1500* (item 277), pp.247-57.

801   ————. *Symbolic Images.* London: Phaidon, 1972.

802   ————. "The Early Medici as Patrons of Art." *Italian
      Renaissance Studies* (item 289), pp.279-311.

803   Hatfield, Rab. "The Compagnia de' Magi." *JWCI,* 33
      (1970): 107-61.

804   Hughes, A., and G. Abrahams, eds. *Ars Nova and the
      Renaissance, 1300-1540.* Oxford History of Music, 3.
      New York: Oxford University Press, 1960.

805   Jenkins, A.D. Fraser. "Cosimo de' Medici's Patronage of
      Architecture and the Theory of Magnificence." *JWCI,*
      33 (1970): 162-70.

806   Kiefer, Frederick. "The Conflation of Fortuna and
       Occasio in Renaissance Thought and Iconography."
       JMRS, 9 (1979): 1-27.

807   Kristeller, Paul Oskar. "The Modern System of the Arts:
       A Study in the History of Aesthetics." *JHI,* 12
       (1951): 496-527; 13 (1952): 17-46; repr. in *Renais-
       sance Thought II* (item 193), pp.163-227.

808   ———. "Music and Learning in the Early Italian
       Renaissance." *Journal of Renaissance and Baroque
       Music,* 1 (1946-1947): 255-74; repr. *Renaissance
       Thought II* (item 193), pp.142-62.

809   Lee, Rensselaer W. *Ut pictura poesis*: *The Humanistic
       Theory of Painting.* New York: Norton, 1963.

810   Lowinsky, Edward E. "Music in the Culture of the
       Renaissance." *JHI,* 15:4 (1954): 509-53; repr. *Renais-
       sance Essays* (item 290), pp.337-81.

811   Panofsky, Dora and Erwin. *Pandora's Box, The Changing
       Aspects of a Mythical Symbol.* 2nd ed. New York:
       Harper and Row, 1965.

812   Panofsky, Erwin. *Meaning in the Visual Arts.* Garden
       City, N.Y.: Doubleday, 1955.

813   ———. *Renaissance and Renascences in Western Art.*
       Stockholm: Almqvist and Wisell, 1960; repr. New York:
       Harper and Row, 1971.

814   ———. *Studies in Iconology: Humanistic Themes in the
       Art of the Renaissance.* New York: Oxford University
       Press, 1939; repr. New York: Harper and Row, 1962.

815   Parronchi, Alessandro. "The Language of Humanism and
       the Language of Sculpture." *JWCI,* 27 (1964): 108-36.

816   Partridge, Loren, and Randolph Starn. *A Renaissance
       Likeness: Art and Culture in Raphael's Julius II.*
       Berkeley: University of California Press, 1980.

817   Pignatti, Terisio. "The Relationship between German and
       Venetian Painting in the Late Quattrocento and Early
       Cinquecento." *Renaissance Venice* (item 284), pp.244-
       73.

818   Reese, Gustav. *Music in the Renaissance*, rev. ed.
        New York: Norton, 1959.

819   Riess, Jonathan B. "The Civic View of Sculpture in
        Alberti's *De re aedificatoria*." *RQ*, 32 (1979): 1-17.

820   Saxl, Fritz. *Lectures*, 2 vols. London: The Warburg
        Institute, 1957.

821   Scott, Geoffrey. *The Architecture of Humanism*. 2nd ed.
        London: Constable, 1924.

822   Seznec, Jean. *The Survival of the Pagan Gods: The
        Mythological Tradition and Its Place in Renaissance
        Humanism and Art,* trans. Barbara F. Sessions. New
        York: Pantheon Books, 1953; repr. New York: Harper
        Torch, 1961.

823   Snyder, Susan. "The Left Hand of God: Despair in
        Medieval and Renaissance Tradition." *Studies in the
        Renaissance,* 12 (1965): 18-59.

824   Sternfeld, F.W., ed. *Music from the Middle Ages to the
        Renaissance*. New York: Praeger, 1973.

825   Sypher, Wylie. *Four Stages of Renaissance Style: Trans-
        formation in Art and Literature, 1400-1700*. Garden
        City, N.Y.: Doubleday, 1955.

826   Walker, D.P. *Studies in Musical Science in the Late
        Renaissance*. London: Warburg Institute, University
        of London, 1978.

827   Westfall, Carroll W. "Society, Beauty, and the Human-
        ist Architect in Alberti's 'De re aedificatoria.'"
        Studies in the Renaissance, 16 (1969): 61-79.

828   White, John. *The Birth and Rebirth of Pictorial Space*.
        London: Faber & Faber, 1957; repr. New York: Harper
        and Row, 1967.

829   ————. "Developments in Renaissance Perspective."
        JWCI, 12 (1949): 58-79.

830   Wind, Edgar. *Pagan Mysteries in the Renaissance,* rev.
        ed. New York: W.W. Norton and Co., 1968.

831   Wittkower, Rudolf. "Alberti's Approach to Antiquity in
      Architecture." *JWCI,* 4 (1940-1941): 1-18.

832   ————. *Allegory and the Migration of Symbols.* London:
      Thames and Hudson, 1977.

833   ————. *Architectural Principles in the Age of Human-
      ism,* 3rd ed. London: A. Tirandi, 1962.

834   ————. "Individualism in Art and Artist: A Renais-
      sance Problem." *JHI,* 22 (1961): 291-302.

See also items 132, 381, 384, 1047, 1181, 1247, 1398, 1424,
      1573-74, 1774-75, 2072, 2181, 2985.

G.   MANUSCRIPTS AND HANDWRITING

835   Coulter, Cornelia Catilin. "The Library of the Angevin
      Kings at Naples." *TAPA,* 75 (1944): 141-55.

836   De la Mare, A.C. *The Handwriting of Italian Humanists,*
      vol.1, fasc.1. Oxford: Association Internationale de
      Bibliophilie, 1973. From Petrarch to Giorgio Antonio
      Vespucci with plates, and discussions of changes in
      hand. Includes Boccaccio, Salutati, and Poggio.

837   ————, and D.F.S. Thomson. "Poggio's Earliest Manu-
      script?" *IMU,* 16 (1973): 179-96.

838   Diller, A. "The Autographs of Georgius Pletho."
      Scriptorium, 10 (1956): 27-41.

839   Dunston, A.J. "The Hand of Poggio." *Scriptorium,* 19
      (1965): 63-70.

840   Elder, John P. "Clues for Dating Florentine Humanistic
      Manuscripts." *Studies in Philology,* 44 (1947): 127-
      39.

841   Grant, Leonard W. "Neo-Latin Materials at St. Louis."
      Manuscripta, 4 (1960): 3-18.

842   Kristeller, Paul O. "Tasks and Experiences in the Study
      of Humanist Manuscripts." *Renaissance News,* 2 (1954):
      75-84.

843   ———. "Renaissance Research in Vatican Manuscripts."
         Manuscripta, 1 (1957): 67-80.

844   ———. "Methods of Research in Renaissance Manuscripts."
         Manuscripta, 19 (1975): 3-14.

845   Morison, Stanley. "Early Humanistic Script and the
         First Roman Type." *The Library,* ser.4, 24 (1943-1944):
         1-29.

846   Robathan, Dorothy M. "The Catalogues of the Princely
         and Papal Libraries of the Italian Renaissance."
         TAPA, 64 (1933): 138-49.

847   ———. "Libraries of the Italian Renaissance." *The
         Medieval Library,* ed. J.W. Thompson. Chicago: Uni-
         versity of Chicago Press, 1939, pp.509-89.

848   Saenger, Paul. "Silent Reading: Its Impact on the Late
         Medieval Script and Society." *Viator,* 13 (1982):
         367-414. On the new form of the manuscript book
         brought about by silent reading.

849   Ullman, B.L. "More Humanistic Manuscripts." *Callig-
         raphy and Paleography, Essays Presented to Alfred
         Fairbank.* London: Faber and Faber, 1965, pp.47-53.

850   ———. *The Origin and Development of Humanistic
         Script.* Rome: Storia e Letteratura, 1960.

851   Wardrop, James. *The Script of Humanism.* Oxford:
         Clarendon Press, 1963.

See also items 114-16, 448-49, 458, 480, 484, 560, 563, 566,
         1167, 1188, 1197, 1236-37, 1317, 1340, 1442, 1477, 1493,
         1505-6, 2725.

                              H. PRINTING

852   Brown, Horatio R.F. *The Venetian Printing Press.*
         London: J.C. Nimmo, 1891.

853   Bühler, Curt F. *Early Books and Manuscripts.* New York:
         Pierpont Morgan Library, 1973.

854   ———. *The Fifteenth-Century Book: The Scribes, the Printers, the Decorators*. Philadelphia: University of Pennsylvania Press, 1960.

855   ———. *The University and the Press in Fifteenth-Century Bologna*. Notre Dame: Mediaeval Institute, University of Notre Dame, 1958.

856   Butler, Pierce. *The Origin of Printing in Europe*. Chicago: University of Chicago Press, 1940.

857   Eisenstein, Elizabeth L. *The Printing Press as an Agent of Change*, 2 vols. Cambridge: Cambridge University Press, 1979.

858   ———. "The Advent of Printing and the Problem of the Renaissance." *Past and Present*, 45 (1969): 19-89.

859   Febvre, Lucien P.V., and H.J. Martin. *The Coming of the Book: The Impact of Printing, 1450-1900*, trans. D. Gerard. London: N.L.B., 1976.

860   Gerulaitis, Leonardas V. "The Ancestry of Aldus Manutius." *Renaissance News*, 19 (1966): 1-12.

861   ———. *Printing and Publishing in Fifteenth-Century Venice*. Chicago: American Library Association, 1976.

862   Goldschmidt, E.P. *Medieval Texts and Their First Appearance in Print*. London: Bibliographical Society, 1943.

863   ———. *Printed Book of the Renaissance*. Cambridge: Cambridge University Press, 1950.

864   Grendler. Paul F. *The Roman Inquisition and the Venetian Press, 1540-1605*. Princeton: Princeton University Press, 1977.

865   *Gutenburg Documents*, ed. Karl Schorbach, trans. Douglas C. McMurtie. New York: Oxford University Press, 1941.

866   Hirsch, Rudolph. *Printing, Selling and Reading 1450-1550*. Wiesbaden: Harrassowitz, 1967.

867   Lowry, M.L.C. *The World of Aldus Manutius, Business and Scholarship in Renaissance Venice*. Oxford: Blackwell, 1979.

868   ————. "Two Great Venetian Libraries in the Age of
       Aldus Manutius." *BJRL*, 57 (1974): 128-66.

869   ————. "The New Academy of Aldus Manutius, A Renais-
       sance Dream." *BJRL*, 58 (1976): 378-420.

870   Noakes, Susan. "The Development of the Book Market in
       Late Quattrocento Italy: Printer's Failures and the
       Role of the Middleman." *JMRS*, 11 (1981): 23-55.

871   Pettas, W. "Niklaos Sophianos and Greek Printing in
       Rome." *The Library*, ser.5, 29 (1974): 206-13.

872   Proctor, Robert George Collier. *The Printing of Greek
       in the Fifteenth Century*. Oxford: Clarendon Press,
       1900; repr. Hildesheim: George Olms, 1966.

873   Rabb, Theodore K. "The Advent of Printing and the
       Problem of the Renaissance: A Comment." *Past and
       Present*, 52 (August, 1971): 135-40.

874   Robertson, E. "Aldus Manutius, the Scholar-Printer,
       1450-1515." *BJRL*, 33 (1950): 57-73.

875   Root, P.K. "Publication before Printing." *PMLA*, 28
       (1913): 417-31.

876   Scholderer, Victor. "Printers and Readers in Italy in
       the Fifteenth Century." *Proceedings of the British
       Academy*, 35 (1949): 25-47.

877   ————. *Fifty Essays on Fifteenth-and-Sixteenth-Century
       Bibliography*. Amsterdam: Menno Hertzberger, 1966.

878   Schutte, Anne Jacobsen. "Printing, Piety, and the
       People in Italy: The First Thirty Years." *ARG*, 71
       (1980): 5-20.

879   Stillwell, Margaret B. *The Beginning of the World of
       Books, 1450 to 1470*. New York: Bibliographical
       Society of America, 1972.

See also items 351, 357, 520, 524-25, 742, 1437, 2831.

I. *SCHOOLS AND UNIVERSITIES*

880   Baldwin, John W., and Richard A. Goldthwaite, eds.
       Universities in Politics, Case Studies from the Late
       Middle Ages and Early Modern Period. Baltimore: Johns
       Hopkins Press, 1972.

881   Brucker, Gene. "A Civic Debate on Florentine Higher
       Education." *RQ,* 34 (1981): 517-33.

882   Cobban, Alan B. "Medieval Student Power." *Past and*
       Present, 53 (November 1971): 28-66.

883   ————. *The Medieval Universities: Their Development*
       and Organization. London: Methuen, 1975.

884   Courtenay, William J. "The Effect of the Black Death
       on English Higher Education." *Speculum,* 55 (1980):
       696-714.

885   Daly, L.J. *The Medieval University, 1200-1400.* New
       York: Sheed and Ward, 1961.

886   Gabriel, Astrik L. "The Ideal Master of the Mediaeval
       University." *Catholic Historical Review,* 60 (1974):
       1-40.

887   Gross, Charles. "The Political Influence of the Uni-
       versity of Paris in the Middle Ages." *American His-*
       torical Review, 6 (1900/1901): 440-45.

888   *History of Universities.* Avebury, England: 1981-.
       Annual edited by Charles Schmitt of the Warburg
       Institute; includes essays and review articles on
       recent work.

889   Jacob, E.F. "On the Promotion of English University
       Clerks in the Later Middle Ages." *Journal of Eccles-*
       iastical History, 1 (1950): 172-86.

890   Kagan, Richard L. *Students and Society in Early Modern*
       Spain. Baltimore: Johns Hopkins University Press,
       1974.

891   ————. "Universities in Castile 1500-1700." *Past and*
       Present, 49 (November 1970): 44-71.

892   Kibre, Pearl. *Scholarly Privileges in the Middle Ages.*
       Cambridge, Mass.: Mediaeval Academy of America, 1962.

893   Kristeller, Paul Oskar. "Learned Women of Early Modern
       Europe: Humanists and University Scholars." *Beyond
       Their Sex* (item 291), pp.91-116.

894   ————. "The School of Salerno: Its Development and
       Its Contribution to the History of Learning." *Bulle-
       tin of the History of Medicine,* 17 (1945): 138-94.

895   ————. "The University of Bologna and the Renaissance."
       *Studi e memorie per la storia dell' Università di
       Bologna,* n.s. 1 (1956): 313-23.

896   Mead, H.R. "Fifteenth-Century Schoolbooks." *The
       Huntington Library Quarterly,* 3 (1939/1940): 37-42.

897   Paetow, Louis J. *The Arts Course at Medieval Universi-
       ties with Special Reference to Grammar and Rhetoric.*
       Champaign, Ill.: University of Illinois Press, 1910.

898   Park, Katharine. "The Readers at the Florentine Studio
       According to Communal Fiscal Records (1357-1380,
       1413-1446)." *Rinascimento,* 20 (1980): 249-310.

899   Radcliff-Umstead, Douglas, ed. *The University World, A
       Synoptic View of Higher Education in the Middle Ages
       and Renaissance.* Pittsburg: Medieval and Renaissance
       Studies Committee, University of Pittsburg, 1973.

900   Rashdall, Hastings. *Universities of Europe in the
       Middle Ages,* ed. F.M. Powicke and A.B. Emden, 3 vols.
       Oxford: Clarendon Press, 1936.

901   Rouse, Richard H. "The Early Library of the Sorbonne."
       Scriptorium, 21 (1967): 42-71; 227-51.

902   Schmitt, Charles B. "Philosophy and Science in Six-
       teenth-Century Universities: Some Preliminary Comments."
       The Cultural Context of Medieval Learning (item 297),
       pp.485-537.

903   Siraisi, Nancy G. *Arts and Sciences at Padua: The
       Studium of Padua before 1350.* Toronto: Pontifical
       Institute of Mediaeval Studies, 1973.

904   Swanson, R.N. *Universities, Academics and the Great
       Schism.* Cambridge: Cambridge University Press, 1979.

905   Woodward, William H. *Studies in Education during the
       Age of the Renaissance, 1400-1600.* Cambridge: At the
       University Press, 1906; repr. New York: Columbia
       Teachers' College, 1967.

See also items 338, 741, 855, 869, 955, 980, 1296, 1322, 1335,
       1404, 1461, 1475, 1514, 1519, 1538, 1543, 1548, 1620,
       1665, 1674, 2518-19, 2599-2601, 2646, 2776, 3034.

IX. THE MEDIEVAL BACKGROUND

Any worthwhile study of Renaissance humanism must be made
against developments in medieval intellectual life, especially
the movement known as the Renaissance of the twelfth century.
In this section are listed the English translations of the
principal medieval antecedents of Renaissance humanism, including Alan of Lille, John of Salisbury, and Richard of Bury.
I have also included several volumes of translation of medieval Latin verse. For background studies of medieval culture,
the reader should turn to studies by Artz, Baldwin, Gilson
and Southern, and, perhaps, consult older works by Rand and
H.O. Taylor. The Carolingian Renaissance is well treated by
Laistner, Munz and Riché, while, for the twelfth century, see
works by Haskins, Brooke, Southern, and Liebeschütz. For
Latin poetry, consult the standard studies of Raby, Dronke,
Stock, and Wetherbee. Study in the sources and scholarship
on the Carolingian period, the twelfth century, Latin poetry
and learning should prepare one well for understanding the
dawn of humanism in Italy at the beginning of the fourteenth
century.

A. SOURCES

906   Alan of Lille. *The Complaint of Nature,* trans. Douglas
      M. Moffat. New York: Henry Holt & Co., 1908.

907   ———. *The Plaint of Nature,* trans. James J. Sheridan.
      Mediaeval Sources in Translation, 26. Toronto: Pon-
      tifical Institute of Mediaeval Studies, 1980.

908   ———. *The Anticlaudian of Alain de Lille: Prologue,
      Argument, and Nine Books,* trans. William Hafner Cornog.
      Philadelphia: University of Pennsylvania Press, 1935.

909   ———. *Anticlaudianus: or The Good and Perfect Man by
      Alan of Lille,* trans. James J. Sheridan. Toronto:
      Pontifical Institute of Mediaeval Studies, 1973.

910   Andeli, Henri d'. *The Battle of the Seven Arts,* trans.
      L.J. Paetow. Berkeley: University of California
      Press, 1914.

911   Andreas Capellanus. *The Art of Courtly Love,* trans.
      J.J. Parry. New York: Columbia University Press,
      1941; repr. New York: Norton, 1969.

912   Bernardus Silvestris. *The Cosmographia of Bernardus
      Silvestris,* trans. with introd. Winthrop Wetherbee.
      New York: Columbia University Press, 1973.

913   Boncompagno da Signa. *Rota Veneris,* repr. of the
      Strassburg Incunabulum with introd., trans., and
      notes by J. Purket. Delmar, N.Y.: Scholars' Fac-
      similes and Reprints, 1975.

914   Hugh of St. Victor. *The Didascalicon, A Medieval Guide
      to the Arts,* trans. Jerome Taylor. New York: Columbia
      University Press, 1961.

915   Joannes de Garlandia. *Morale scolarium of John of
      Garland*, trans. Louis John Paetow. Berkeley: Uni-
      versity of California Press, 1927.

916   John of Salisbury. *Letters*, ed. and trans. W.J.
      Millor, S.J., H.E. Butler, and C.N.L. Brooke.
      2 vols. London: Nelson, 1955; Oxford: Oxford Uni-
      versity Press, 1979.

917   ————. *Memoirs of the Papal Court*, ed. and trans.
      M. Chibnall. London: Nelson, 1956.

918   ————. *Metalogicon*, trans. D. McGarry. Berkeley and
      Los Angeles: University of California Press, 1955;
      repr. Westport, Ct.: Greenwood, 1982.

919   ————. *Frivolities of Courtiers and Footprints of
      Philosophers, Being a Translation of the First, Sec-
      ond, and Third Books and Selections from the Seventh
      and Eighth Books of the Policraticus of John of
      Salisbury*, trans. Joseph B. Pike. Minneapolis: Uni-
      versity of Minnesota Press, 1938; repr. New York:
      Octagon Books, 1972. Together with the *Statesman's
      Book*, comprises a complete translation of the *Poli-
      craticus*.

920   ————. *The Statesman's Book of John of Salisbury,
      Being the Fourth, Fifth, and Sixth Books, and Selec-
      tions from the Seventh and Eighth Books, of the
      Policraticus*, trans. John Dickenson. New York:
      Knopf, 1927; repr. New York: Russell and Russell,
      1963.

921   ————. *Statesman's Book (Policraticus)*, ed. and
      abridged M.F. Markland. New York: Ungar, 1980.

922   Nigel Longchamp. *The Book of Daun Burnel the Ass,
      Nigellus Wireker's Speculum stultorum*, trans. with
      introd. G.W. Regenos. Austin: University of Texas
      Press, 1959.

923   ————. *A Mirror of Fools (Speculum stultorum)*, ed.
      and trans. John Henry Mozley. Notre Dame, Ind.:
      University of Notre Dame Press, 1963.

924   Richard of Bury. *The Philobiblon*, trans. E.C. Thomas
      with Latin text. New York: Lockwood and Coombe,
      1889; repr. without Latin text, London: Chatto and

Windus, 1911 and 1925. *Richard de Bury, Philobiblon, Latin text and translation,* ed. E.C. Thomas with introd. M. Maclagan. Oxford: Blackwell, 1960.

925   Whicher, George F., trans. *The Goliard Poets, Medieval Latin Songs and Satires.* Cambridge, Mass.: Privately Printed, 1949.

926   Zeydel, Edwin H., trans. *Vagabond Verse, Secular Poems of the Middle Ages.* Detroit: Wayne State University Press, 1966.

B. STUDIES

927   Allen, Judson Boyce. *The Ethical Poetic in the Later Middle Ages: A Decorum of Convenient Distinction.* Toronto: University of Toronto Press, 1982.

928   ————. *The Friar as Critic: Literary Attitudes in the Later Middle Ages.* Nashville: Vanderbilt University Press, 1971.

929   Allen, Philip Schuyler. *Medieval Latin Lyric.* Chicago: University of Chicago Press, 1931.

930   Artz, Frederick Binkerd. *The Mind of the Middle Ages: An Historical Survey.* 3rd ed. rev. New York: Knopf, 1958.

931   Atkins, J.W.H. *English Literary Criticism: The Medieval Phase.* London: Methuen, 1952.

932   Baldwin, John W. "Masters at Paris from 1179 to 1215: A Social Perspective." *Renaissance and Renewal in the Twelfth Century* (item 935), pp. 138-72.

933   ————. *The Scholastic Culture of the Middle Ages, 1000-1300.* Lexington, Mass.: Heath, 1971.

934   Benson, Robert L. "Political *Renovatio*: Two Models from Roman Antiquity." *Renaissance and Renewal in the Twelfth Century* (item 935), pp.339-86.

935   ———, and Giles Constable, eds. *Renaissance and Re-
       newal in the Twelfth Century.* Cambridge, Mass.:
       Harvard University Press, 1982.

936   Benton, John F. "Consciousness of Self and Perceptions
       of Individuality." *Renaissance and Renewal in the
       Twelfth Century* (item 935), pp.263-95.

937   Berrigan, Joseph R. *Medieval Intellectual History: A
       Primer.* Lawrence, Kan.: Coronado Press, 1974.

938   Bloch, Herbert. "The New Fascination with Ancient Rome."
       Renaissance and Renewal in the Twelfth Century (item
       935), pp.615-36.

939   Bloomfield, Morton W. *The Seven Deadly Sins: An Intro-
       duction to the History of a Religious Concept, with
       Special Reference to Medieval English Literature.*
       East Lansing, Mich.: Michigan State College Press,
       1952.

940   Breen, Quirinus. "The Twelfth-Century Revival of the
       Roman Law." *Christianity and Humanism* (item 218),
       pp.131-82.

941   Brooke, C. *The Twelfth Century Renaissance.* London:
       Thames and Hudson, 1969.

942   Chaytor, Henry John. "The Medieval Reader and Textual
       Criticism." *BJRL,* 26 (1941): 49-56.

943   Chenu, Marie-Dominique. *Nature, Man, and Society in the
       Twelfth Century. Essays on New Theological Perspec-
       tives in the Latin West,* trans. Jerome Taylor and
       Lester K. Little. Chicago: University of Chicago
       Press, 1968. Especially Chapter I. Nature and Man--
       The Renaissance of the Twelfth Century, pp.1-48.

944   Clagett, M., et al, eds. *Twelfth-Century Europe and the
       Foundations of Modern Society.* Madison: University of
       Wisconsin Press, 1961.

945   Clarke, Maude Violet. *The Medieval City-State: an
       Essay on Tyranny and Federation in the Later Middle
       Ages.* London: Methuen, 1926.

946   Classen, Peter. "*Res gestae,* Universal History, Apoc-
       alypse: Visions of Past and Future." *Renaissance and
       Renewal in the Twelfth Century* (item 935), pp.387-417.

947   Constable, Giles. "The Popularity of Twelfth-Century
       Spiritual Writers in the Late Middle Ages." *Renais-
       sance Studies in Honor of Hans Baron* (item 296),
       pp.3-28.

948   Courcelle, Pierre. *Late Latin Writers and Their Greek
       Sources,* trans. H.E. Wedeck. Cambridge, Mass.:
       Harvard University Press, 1969.

949   Curtius, Ernst Robert. *European Literature and the
       Latin Middle Ages,* trans. W.R. Trask. New York:
       Pantheon Books, 1953; repr. New York: Harper Torch-
       books, 1963.

950   ————. "The Medieval Basis of Western Thought."
       Gesammelte Aufsätze zur romanischen Philologie.
       Bern and Munich: Francke, 1960, pp.28-39.

951   Dronke, Peter. *Medieval Latin and the Rise of the
       European Love-Lyric,* 2 vols. New York: Oxford Uni-
       versity Press, 1968.

952   Duckett, E.S. *Carolingian Portraits, A Study in the
       Ninth Century.* Ann Arbor: University of Michigan
       Press, 1962. Vignettes of leaders of the Carolingian
       Renaissance.

953   Economou, George D. *The Goddess Natura in Medieval
       Literature.* Cambridge, Mass.: Harvard University
       Press, 1972.

954   Friedman, John Block. *Orpheus in the Middle Ages.*
       Cambridge, Mass.: Harvard University Press, 1970.

955   Gabriel, Astrik. *The Educational Ideas of Vincent of
       Beauvais.* Notre Dame: Mediaeval Institute of the
       University of Notre Dame, 1956.

956   Gilson, Etienne Henri. *History of Christian Philosophy
       in the Middle Ages.* New York: Random House, 1955.

957   Graus, F. "Social Utopias in the Middle Ages." *Past
       and Present,* 38 (December 1967): 3-19.

958   Häring, Nikolaus M. "Commentary and Hermeneutics."
       Renaissance and Renewal in the Twelfth Century (item
       935), pp.173-200.

959   Haskins, Charles Homer. *The Renaissance of the Twelfth Century*. Cambridge, Mass.: Harvard University Press, 1927.

960   ———. *Studies in Medieval Culture*. Oxford: Oxford University Press, 1929.

961   Helin, Maurice. *A History of Medieval Latin Literature*, rev. ed. and trans. Jean Chapman Snow. New York: Salloch, 1949.

962   Hendley, Brian. "John of Salisbury and the Problem of Universals." *Journal of the History of Philosophy*, 8 (1970): 289-302.

963   Hunt, R.W. "English Learning in the Late Twelfth Century." *Transactions of the Royal Historical Society*, ser.4, 19 (1936): 19-35.

964   Jackson, William Thomas Hobdell. *The Literature of the Middle Ages*. New York: Columbia University Press, 1960.

965   ———. "The *De Amore* of Andreas Capellanus and the Practice of Love at Court." *Romanic Review*, 49 (1958): 243-51.

966   ———. "The Politics of a Poet: The Archipoeta as Revealed in His Imagery." *Philosophy and Humanism* (item 293), pp.320-38.

967   Kitzinger, Ernst. "The Arts as Aspects of a Renaissance: Rome and Italy." *Renaissance and Renewal in the Twelfth Century* (item 935), pp. 637-70.

968   Knowles, Dom David. *The Evolution of Medieval Thought*. Baltimore: Helicon Press, 1962.

969   ———. *The Historian and Character*. Cambridge: Cambridge University Press, 1963. Important essays on medieval humanism and figures of the twelfth century Renaissance.

970   Ladner, Gerhart B. "Terms and Ideas of Renewal." *Renaissance and Renewal in the Twelfth Century* (item 935), pp.1-33.

971   Laistner, Max Ludwig Wolfram. *Thought and Letters of*
       Western Europe, A.D. 500 to 900, rev. ed. Ithaca:
       Cornell University Press, 1957.

972   Leclercq, Dom Jean. *The Love of Learning and the Desire*
       for God. New York: New American Library, 1961.

973   Leff, Gordon. *Heresy in the Later Middle Ages,* 2 vols.
       New York: Barnes and Noble, 1967.

974   Lerar, Seth. "John of Salisbury's Virgil." *Vivarium,*
       20 (1982): 24-39.

975   Lewis, C.S. *The Discarded Image.* Cambridge: Cambridge
       University Press, 1964.

976   Liebeschütz, Hans. *Medieval Humanism in the Life and*
       Writings of John of Salisbury. Studies of the
       Warburg Institute, vol.17. London: University of
       London Press, 1950; repr. with additions, New York:
       Kraus, 1968.

977   ————. "John of Salisbury and Pseudo-Plutarch." *JWCI,*
       6 (1943): 33-39.

978   Linder, A. "The Knowledge of John of Salisbury in the
       Late Middle Ages." *Studi medievali,* ser.3, 18.2
       (1977): 315-66.

979   Lutz, Cora E. "Remigius' Ideas on the Classification of
       the Seven Liberal Arts." *Traditio,* 12 (1956): 65-86.

980   McCarthy, Joseph M. *Humanistic Emphases in the Educa-*
       tional Thought of Vincent of Beauvais. Leiden: Brill,
       1976.

981   McKeon, Richard. "The Organization of Sciences and the
       Relations of Cultures in the Twelfth and Thirteenth
       Centuries." *The Cultural Context of Medieval Learn-*
       ing (item 297), pp.151-92.

982   ————. "Poetry and Philosophy in the Twelfth Century:
       The Renaissance of Rhetoric." *Modern Philology,* 43
       (1946): 217-34.

983   Martin, Janet. "Classicism and Style in Latin Litera-
       ture." *Renaissance and Renewal in the Twelfth Cen-*
       tury (item 935), pp.537-68.

984   Mierow, Charles Christopher. "Mediaeval Latin Vocabu-
      lary, Usage, and Style as Illustrated by the *Philo-
      biblon* (1345) of Richard de Bury." *Classical Philology*,
      25 (1930): 343-57.

985   Minnis, Alistair. *Medieval Theory of Authorship: Scho-
      lastic Literary Attitudes in the Later Middle Ages*.
      Berkeley and Los Angeles: University of California
      Press, 1982.

986   Morris, Colin. *The Discovery of the Individual, 1050-
      1200*. New York: Harper and Row, 1972.

987   Munz, Peter. *Life in the Age of Charlemagne*. London:
      Batsford, 1969.

988   Murdoch, John E. "From Social into Intellectual Factors:
      An Aspect of the Unitary Character of Late Medieval
      Learning." *The Cultural Context of Medieval Learning*
      (item 297), pp.271-348.

989   Murray, Alexander. *Reason and Society in the Middle
      Ages*. Oxford: Clarendon Press, 1978.

990   Mynors, R.A.B. "The Latin Classics Known to Boston of
      Bury." *Fritz Saxl, 1890-1948* (item 283), pp.199-217.

991   Patch, Howard R. *The Other World*. Cambridge, Mass.:
      Harvard University Press, 1950.

992   ————. *The Goddess Fortuna in Medieval Literature*.
      Cambridge, Mass.: Harvard University Press, 1927.

993   Piehler, Paul. *The Visionary Landscape, A Study in
      Medieval Allegory*. London: Edward Arnold, 1971.
      Perceptive essay on twelfth-century Latin poetry.

994   Poole, Reginald Lane. *Illustrations of the History of
      Medieval Thought and Learning*, 2nd ed. London:
      Society for Promoting Christian Knowledge, 1920.

995   Raby, F.J.E. *A History of Christian-Latin Poetry from
      the Beginning to the Close of the Middle Ages*, 2nd
      ed. Oxford: Clarendon Press, 1953.

996   ————. *A History of Secular Latin Poetry in the Middle
      Ages*, 2 vols. Oxford: Clarendon Press, 1934. 2nd ed.
      Oxford: Clarendon Press, 1957.

997   Rand, E.K. *Founders of the Middle Ages.* Cambridge,
       Mass.: Harvard University Press, 1928; repr. New
       York: Dover, 1958.

998   Riché, Pierre. *Education and Culture in the Barbarian
       West, Sixth through Eighth Centuries,* trans. J.J.
       Contreni. Columbia: University of South Carolina
       Press, 1976.

999   Robertson, D.W., Jr. "The Subject of *De Amore* of
       Andreas Capellanus." *Modern Philology,* 50 (1953):
       145-61.

1000   Saxl, Fritz, with appendices by O. Kurz. "A Spiritual
       Encyclopaedia of the Later Middle Ages." *JWCI,* 5
       (1942): 83-142.

1001   Setton, Kenneth M. "From Medieval to Modern Library."
       *Proceedings of the American Philosophical Associa-
       tion,* 104 (1960): 371-90.

1002   Smalley, Beryl. *The Study of the Bible in the Middle
       Ages.* Oxford: Blackwell, 1952.

1003   Southern, R.W. *The Making of the Middle Ages.* New
       Haven: Yale University Press, 1953.

1004   ———. *Medieval Humanism and Other Studies.* Oxford:
       Blackwell, 1970.

1005   ———. "The Schools of Paris and the Schools of
       Chartres." *Renaissance and Renewal in the Twelfth
       Century* (item 935), pp.113-37.

1006   Stock, Brian. *Myth and Science in the Twelfth Century,
       A Study of Bernard Sylvester.* Princeton: Princeton
       University Press, 1972.

1007   Summers, Walter C. "John of Salisbury and the Classics."
       Classical Quarterly, 4 (1910): 103-05.

1008   Thompson, James Westfell, et al. *The Medieval Library.*
       Chicago: University of Chicago Press, 1938.

1009   Ullmann, W. "John of Salisbury's *Policraticus* in the
       Later Middle Ages." *Geschichtsschreibung und Geist-
       iges Leben im Mittelalter: Festschrift für Heinz
       Löwe,* ed. K. Hauck and H. Mordek. Cologne and Vienna,
       Böhlau, 1978, pp.519-45.

1010   Waddell, Helen. *The Wandering Scholars*, 6th ed.
         London: Constable, 1932.

1011   Wallach, Luitpold. *Alcuin and Charlemagne: Studies in
         Carolingian History and Literature*. Ithaca: Cornell
         University Press, 1959.

1012   Webb, Clement. *John of Salisbury*. London: Methuen,
         1932.

1013   Wetherbee, Winthrop. *Platonism and Poetry in the
         Twelfth Century*. Princeton: Princeton University
         Press, 1972.

1014   ————. "The Function of Poetry in *De planctu naturae*
         of Alain of Lille." *Traditio*, 25 (1969): 96-99.

See also items 349, 364, 370, 437, 444, 469, 492, 502-3,
     531-32, 629, 1264, 1328.

X.   THE DAWN OF HUMANISM IN ITALY

Humanism was born in Italy in the cities of Padua, Bologna, and Verona at the beginning of the fourteenth century, fostered by amateur classicists and manuscript hunters, who were drawn from the professional classes, lawyers, notaries, and merchants of the Italian middle class. The principal investigator of early Italian humanism has been Roberto Weiss, an Italian literary scholar who became an Oxford don; his brilliant sketch, *The Dawn of Humanism in Italy*, is the starting point for further study. Consult also the important studies of J.R. Berrigan on humanism in Verona, of C.T. Davis on Florence, and for background and the social context, the works of J.K. Hyde.

A. SOURCES

1015   Colonne, Guido delle. *Historia Destructionis Troia,*
       trans. Mary Elizabeth Meek. Bloomington: Indiana
       University Press, 1974.

1016   Legnano, Giovanni da. *Tractatus de bello, de repre-*
       saliis et de duello by Giovanni da Legnano, ed.
       Thomas Erskine Holland. Oxford: Oxford University
       Press, 1917.

1017   Mussato, Albertino. *Eccerinis, Albertino Musatto/*
       Antonio Loschi, Achilles, trans. J.R. Berrigan.
       Munich: W. Fink, 1975. Reprint of the 1903 edition
       of L. Padrin of Mussato's first Latin tragedy of the
       Renaissance played for the first time in 1315 with
       Berrigan's translation on facing pages.

1018   Virgilio, Giovanni del. "Eclogues," trans. in *Dante*
       and Giovanni del Virgilio (item 1078).

B. STUDIES

1019   Andrews, R.A. "A Note on the Text of Antonio da
       Tempo's 'Summa Artis Rithmici Vulgaris Dictaminis.'"
       Italian Studies, 20 (1970): 30-39.

1020   Aquilecchia, G. "Dante and the Florentine Chroniclers."
       BJRL, 48 (1965-66): 30-55.

1021   Banker, James R. "The *Ars Dictaminis* and Rhetorical
       Textbooks at the Bolognese University in the Four-
       teenth Century." *MH,* n.s. 5 (1974): 153-68.

1022   ————. "Giovanni di Bonandrea and Civic Values in
        the Context of the Italian Rhetorical Tradition."
        Manuscripta, 18 (1974): 3-20.

1023   Baxandall, Michael. *Giotto and the Orators, Humanist
        Observers of Painting in Italy and the Discovery of
        Pictorial Composition 1350-1450.* Oxford-Warburg
        Studies, 6. Oxford: Clarendon Press, 1971.

1024   Berrigan, Joseph R. "Benzo D'Alessandria and the
        Cities of Northern Italy." *SMRH,* 4 (1967): 125-93.

1025   ————. "The Prehumanism of Benzo D'Alessandria."
        Traditio, 25 (1969): 249-63.

1026   ————. "The *Eccerinis.* A Prehumanist View of Tyranny."
        Delta Epsilon Sigma Bulletin, 12 (October 1967):
        71-86.

1027   Bowsky, William. *Henry VIII in Italy: The Conflict of
        Empire and City-State, 1310-1313.* Lincoln: Univer-
        sity of Nebraska Press, 1960.

1028   Carmody, F.J. "Latin Sources of Brunetto Latini's
        World History." *Speculum,* 11 (1936): 359-69.

1029   Coopland, G.W. "An Unpublished Work of John of Legnano:
        The 'Somnium' of 1373." *Nuovi Studi Medievali,* 2
        (1926): 65-88. Includes an edition of the work.

1030   Davis, Charles T. "An Early Florentine Political
        Theorist: Fra Remigio De' Girolamo." *Proceedings
        of the American Philosophical Society,* 104 (1960):
        662-77.

1031   ————. "Education in Dante's Florence." *Speculum,*
        40 (1965): 415-35.

1032   ————. "Ptolemy of Lucca and the Roman Republic."
        Proceedings of the American Philosophical Society,
        118 (1974): 30-50.

1033   ————. "Roman Patriotism and Republican Propaganda:
        Ptolemy of Lucca and Pope Nicholas III." *Speculum,*
        50 (1975): 411-33.

1034   Dean, Ruth J. "Cultural Relations in the Middle Ages:
        Nicholas Trevet and Nicholas of Prato." *Studies in
        Philology*, 44 (1947): 541-64.

1035   Ermatinger, Charles J. "Averroism in Early Fourteenth
        Century Bologna." *Mediaeval Studies*, 16 (1954): 35-
        56.

1036   Fisher, Craig B. "The Pisan Clergy and an Awakening
        of Historical Interest in a Medieval Commune."
        SMRH, 3 (1966): 141-221.

1037   Hankey, A.T. "Domenico di Bandino of Arezzo." *Italian
        Studies*, 12 (1957): 110-28.

1038   ————. "The Library of Domenico di Bandino." *Rinas-
        cimento*, 8.2 (1957): 177-208.

1039   ————. "Riccobaldo of Ferrara, Boccaccio and Domen-
        ico di Bandino." *JWCI*, 21 (1958): 507-23.

1040   ————. "The Successive Revisions and Surviving
        Codices of the *Fons Memorabilium Universi* of Domen-
        ico di Bandino." *Rinascimento*, 11 (1960): 3-50.

1041   Hyde, J.K. "Contemporary Views on Faction and Civil
        Strife in Thirteenth and Fourteenth Century Italy."
        *Violence and Civil Disorder in Italian Cities, 1200-
        1500*, ed. L. Martines. Berkeley and Los Angeles:
        University of California Press, 1972, pp.273-307.

1042   ————. "Medieval Descriptions of Cities." *BJRL*, 48
        (1965-1966): 308-40.

1043   ————. *Padua in the Age of Dante*. New York: Barnes
        and Noble, 1966. Chapter 10 on the dawn of the
        Renaissance.

1044   ————. *Society and Politics in Medieval Italy: The
        Evolution of the Civil Life*. London: Macmillan,
        1973. Excellent introduction to the political and
        cultural context of the early Italian Renaissance.

1045   ————. "Some Uses of Literacy in Venice and Florence
        in the Thirteenth and Fourteenth Centuries." *TRHS*,
        ser.5, 29 (1979): 109-28.

1046   Kristeller, Paul Oskar. "A Philosophical Treatise
        from Bologna Dedicated to Guido Cavalcanti: Magis-
        ter Jacobus de Pistorio and His 'Questio de Feli-
        citate.'" *Medioevo e Rinascimento* (item 294), vol.1,
        pp.427-63.

1047   Larner, John. "The Artist and the Intellectuals in
        Fourteenth Century Italy." *History*, 54 (1969): 13-
        30.

1048   ————. "Boccaccio and Lovato Lovati." *Cultural
        Aspects of the Italian Renaissance* (item 280), pp.22-
        32.

1049   Leff, Gordon. "The Changing Pattern of Thought in the
        Early Fourteenth Century." *BJRL*, 43 (1960-1961):
        354-72.

1050   ————. *The Dissolution of the Medieval Outlook: An
        Essay on Intellectual and Spiritual Change in the
        Fourteenth Century*. New York: Harper and Row, 1976.

1051   ————. "Faith and Reason in the Thought of Gregory
        of Rimini." *BJRL*, 42 (1959-1960): 88-112.

1052   ————. "The Fourteenth Century and the Decline of
        Scholasticism." *Past and Present*, 9 (April 1956):
        30-39.

1053   ————. *William of Ockham: The Metamorphosis of Scho-
        lastic Discourse*. Manchester: Manchester University
        Press; Totowa, N.J.: Rowman and Littlefield, 1975.

1054   McCall, John P. "Chaucer and John of Legnano." *Spec-
        ulum*, 40 (1965): 484-89.

1055   Minio-Paluello, L. "Remigio Girolami's 'De Bono Com-
        muni.'" *Italian Studies*, 11 (1956): 56-71.

1056   Oberman, Heiko A. "Fourteenth-Century Religious
        Thought: A Premature Profile." *Speculum*, 53 (1978):
        80-93.

1057   Patt, William D. "The Early Ars dictaminis as Res-
        ponse to a Changing Society." *Viator*, 9 (1978):
        133-55.

1058   Ross, W. Braxton, Jr. "Giovanni Colonna, Historian at
        Avignon." *Speculum,* 45 (1970): 533-63.

1059   Rubinstein, Nicolai. "The Beginnings of Political
        Thought in Florence." *JWCI,* 5 (1942): 298-327.

1060   ————. "Marsilius of Padua and Italian Political
        Thought of His Time." *Europe in the Later Middle
        Ages* (item 285), pp.44-75.

1061   ————. "Some Ideas of Municipal Progress and Decline
        in the Italy of the Communes." *Fritz Saxl, 1890-1948*
        (item 283), pp.165-83.

1062   Schlam, Carl C. "Graduation Speeches of Gentile da
        Foligno." *Mediaeval Studies,* 40 (1978): 96-119.

1063   Schork, Joseph R., and John P. McCall. "A Lament on
        the Death of John Legnano." *Studies in the Renais-
        sance,* 19 (1972): 180-95.

1064   Setton, Kenneth Meyer. "The Byzantine Background to
        the Italian Renaissance." *Proceedings of the American
        Philosophical Society,* 100 (1956): 1-76.

1065   Sheedy, Anna T. *Bartolus on Social Conditions in the
        Fourteenth Century.* New York: Columbia University
        Press, 1942.

1066   Smalley, B. *English Friars and Antiquity in the Early
        Fourteenth Century.* Oxford: Blackwell, 1960. Con-
        tains important chapter on early Italian humanism.

1067   Sullivan, James. "Marsiglio of Padua and William of
        Ockham." *American Historical Review,* 2 (1896/97):
        593-610.

1068   Trapp, D. "Augustinian Theology of the Fourteenth
        Century." *Augustiniana,* 6 (1956): 146-274.

1069   Ullman, B.L. "Some Aspects of the Origin of Italian
        Humanism." *Philological Quarterly,* 20 (1941): 212-23;
        repr. in his *Studies in the Italian Renaissance* (item
        203).

1070   Ullmann, Walter. "The Rebirth of the Citizen on the Eve
        of the Renaissance Period." *Aspects of the Renais-
        sance* (item 292), pp.5-25.

1071   Vittorini, Domenico. *The Age of Dante, A Concise
        History of Italian Culture in the Years of the
        Early Renaissance.* Syracuse: Syracuse University
        Press, 1957.

1072   Waley, D.P. *The Italian City-Republics.* London:
        Weidenfeld and Nicolson, 1969.

1073   Weiss, Roberto. *The Dawn of Humanism in Italy.*
        London: Inaugural Lecture, 1947; repr. New York:
        Haskell House, 1970.

1074   ————. "The Dawn of Humanism in Italy." *BIHR,* 42
        (1969): 1-16. Updated version of the Inaugural
        Lecture of 1947.

1075   ————. "Greek Culture of South Italy in the Later
        Middle Ages." *Proceedings of the British Academy,*
        37 (1951): 23-50; repr. in *Medieval and Humanist
        Greek* (item 206).

1076   ————. "Notes on Dionigi da Borgo San Sepolcro."
        Italian Studies, 10 (1955): 40-42.

1077   ————. "The Translators from the Greek of the Angevin
        Court of Naples." *Rinascimento,* 1.3-4 (1950-1951):
        195-226; repr. in *Medieval and Humanist Greek* (item
        206).

1078   Wickstead, Philip H., and E.G. Gardner. *Dante and
        Giovanni del Virgilio, Including a Critical Edition
        of the Text of Dante's "Eclogae Latinae" and the
        Poetic Remains of Giovanni del Virgilio.* West-
        minster: Constable, 1902.

1079   Wieruszowski, Helene. "Ars Dictaminis in the Time of
        Dante." *MH,* 1 (1943): 95-108; repr. in *Politics and
        Culture in Medieval Spain and Italy* (item 1080).

1080   ————. *Politics and Culture in Medieval Spain and
        Italy.* Rome: Storia e Letteratura, 1971. Includes
        her important essays on the *Ars dictaminis.*

1081   Witt, Ronald G. "Medieval 'Ars Dictaminis' and the
        Beginnings of Humanism: A New Construction of the
        Problem." *RQ,* 35 (1982): 1-35.

See also items 419, 424, 438, 653.

XI. THE AGE OF BOCCACCIO AND PETRARCH, 1340-1375

Italian prose and poetry as well as Latin learning was dominated in the middle decades of the fourteenth century by two
great figures: the poet and humanist, Francesco Petrarca
(1304-1374), and his younger contemporary, Giovanni Boccaccio
(1313-1375), famed as the author of Europe's first great novel,
the *Decameron*. Together, these two men defined and gave substance to European humanism as the investigation of history,
poetics and moral philosophy as well as classical studies and
textual criticism. Unfortunately, only a portion of Petrarch's
Latin works are available in translation; consult several excellent selections of the letters, and two major philosophical
works: *De remediis utriusque fortune,* available in an Elizabethan version as *Phisicke against Fortune,* and the interior
dialogue between Petrarch and St. Augustine, the *Secretum*.
Ample bibliographical orientation is to be found in the catalogues of the great Cornell University collection of Petrarch-
iana as well as several essays by E.H. Wilkins. Morris
Bishop, Thomas Bergin, and Wilkins have provided valuable
biographies of Petrarch and Boccaccio, while important intro-
ductions to Petrarch's thought are found in studies by Hans
Baron and Charles Trinkaus.

A. BIBLIOGRAPHY

1082   *Catalogue of the Petrarch Collection in Cornell University Library,* introd. M. Bishop and index by L. Jennings. Millwood, N.Y.: Kraus, 1974.

1083   *Cornell University Library, Catalogue of the Petrarch Collection Bequeathed by Willard Fisk,* compiled Mary Fowler. New York: Oxford University Press, 1916.

1084   Corrigan, Beatrice. "Petrarch in English." *Italica,* 50 (1973): 400-07.

1085   Fucilla, Joseph C. "The Present State of Petrarchan Studies." *Francis Petrarch, Six Centuries Later* (item 1218), pp. 25-55.

1086   Gathercole, Patricia M. "Boccaccio in English." *Studi sul Boccaccio,* 7 (1973): 353-68. A bibliography of English translations of Boccaccio's works from the fourteenth century to 1970.

1087   Lepsky, Anna Laura. "Boccaccio Studies in English, 1945-1969." *Studi sul Boccaccio,* 6 (1971): 211-29.

1088   Luciani, Vincent. "Medieval Italian Literature." *The Medieval Literature of Western Europe, A Review of Research, Mainly 1930-1960,* ed. J.H. Fisher. New York: New York University Press, 1966, pp.281-327. Valuable for Petrarch and Boccaccio.

1089   Weinberg, Bernard. "Recent Studies on Petrarch." *Renaissance News,* 17 (1964): 61-65.

1090   Wilkins, Ernest H. "A Chronological Conspectus of the Writings of Petrarch." *The Romanic Review,* 39 (1948): 89-101.

1091   ————. "An Introductory Boccaccio Bibliography."
        Philological Quarterly, 6 (1927): 111-22.

1092   ————. "An Introductory Petrarch Bibliography."
        Philological Quarterly, 27 (1948): 27-36.

1093   ————. "Recent Petrarch Publications." *Studies in
        the Renaissance,* 1 (1954): 13-21.

                    B. WORKS BY BOCCACCIO

1094   *Concerning Famous Women,* trans. Guido A. Guarino. New
        Brunswick, N.J.: Rutgers University Press, 1963.

1095   *The Fall of Princes (De casibus virorum illustrium),*
        trans. John Lydgate (from a French version, A.D.
        1420). London: Pynson, 1494, new ed. Henry Bergen,
        Early English Text Society, E.S.121-24. Washington,
        D.C. and London: Oxford University Press, 1923-27.

1096   *The Fates of Illustrious Men,* trans. Louis B. Hall.
        New York: Ungar, 1965.

1097   *Forty-six Lives (De claris mulieribus),* trans. Henry
        Parker, Lord Morely. London: Oxford University
        Press, 1943.

1098   *Boccaccio on Poetry, Being the Preface and the Four-
        teenth and Fifteenth Books of Boccaccio's Genealogia
        deorum gentilium,* trans. Charles G. Osgood. Prince-
        ton: Princeton University Press, 1930; repr.
        Indianapolis: Bobbs-Merrill, 1956.

1099   Prowse, A.M. "The First Eclogue of Boccaccio."
        Allegorica, 2 (1977): 172-81. Text and translation.

1100   "Letter of Nov. 7, 1374 on Death of Petrarch," in
        Hutton, *Boccaccio* (item 1189), pp.282-88.

C.   WORKS BY PETRARCH

1.   LETTERS

1101   Bernardo, Aldo S., trans. *Rerum familiarium libri
        I-VIII*. Albany: State University of New York Press,
        1975.

1102   ————. *Letters on Familiar Matters, Rerum familiar-
        ium libri IX-XVI*. Baltimore: Johns Hopkins Univer-
        sity Press, 1982.

1103   Bishop, Morris. *Letters from Petrarch*. Bloomington:
        Indiana University Press, 1966. An ample selection
        from all periods of Petrarch's life gracefully trans-
        lated.

1104   Cosenza, Mario Emilio. *Francesco Petrarca and the
        Revolution of Cola di Rienzo*. Chicago: University of
        Chicago Press, 1913. Includes translations of the
        letters to Cola and his contemporaries.

1105   ————. *Petrarch's Letters to Classical Authors*.
        Chicago: University of Chicago Press, 1910.

1106   Lohse, J., trans. *Thoughts from the Letters of
        Petrarch*. London: J.M. Dent and Co., 1901.

1107   Robinson, James Harvey, and J.C. Rolfe, trans.
        *Petrarch, the First Modern Man of Letters: A Selec-
        tion from His Correspondence with Boccaccio and
        Other Friends (Epistolae)*, 2nd ed. New York: G.P.
        Putnam's Sons, 1914; repr. Westport, Ct.: Greenwood,
        1978.

1108   Thompson, David, ed. *Petrarch: A Humanist among
        Princes. An Anthology of Petrarch's Letters and of
        Selections from His Other Works*. New York: Harper
        and Row, 1971.

1109   Wilkins, Ernest H., trans. *Petrarch at Vauclus*.
        Chicago: University of Chicago Press, 1958.

2. *De remediis utriusque fortune*

1110   *Phisicke against Fortune,* trans. Thomas Twyne. London:
        Richard Watkins, 1579; repr. with introd. and bib-
        liog. B.G. Kohl. Delmar, N.Y.: Scholars' Facsimiles
        and Reprints, 1980.

1111   Dobson, Susannah Dawson. *Petrarch's View of Human Life.*
        London: J. Stockdale, 1791. Selections from Twyne's
        translation of *De remediis.*

1112   *A Dialogue Between Reason and Adversity: A Late Middle
        English Version of Petrarch's "De Remediis,"* ed.
        F.N.M. Diekestra. New York: Humanities Press; Assen:
        Van Gorcum, 1968. Selected dialogues in fifteenth-
        century translations.

1113   "On the Remedies of Good and Bad Fortune. Book 1,
        dialogues 1, 2, 49, 92, 108, 121." *Renaissance Phil-
        osophy, vol.1, The Italian Philosophers* (item 316),
        pp. 3-26.

1114   Rawski, Conrad H., trans. *Petrarch: Four Dialogues for
        Scholars.* Cleveland: Press of Western Reserve Uni-
        versity, 1967. Translation of 1.43-46 of *De remediis.*

1115   ————. "Petrarch's Dialogue on Music." *Speculum,*
        46 (1971): 302-17. Translation and Latin text of
        De remediis, 1.23.

3. OTHER LATIN WORKS

1116   Bergin, Thomas G., trans. *Petrarch's Bucolicum Car-
        men.* New Haven: Yale University Press, 1974.
        English translation in hexameter with Latin text
        based on Avena's edition of 1906.

1117   ————. "An Annotated Translation of Petrarch's
        Epistola metrica II.10." *Dante, Petrarch, Boccaccio,
        Studies in the Italian Trecento in Honor of Charles
        S. Singleton,* ed. A.S. Bernardo and A.L. Pellegrini.
        Binghamton, N.Y.: Center for Medieval and Early
        Renaissance Studies, 1983, pp.183-219.

1118   ————. *"Epistola metrica* II.1: An Annotated Transla-
        tion." *Francis Petrarch: Six Centuries Later* (item
        1218), pp.56-66.

1119   ————, and Alice S. Wilson, trans. *Petrarch's Africa.*
        New Haven: Yale University Press, 1977.

1120   Draper, William H., trans. *Petrarch's Secret: or, The
        Soul's Conflict with Passion (Secretum).* London:
        Chatto and Windus, 1911; repr. Westport, Ct.:
        Hyperion Press, 1977.

1121   Gilbert, Allan H., ed. and trans. "Petrarch's Confes-
        sional Psalms *(Psalmi)." Romanic Review,* 2 (1911):
        429-43.

1122   Kadish, Emilie P. "Petrarch's Griselda: An English
        Translation." *Mediaevalia,* 3 (1977): 1-24.

1123   Kohl, B.G. "How a Ruler Ought to Govern His State
        (Seniles 14.1)." *The Earthly Republic* (item 322),
        pp.35-78.

1124   ————. "Petrarch's Prefaces to *De viris illustribus."
        History and Theory,* 13 (1974): 132-44.

1125   Mommsen, Theodor E. *Petrarch's Testament.* Ithaca:
        Cornell University Press, 1957. Critical Latin
        edition with facing English translation and notes.

1126   Nachod, Hans, trans. "The Ascent of Mount Ventoux."
        The Renaissance Philosophy of Man (item 311), pp.36-
        46.

1127   ————. "On His Own Ignorance and That of Many Others."
        The Renaissance Philosophy of Man (item 311), pp.47-
        133.

1128   Wilkins, Ernest H., trans. "Petrarch's Coronation
        Oration." *PMLA,* 68 (1953): 1242-50; repr. in E.H.
        Wilkins, *Studies in the Life and Works of Petrarch.*
        Cambridge, Mass.: Mediaeval Academy of America, 1955,
        pp.300-13.

1129   ————. *The Triumphs of Petrarch.* Chicago: University
        of Chicago Press, 1962.

1130   Zacour, Norman P., trans. *Petrarch's Book without a*
       Name. A Translation of the "Liber sine nomine."
       Toronto: Pontifical Institute of Mediaeval Studies,
       1973.

1131   Zeitlin, Jacob, trans. *The Life of Solitude.* Urbana,
       Ill.: University of Illinois Press, 1924; repr.
       Westport, Ct.: Hyperion Press, 1977.

                           D. STUDIES

1132   Allen, Shirley S. "The Griselda Tale and the Portrayal
       of Women in the *Decameron.*" *Philological Quarterly,*
       56 (1977): 1-26.

1133   Baron, Hans. *From Petrarch to Leonardo Bruni.* Chicago:
       University of Chicago Press, 1968, chaps.1-2.

1134   ————. "Petrarch: His Inner Struggle and the Human-
       istic Discovery of Man's Nature." *Florilegium
       Historiale* (item 302), pp.19-51.

1135   Bayley, C.C. "Petrarch, Charles IV and the 'Renovatio
       Imperii.'" *Speculum,* 17 (1942): 323-41.

1136   Bennett, J.A.W. "Chaucer, Dante, and Boccaccio."
       Medium Aevum, 22 (1953): 114-15.

1137   Bergin, Thomas G. *Boccaccio.* New York: Viking Press,
       1981.

1138   ————. *Petrarch.* Boston: Twayne, 1970.

1139   Bernardo, Aldo S. "Letter-Splitting in Petrarch's
       'Familiares.'" *Speculum,* 33 (1958): 236-41.

1140   ————. "Petrarch and the Art of Literature."
       *Petrarch to Pirandello: Studies in Italian Litera-
       ture in Honor of Beatrice Corrigan,* ed. Julius
       Molinaro. Toronto: University of Toronto Press,
       1973, pp.19-43.

1141   ————. *Petrarch, Laura and the "Triumphs."* Albany:
       State University of New York Press, 1974.

1142   ———. "Petrarch on the Education of a Prince: Fami-
        liares XII, 2." *Medievalia*, 6 (1980): 135-50.

1143   ———. *Petrarch, Scipio and the "Africa."* Baltimore:
        Johns Hopkins University Press, 1962.

1144   ———. "Petrarch's Attitude towards Dante." *PMLA*,
        70 (1955): 488-517.

1145   ———. "Petrarch's Laura: The Convolutions of a
        Humanistic Mind." *The Role of Women in the Middle
        Ages*, ed. Rosemarie Thee Morewedge. Albany: State
        University of New York Press, 1975, pp.65-89.

1146   ———. "The Selection of Letters in Petrarch's 'Fami-
        liares.'" *Speculum*, 35 (1960): 280-88.

1147   ———, ed. *Francesco Petrarca, Citizen of the World,
        Proceedings of the World Petrarch Congress, Washing-
        ton, D.C., April 6-13, 1974.* Padua: Antenore; Albany:
        State University of New York Press, 1980. Contains
        important essays by Trinkaus and Mann on Petrarch as
        humanist.

1148   Berrigan, Joseph R. "The Myth of Rome: Dante and
        Petrarch." *Classical Folia*, 27 (1973): 230-51.

1149   Bettridge, William Edwin, and Francis Lee Utley. "New
        Light on the Origin of the Griselda Story." *Texas
        Studies in Literature and Language*, 13.2 (1971):
        153-208.

1150   Billanovich, G. "Petrarch and the Textual Tradition of
        Livy." *JWCI*, 14 (1951): 137-208.

1151   Bishop, Morris. *Petrarch and His World*. Bloomington:
        Indiana University Press, 1963.

1152   Boitan, Piero. "Boccaccio's Triumph." *Medium Aevum*,
        47 (1978): 312-17.

1153   ———. *Chaucer and Boccaccio*. Oxford: Blackwell,
        1977.

1154   ———. *"The Monk's Tale*: Dante and Boccaccio."
        Medium Aevum, 45 (1976): 50-69.

1155   Born, Lester K.   "The Perfect Prince: A Study in
        Thirteenth and Fourteenth Century Ideals." *Speculum,*
        3 (1928): 470-504. Includes a discussion of
        Petrarch's letter to Francesco il Vecchio da
        Carrara (1373).

1156   Branca, Vittore. *Boccaccio: The Man and His Work,*
        trans. R. Monges. New York: New York University
        Press, 1976.

1157   Brink, Joel. "Simone Martini, Francesco Petrarca and
        the Humanistic Program of the Virgil Frontispiece."
        Medievalia, 3 (1977): 83-117.

1158   Bruère, R.T. "Lucan and Petrarch's 'Africa.'" *Clas-
        sical Philology,* 56 (1961): 83-99.

1159   Cary, George. "Petrarch and Alexander the Great."
        Italian Studies, 5 (1950): 43-55.

1160   Cassell, Anthony K. "*Il Corbaccio* and the Secundus
        Tradition." *Comparative Literature,* 25 (1973): 352-
        60. Traces the source of Boccaccio's misogyny to
        Secundus the Silent, philosopher.

1161   Cioffari, Vincent. "The Function of Fortune in Dante,
        Boccaccio and Machiavelli." *Italica,* 24 (1947):
        111-13.

1162   Cipolla, Gaetano. "Labyrinthine Imagery in Petrarch."
        Italica, 54 (1979): 263-89.

1163   Coogan, Robert. "Petrarch's *Liber sine nomine* and a
        Vision of Rome in the Reformation." *Renaissance and
        Reformation,* 19 (1983): 1-12.

1164   Cook, Albert Stanburrough. "The First Two Readers of
        Petrarch's *Tale of Griselda*." *Modern Philology,* 15
        (1917-1918): 633-43.

1165   Cool, Kenneth E. "The Petrarchan Landscape as Palimp-
        sest." *JMRS,* 11 (1981): 83-100.

1166   Copland, Murray. "*The Shipman's Tale*: Chaucer and
        Boccaccio." *Medium Aevum,* 35 (1966): 11-28.

1167   Coulter, Cornelia Catlin. "Boccaccio and the Cassinese
        Manuscripts of the Laurentian Library." *Classical
        Philology,* 43 (1948): 217-30.

1168   ————. "Boccaccio's Knowledge of Quintilian."
        Speculum, 33 (1958): 490-96.

1169   ————. "The Genealogy of the Gods." *Vassar Mediae-
        val Studies,* ed. C.F. Fiske. New Haven: Yale Uni-
        versity Press, 1923, pp.317-41. On Boccaccio's
        work of the same name.

1170   Deligiorgis, Stavros. "Boccaccio and the Greek
        Romances." *Comparative Literature,* 19.2 (1967): 97-
        113.

1171   Dempster, Germaine. "Chaucer's Manuscript of
        Petrarch's Version of the Griselda Story." *Modern
        Philology,* 41 (1943-1944): 6-16.

1172   Dziedzic, Margarita, Richard Huling and Chris Ferguson.
        "The Binghamton Manuscript of Petrarch." *Manuscripta,*
        25 (1981): 35-42.

1173   Farquhar, James Douglas. "Don Simone da Siena: A
        Comment on the Author Portrait of Boccaccio's *Gene-
        alogia Deorum* in the University of Chicago Library."
        Manuscripta, 24 (1980): 114-18.

1174   Folts, James D., Jr. "Senescence and Renascence:
        Petrarch's Thoughts on Growing Old." *JMRS,* 10 (1980):
        207-37.

1175   Forster, Leonard. *The Icy Fire: Five Studies in Euro-
        ean Petrarchism.* London: Cambridge University Press,
        1969.

1176   ————. "On Petrarchism in Latin and the Role of An-
        thologies." *Acta Conventus Neo-latini Lovaniensis*
        (item 288), pp.235-44.

1177   Françon, Marcel. "Petrarch, Disciple of Heraclitus."
        Speculum, 11 (1936): 265-71.

1178   Frasso, Giuseppe. *Travels with Francesco Petrarca,*
        trans Nicholas Mann. Padua: Antenore, 1974.
        Brilliant photographic presentation of Petrarch's
        fourteenth-century world.

1179   Freccero, John. "The Fig Tree and the Laurel: Pe-
        trarch's Poetics." *Diacritics,* 5.1 (1975): 34-40.

1180   Gathercole, Patricia May. "Laurent de Premierfait:
        The Translator of Boccaccio's *De casibus virorum
        illustrium.*" *The French Review,* 27 (1954): 245-52.

1181   ————. *Tension in Boccaccio: Boccaccio and the Fine
        Arts.* University, Miss.: Mediaeval Studies, Romance
        Monographs, 1975.

1182   ————. "Two Old French Translations of Boccaccio's
        De casibus virorum illustrium." *Modern Language
        Quarterly,* 27 (1956): 304-09.

1183   Grant, W. Leonard. "Petrarch's *Africa* I 4-6." *Philo-
        logical Quarterly,* 34 (1955): 75-81.

1184   Greene, Thomas M. "Petrarch and the Humanist Hermeneu-
        tic." *Italian Literature: Roots and Branches: Essays
        in Honor of Thomas Goodard Bergin,* ed. Giose Riman-
        elli and Kenneth John Atchity. New Haven: Yale
        University Press, 1976, pp.201-24.

1185   Hendrickson, G.L. "Chaucer and Petrarch: Two Notes on
        The Clerkes Tale." *Modern Philology,* 4 (1906-1907):
        179-92.

1186   Holloway-Calthrop, H.C. *Petrarch, His Life and Times.*
        London: Methuen, 1907.

1187   Hornstein, L.H. "Petrarch's Laelius, Chaucer's Lollius?"
        PMLA, 63 (1948): 64-84.

1188   Howard, Donald R. "A New Manuscript for Petrarch's
        De Vita Solitaria: Cod. lat. 5151." *Manuscripta,*
        5 (1961): 169-70.

1189   Hutton, Edward. *Giovanni Boccaccio: A Biographical
        Study.* London: John Lane, 1910.

1190   Jack, R.D.S. "Petrarch in English and Scottish Renais-
        sance Literature." *Modern Language Review,* 71 (1976):
        801-11.

1191   Jerrold, Maud F. *Francesco Petrarca, Poet and Human-
        ist.* London: Dent, 1909.

1192   Kessler, Eckhard. "Petrarch's Contribution to Renais-
        sance Historiography." *Res Publica Litterarum,* 1
        (1978): 129-49.

1193　Kristeller, Paul Oskar. "Petrarch's 'Averroists': A
　　　Note on the History of Aristotelianism in Venice,
　　　Padua and Bologna." *BHR,* 14 (1952): 59-65.

1194　————. "Petrarch, Francesco." *The Encyclopedia of
　　　Philosophy.* New York: Macmillan and the Free Press,
　　　1967. Vol.6, pp.126-28.

1195　Luttrell, Anthony. "Capranica before 1337: Petrarch
　　　as Topographer." *Cultural Aspects of the Italian
　　　Renaissance* (item 280), pp.9-21.

1196　Mann, N. "The Making of Petrarch's 'Bucolicum Car-
　　　men': A Contribution to the History of the Text."
　　　IMU, 20 (1977): 127-84.

1197　————. "The Manuscripts of Petrarch's 'De remediis':
　　　A Checklist." *IMU,* 14 (1971): 57-90.

1198　————. "New Light on a Recently Discovered Manu-
　　　script of the 'De remediis.'" *IMU,* 12 (1969): 317-
　　　22.

1199　————. "'O Deus, qualis epistola!' A New Petrarch
　　　Letter." *IMU,* 17 (1974): 207-43.

1200　————. "Petrarch and the Transmission of Classical
　　　Elements." *Classical Influences on European Culture
　　　A.D. 500-1500* (item 277), pp.217-24.

1201　Marsh, David. "Boccaccio in the Quattrocento: Manetti's
　　　Dialogus in symposio." *RQ,* 33 (1980): 337-51.

1202　Mazzocco, A. "The Antiquarianism of Francesco
　　　Petrarca." *JMRS,* 7 (1977): 203-24.

1203　Milde, Wolfgang. "Petrarch's List of Favorite Books."
　　　Res Publica Litterarum, 2 (1979): 229-32.

1204　Minta, Stephen. *Petrarch and Petrarchism, The English
　　　and French Traditions.* New York: Barnes and Noble,
　　　1980.

1205　Momigliano, Arnaldo, and H. Liebeschütz. "Notes on
　　　Petrarch, John of Salisbury, and the Institutio Trai-
　　　ani." *JWCI,* 12 (1949): 189-90.

1206   Mommsen, Theodor E. *Medieval and Renaissance Studies,*
       ed. E.F. Rice, Jr. Ithaca: Cornell University Press,
       1959; repr. Westport, Ct.: Greenwood, 1980. Includes
       Mommsen's essays on Petrarch and the Dark Ages, and
       the decoration of the Sala Virorum Illustrium in
       Padua, as well as several minor pieces.

1207   Montano, Rocco. "Italian Humanism: Dante and Petrarch."
       Italica, 50 (1973): 205-21.

1208   Nolhac, Pierre de. *Petrarch and the Ancient World,*
       trans. D.B. Updike. Boston: Merrymount Press, 1907.

1209   Oliver, R.P. "Petrarch's Prestige as a Humanist."
       *Classical Studies in Honor of William Abbott Old-
       father.* Urbana: University of Illinois Press, 1943,
       pp.134-53.

1210   ————. "Salutati's Criticism of Petrarch." *Italica,*
       16 (1939): 49-57.

1211   Osgood, Charles G. "Boccaccio's Knowledge of the Life
       of Virgil." *Classical Philology,* 25 (1930): 27-36.

1212   Peebles, Bernard M. "The *Ad Maronis Mausoleum*: Pe-
       trarch's Virgil and Two Fifteenth-Century Manuscripts."
       *Classical, Mediaeval and Renaissance Studies in Honor
       of Berthold Louis Ullman* (item 287). Vol.2, pp.169-
       98.

1213   Phillips, Dayton. "Petrarch's Ethical Principles."
       Italica, 24 (1947): 219-32.

1214   Post, Gaines. "Petrarch and Heraclitus Once More."
       Speculum, 12 (1927): 343-50.

1215   Praz, Mario. "Chaucer and the Great Italian Writers of
       the Trecento." *The Flaming Heart: Essays on Crashaw,
       Machiavelli and Other Studies of the Relations between
       Italian and English Literature from Chaucer to T.S.
       Eliot.* New York: Doubleday Anchor Books, 1958,
       pp.29-89.

1216   Radcliff-Umstead, Douglas. "Boccaccio's Adaptation of
       Some Latin Sources for the *Decameron*." *Italica,* 45
       (1968): 174-94.

1217   Robathan, D.M. "Boccaccio's Accuracy as a Scribe."
        Speculum, 13 (1938): 458-60.

1218   Scaglione, Aldo, ed. *Francis Petrarch, Six Centuries
        Later.* Chapel Hill: University of North Carolina
        Press and Chicago: Newberry Library, 1975.

1219   ————. *Nature and Love in the Late Middle Ages.*
        Berkeley and Los Angeles: University of California
        Press, 1963. On Boccaccio; especially valuable for
        appendix on naturalism and classicism in Renaissance
        art.

1220   Seigel, Jerrold E. "Ideals of Eloquence and Silence in
        Petrarch." *JHI,* 26 (1965): 147-74.

1221   Severs, J. Burke. *The Literary Relationships of
        Chaucer's "Clerk's Tale."* New Haven: Yale Univer-
        sity Press, 1942; repr. Greenwood, Ct.: Archon, 1972.

1222   Simpson, W. "A New Codex of Petrarch's *De viris illus-
        tribus.*" *IMU,* 3 (1960): 267-70.

1223   Sinclair, K.U. "A New Fragment of Petrarch's 'Episto-
        lae Seniles.'" *Speculum,* 40 (1965): 323-25.

1224   Smarr, Janet. "Petrarch: A Vergil without a Rome."
        Rome in the Renaissance (item 300), pp.133-40.

1225   Stadter, P.A. "Planudes, Plutarch, and Pace of
        Ferrara." *IMU,* 16 (1973): 137-62.

1226   Starn, Randolph. "Petrarch's Consolation of Exile: A
        Humanist Use of Adversity." *Essays Presented to
        Myron P. Gilmore* (item 275), vol.1, pp.241-54.

1227   Steiner, Appad. "Petrarch's *Optimus Princeps.*" *The
        Romanic Review,* 25 (1934): 99-111. Discussion of
        Petrarch's letter of 1373 to Francesco il Vecchio da
        Carrara.

1228   Stuart, D.R. "Petrarch's Indebtedness to the *Libellus*
        of Catullus." *TAPA,* 48 (1917): 3-27.

1229   ————. "The Sources and the Extent of Petrarch's
        Knowledge of the Life of Vergil." *Classical Phil-
        ology,* 12 (1917): 365-404.

1230   Tatham, Edward H.R. *Francesco Petrarca, The First
        Modern Man of Letters, His Life and Correspondence,
        A Study of the Early Fourteenth Century (1304-1374)*,
        2 vols. London: The Sheldon Press, 1925-1926.

1231   Tournoy, Gilbert, ed. *Boccaccio in Europe, Proceed-
        ings of the Boccaccio Conference, Louvain, December
        1975*. Leuven: University Press, 1977. Collabora-
        tive volume mainly on the influence of Boccaccio in
        western literature and culture.

1232   Trinkaus, Charles. "Petrarch's Views on the Individual
        and His Society." *Osiris*, 11 (1954): 168-98.

1233   ————. "Humanist Treatises on the Status of the Reli-
        gious: Petrarch, Salutati, Valla." *Studies in the
        Renaissance*, 11 (1964): 7-45.

1234   ————. *The Poet as Philosopher: Petrarch and the
        Formation of Renaissance Consciousness*. New Haven:
        Yale University Press, 1979.

1235   Tusiani, Joseph. "The Poetry of Giovanni Boccaccio."
        Thought, 50 (1975): 339-50.

1236   Ullman, Berthold Louis. "The Composition of Pe-
        trarca's *De vita solitaria* and the History of the
        Vatican Manuscript." *Miscellanea Giovanni Mercati*
        (item 295), pp.107-42.

1237   ————. "Petrarch Manuscripts in the United States."
        IMU, 5 (1962): 443-76.

1238   ————. "Petrarch's Favorite Books." *TAPA*, 54
        (1923): 21-38; repr. in *Studies in the Italian
        Renaissance* (item 203).

1239   Waller, Marguerite. *Petrarch's Poetics and Literary
        History*. Amherst: University of Massachusetts Press,
        1980.

1240   Watkins, Renée Neu. "Petrarch and the Black Death:
        From Fear to Monuments." *Studies in the Renaissance*,
        19 (1972): 196-223.

1241   Weiss, Roberto. "Jacopo Angeli da Scarperia (c.1360-
        1410-11)." *Medioevo e Rinascimento* (item 294), vol.
        2, pp.801-27.

1242   ———. "Notes on Petrarch and Homer." *Rinascimento,*
        4 (1952): 263-76.

1243   ———. "Petrarch the Antiquarian." *Classical,*
        Mediaeval and Renaissance Studies in Honor of Berthold
        Louis Ullman (item 287), vol.2, pp.199-209.

1244   ———. "Some New Correspondence of Petrarch and Bar-
        bato da Sulmona." *Modern Language Review,* 43 (1948):
        60-66.

1245   Wenzel, Siegfried. "The Seven Deadly Sins: Some
        Problems of Research." *Speculum,* 43 (1968): 1-22.

1246   ———. "Petrarch's 'Accidia.'" *Studies in the*
        Renaissance, 8 (1961): 36-48.

1247   White, Lynn, Jr. "Indic Elements in the Iconography of
        Petrarch's 'Trionfo della Morte.'" *Speculum,* 49
        (1974): 201-21.

1248   Whitfield, J.H. "Petrarch and the Birth of Culture."
        Italian Studies, 38 (1983): 39-55.

1249   ———. *Petrarch and the Renascence.* Oxford: Black-
        well, 1943; repr. New York: Russell and Russell,
        1965.

1250   Wilkins, Ernest H. "Boccaccio's Early Tributes to
        Petrarch." *Speculum,* 38 (1963): 79-87.

1251   ———. "The Coronation of Petrarch." *Speculum,* 18
        (1943): 155-97.

1252   ———. "The Dates of Three Letters of Petrarch."
        Speculum, 16 (1941): 485-86.

1253   ———. "The Dates of Transcription of Petrarch's
        Manuscript V.L. 3195." *Modern Philology,* 26 (1928-
        1929): 283-94.

1254   ———. "Descriptions of Pagan Divinities from Pe-
        trarch to Chaucer." *Speculum,* 32 (1957): 511-22.

1255   ———. "'Empedocles et alii' in Filelfo's 'Terza
        Rima.'" *Speculum,* 38 (1963): 318-23.

1256   ————. "Letters in Italian Attributed to Petrarch."
        IMU, 3 (1960): 271-80.

1257   ————. *Life of Petrarch.* Chicago: University of
        Chicago Press, 1961.

1258   ————. *The Making of the "Canzoniere" and Other Pe-*
        trarchan Studies. Rome: Edizioni di Storia e
        Letteratura, 1951.

1259   ————. "On Petrarch's 'Accidia' and His Adamantine
        Chains." *Speculum,* 37 (1962): 589-94.

1260   ————. "On Petrarch's 'Ad Seipsum' and 'I'vo pen-
        sando.'" *Speculum,* 32 (1957): 84-91.

1261   ————. "On Petrarch's Ep. Fam. 6.2." *Speculum,* 38
        (1963): 620-22.

1262   ————. "On Petrarch's Rewriting the Triumph of
        Fame." *Speculum,* 39 (1964): 440-43.

1263   ————. "On the Carriage of Petrarch's Letters."
        Speculum, 35 (1960): 214-23.

1264   ————. "On the Evolution of Petrarch's Letter to
        Posterity." *Speculum,* 39 (1964): 304-08.

1265   ————. "On the Transcription by Petrarch in V.L.
        3195, I and II." *Modern Philology,* 24 (1926-1927):
        261-68, 389-404.

1266   ————. "Petrarch and Giacomo de' Rossi." *Speculum,*
        25 (1950): 374-78.

1267   ————. "Petrarch and Manno Donati." *Speculum,* 35
        (1960): 381-93.

1268   ————. "Petrarch and Roberto di Battifolle." *The*
        Romanic Review, 50 (1959): 3-8.

1269   ————. *Petrarch's Correspondence.* Padua: Antenore,
        1960.

1270   ————. "Petrarch's Ecclesiastical Career." *Speculum,*
        28 (1953): 754-75.

1271   ————. *Petrarch's Eight Years at Milan.* Cambridge,
        Mass.: Mediaeval Academy of America, 1958.

1272   ————. "Petrarch's 'Exul ab Italia.'" *Speculum*, 38
        (1963): 453-60.

1273   ————. "Petrarch's First Collection of His Italian
        Poems." *Speculum,* 7 (1932): 169-80.

1274   ————. "Petrarch's Last Return to Provence." *Spec-
        ulum,* 39 (1964): 75-84.

1275   ————. *Petrarch's Later Years.* Cambridge, Mass.:
        Mediaeval Academy of America, 1959.

1276   ————. "Petrarch's Seventh Eclogue." *MH,* 8 (1954):
        22-31.

1277   ————. "Philipe de Cabassoles on Petrarch." *Specu-
        lum,* 35 (1960): 69-77.

1278   ————. *Studies in the Life and Works of Petrarch.*
        Cambridge, Mass.: Mediaeval Academy of America, 1955.

1279   ————. *Studies on Petrarch and Boccaccio,* ed.
        A.S. Bernardo. Padua: Antenore, 1978.

1280   ————. "A Survey of the Correspondence between
        Petrarch and Boccaccio." *IMU,* 6 (1963): 179-84.

1281   ————. "A Survey of the Correspondence between
        Petrarch and Francesco Nelli." *IMU,* 1 (1958):
        351-58.

1282   ————. *The University of Chicago Manuscript of the
        "Genealogia deorum gentilium" of Boccaccio.*
        Chicago: University of Chicago Press, 1927.

1283   ————. "Works That Petrarch Thought of Writing."
        Speculum, 35 (1960): 563-71.

1284   ————, and Giuseppe Billanovich. "The Miscellaneous
        Letters of Petrarch." *Speculum,* 37 (1962): 226-43.

1285   Woodbridge, E. "Boccaccio's Defense of Poetry as Con-
        tained in the 14th Book of the *Genealogia deorum.*"
        PMLA, 13 (1898): 333-49.

1286   Wright, Herbert C. *Boccaccio in England from Chaucer
        to Tennyson.* London: The Athlone Press, 1957.
        Especially Chapter 1 on the fortuna of the Latin
        works *De casibus virorum illustrium, De Claris
        mulieribus, De genealogia deorum.*

1287   Wrigley, John E. "A Papal Secret Known to Petrarch."
        Speculum, 39 (1964): 613-34.

1288   ————. "A Presumed Lost Petrarch Letter: *Sine nomine
        X."* Medium Aevum, 37 (1968): 293-306.

1289   Zacour, Norman P. "Petrarch and Talleyrand." *Specu-
        lum,* 31 (1956): 683-703.

See also items 354, 377, 450-52, 945, 1039, 1787, 1947, 2415-
        17, 2852.

XII. FLORENCE IN THE AGE OF SALUTATI AND BRUNI, 1375-1440

Under the leadership of Coluccio Salutati and Leonardo Bruni, Florence became the leading center of Italian Renaissance humanism. In an important new study, Ronald G. Witt has demonstrated that the Florentine chancellor, Salutati, gave definition and permanence to the revolution in outlook and values wrought in the earlier generation of Petrarch and Boccaccio. These humanists focussed on questions of the republican origins of Florence, the nature of the good life and just community, and the political destiny of the Arno city, causing Hans Baron to term this movement "civic humanism." In his major work, *Crisis of the Early Italian Renaissance* (item 1304), Baron has seen civic humanism as a response to the successful resistance to the expansionist Duke of Milan, Giangaleazzo Visconti, though later scholars such as G.A. Brucker (item 1321), see the new civic attitudes emerging a decade later. Key documents of civic humanism include Bruni's *Panegyric to the City of Florence* and Renée Watkins' anthology (item 336).

A. *SOURCES*

1290   Bruni, Leonardo. "The Tractate of Lionardo Bruni
        d'Arezzo De studiis et literis." W.H. Woodward,
        Vittorino da Feltre and Other Humanist Educators
        (item 338), pp.119-33.

1291   ————. "Dialogues to Pier Paolo Vergerio (Dialogi
        ad Petrum Paulum Istrum)." *Three Crowns of Florence*
        (item 334), pp.19-56.

1292   ————. "Funeral Oration for Nanni Strozzi," trans.
        R.G. Witt. In Mary Ann F. Witt, et al. *The Humani-
        ties, Cultural Roots and Continuities.* Lexington,
        Mass.: Heath, 1980, vol.1, pp.224-26.

1293   ————. "Panegyric to the City of Florence (*Laudatio
        Florentinae Urbis)*," trans. B.G. Kohl, in *The
        Earthly Republic* (item 322), pp.135-75.

1294   ————. "The History of Florence (selections),"
        Humanism and Liberty (item 336), pp.27-91.

1295   ————. *The Historie of ... the Warres betwene the
        Imperialles and Gothes for the Possession of Italy,*
        trans A. Golding. London: Rouland Hall, 1563.

1296   Dominici, Giovanni. *On the Education of Children,
        Parte Quarta Regola del Governo di cura familiare,*
        trans. with introd. A.B. Cote. Washington, D.C.:
        diss. Catholic University of America, 1927.

1297   Jensen, R.C., and Marie Bahr-Volk. "The Fox and the
        Crab. Coluccio Salutati's Unpublished Fable."
        Studies in Philology, 73 (1976): 162-75. Edition
        and translation of *Fabula de vulpe et cancro* in
        elegiac distichs.

1298   Salutati, Coluccio. "De Tyranno." *Humanism and Tyr-
       anny* (item 315), pp.70-116.

1299   ————. "The Death of Petrarca (Letter of August 16,
       1374)." *Three Crowns of Florence* (item 334), pp.3-13.

1300   ————. "Letter to Pellegrino Zambeccari," trans. R.G.
       Witt. *The Earthly Republic* (item 322), pp.93-114.

1301   ————. "Letter to Caterina di messer Vieri di Donatino
       d' Arezzo," trans. R.G. Witt. *The Earthly Republic*
       (item 322), pp.115-18.

1302   ————. "Letters in Defense of Liberal Studies."
       Humanism and Tyranny (item 315), pp.290-377.

1303   Silvester, Dominico. *The Latin Poetry,* trans. R.C.
       Jenson. Humanische Bibliothek II.20.   Munich:
       Wilhelm Fink Verlag, 1973.   Latin text and English
       translation.

B. STUDIES

1304   Baron, Hans. *The Crisis of the Early Italian Renais-
       sance,* 2 vols.   Princeton: Princeton University
       Press, 1955.   2nd ed., Princeton: Princeton Univer-
       sity Press, 1966.

*   ————. *From Petrarch to Leonardo Bruni.*   Chicago:
       University of Chicago Press, 1968, chaps. 3-6.
       Includes four important studies on Bruni.   Cited
       above as item 1137.

1305   ————. "The Historical Background of the Florentine
       Renaissance." *History,* 22 (1938-1939): 315-27.

1306   ————. *Humanistic and Political Literature in Flor-
       ence and Venice at the Beginning of the Quattro-
       cento.*   Cambridge, Mass.: Harvard University Press,
       1955; repr. with new introd.   New York: Russell and
       Russell, 1968.

1307   ————. "Leonardo Bruni: 'Professional Rhetorician' or
       'Civic Humanist?'" *Past and Present,* 36 (April 1967):
       21-37.

1308   ————. "Progress in Bruni Scholarship: Apropos of
        F.P. Luiso's *Studi su l'Epistolario di Leonardo
        Bruni.*" *Speculum*, 56 (1981): 831-39.

1309   ————. "The Social Background of Political Liberty
        in the Early Italian Renaissance." *Comparative
        Studies in Society and History,* 21 (1960): 440-51.

1310   ————. "A Sociological Interpretation of the Early
        Renaissance in Florence." *The South Atlantic Quar-
        terly,* 38 (1939): 427-48.

1311   ————. "The Year of Leonardo Bruni's Birth and
        Methods for Determining the Ages of Humanists Born
        in the Trecento." *Speculum,* 52 (1977): 582-625.

1312   Bayley, Charles. *War and Society in Renaissance
        Florence: The "De militia" of Leonardo Bruni.*
        Toronto: University of Toronto Press, 1961.

1313   Becker, Marvin B. "An Essay on the Quest for Identity
        in the Early Italian Renaissance." *Florilegium
        Historiale* (item 302), pp.295-312.

1314   ————. *Florence in Transition,* 2 vols. Baltimore:
        The Johns Hopkins Press, 1967-68.

1315   ————. "Individualism in the Early Italian Renais-
        sance: Burden and Blessing." *Studies in the Renais-
        sance,* 19 (1972): 273-97.

1316   ————. "Towards a Renaissance Historiography in
        Florence." *Renaissance Studies in Honor of Hans
        Baron* (item 296), pp.141-72.

1317   Bell, H.I. "A Solinus Manuscript from the Library of
        Coluccio Salutati." *Speculum,* 4 (1929): 451-61.

1318   Bonnell, Robert A. "An Early Humanistic View of the
        Active and Contemplative Life." *Italica,* 43 (1966):
        225-39. On Salutati's *De seculo et religione* and
        other writings on that theme.

1319   ————. "Salutati--A View of Caesar and Rome." *Annu-
        ale Mediaevale,* 8 (1967): 59-69.

1320   Brucker, Gene A. *The Civic World of Early Renaissance
        Florence.* Princeton: Princeton University Press,
        1977.

1321   ————. "Humanism, Politics and the Social Order in
        Early Renaissance Florence." *Florence and Venice*
        (item 276), vol.1, pp.3-12.

1322   ————. "Florence and Its University, 1348-1424."
        Action and Conviction in Early Modern Europe (item
        299), pp.220-36.

1323   ————. *Renaissance Florence*. New York: John Wiley,
        1969; repr. with new bibliog. Berkeley: University of
        California Press, 1983.

1324   Chroust, Anton Hermann, and James A. Corbett. "The
        Fifteenth Century 'Review of Politics' of Laurentius
        of Arezzo." *Mediaeval Studies*, 2 (1949): 62-76.
        On Leonardo Bruni.

1325   Cinquino, J. "Coluccio Salutati, Defender of Poetry."
        Italica, 26 (1949): 131-35.

1326   Crum, Richard H. "A Note on Dominici's Sources." *MH*,
        5 (1947): 42-45.

1327   Denley, Peter. "Giovanni Dominici's Opposition to
        Humanism." *Religion and Humanism* (item 301), pp.
        103-14.

1328   Donovan, Richard B. "Salutati's Opinion of Non-Italian
        Latin Writers of the Middle Ages." *Studies in the
        Renaissance*, 14 (1967): 185-201.

1329   Fryde, Edmund. "The Beginnings of Italian Humanist
        Historiography: The 'New Cicero' of Leonardo Bruni."
        EHR, 95 (1980): 533-52.

1330   Gallacher, Patrick. "Shame and Recognition Scene in
        Coluccio Salutati and Natali Conti." *Acta Conventus
        Neo-latini Amstelodamensis* (item 305), pp.426-39.

1331   Garin, Eugenio. "The Humanist Chancellors of the
        Florentine Republic from Coluccio Salutati to Bar-
        tolomeo Scala." *Portraits from the Quattrocento*,
        trans. V. and E. Velen. New York: Harper and Row,
        1972, pp.1-29.

1332   Gerl, Hanna Barbara. "On the Philosophical Dimension
        of Rhetoric: The Theory of *Ornatus* in Leonardo Bruni."
        Philosophy and Rhetoric, 11 (1978): 178-90.

1333   Gilbert, Neal W.   "The Early Italian Humanists and
        Disputation."   *Renaissance Studies in Honor of Hans
        Baron* (item 296), pp.201-26.

1334   Gilmore, Myron P.   "*Studia Humanitatis* and the Profes-
        sions in Fifteenth-Century Florence."   *Florence and
        Venice* (item 276), vol.1, pp.27-40.

1335   Griffiths, Gordon.   "Leonardo Bruni and the Restora-
        tion of the University of Rome (1406)."   *RQ*, 26
        (Spring 1973): 1-11.

1336   Hammond, E.P.   "Lydgate and Coluccio Salutati."   *Modern
        Philology*, 25 (1927-1928): 49-57.

1337   Hankey, A.T.   "Salutati's Epigrams for the Palazzo
        Vecchio at Florence."   *JWCI*, 22 (1959): 359-60.

1338   Holmes, George.   "The Emergence of an Urban Ideology
        at Florence, c.1250-1450."   *TRHS*, ser.5, 23 (1973):
        111-34.

1339   ————.   *The Florentine Enlightenment*.   New York:
        Pegasus, 1969.

1340   Hunt, R.W.   "A Manuscript from the Library of Coluccio
        Salutati."   *Calligraphy and Paleography, Essays Pre-
        sented to Alfred Fairbank*.   London: Faber and Faber,
        1965, pp.75-79.

1341   Jensen, Richard C.   "Coluccio Salutati's *Lament of
        Phyllis*."   *Studies in Philology*, 65 (1968): 109-23.

1342   ————, and J.T. Ireland.   "Giovanni Moccia on Zanobi
        da Strada and Other Florentine Notables."   *Studies in
        Philology*, 73 (1976): 365-75.

1343   Luttrell, Anthony.   "Coluccio Salutati's Letter to Juan
        Fernandez de Heredia."   *IMU*, 13 (1970): 235-44.

1344   McCormick, Andrew.   "Freedom of Speech in Early Renais-
        sance Florence: Salutati's 'Questio est coram Decem-
        viris.'"   *Rinascimento*, 19 (1979): 235-40.

1345   Marrone, Steven P.   "Domenico Silvestri's Defense of
        Poetry."   *Rinascimento*, 13 (1973): 115-32.

1346   Martines, Lauro. *Lawyers and Statecraft in Renaissance Florence*. Princeton: Princeton University Press, 1968.

1347   ————. *The Social World of the Florentine Humanists, 1390-1460*. Princeton: Princeton University Press, 1963.

1348   ————. "A Way of Looking at Women in Renaissance Florence." *JMRS*, 4 (1974): 15-28.

1349   Molho, Anthony. "The Florentine Oligarchy and the 'Balie' of the Late Trecento." *Speculum*, 43 (1968): 23-51.

1350   ————. "Politics and the Ruling Class in Early Renaissance Florence." *Nuova Rivista Storica*, 52 (1968): 401-20.

1351   Morreale, Margherita. "Coluccio Salutati's *De Laboribus Herculis* (1406) and Enrique de Villena's *Los doze trabajos de Hercules* (1417)." *Studies in Philology*, 51 (1974): 95-106.

1352   O'Donnell, J. Reginald. "Coluccio Salutati on the Poet Teacher." *Mediaeval Studies*, 22 (1960): 240-56.

1353   Oliver, R.P. "Plato and Salutati." *TAPA*, 71 (1940): 315-34.

1354   Patrinelis, C.G. "An Unknown Discourse of Chrysoloras Addressed to Manuel II Palaeologus." *Greek, Roman, and Byzantine Studies*, 13 (1972): 497-502.

1355   Prete, S. "Leonardo Bruni Aretini Carmen." *Classical World*, 56 (1963): 180-83.

1356   Reynolds, B. "Bruni and Perotti Present a Greek Historian." *BHR*, 16 (1954): 108-18.

1357   Rich, T.I. "Giovanni da Sanminiato and Coluccio Salutati." *Speculum*, 11 (1936): 386-90.

1358   Robinson, Rodney. "The Inventory of Niccolò Niccoli." *Classical Philology*, 16 (1921): 251-55.

1359   Rubinstein, Nicolai. "Florence and the Despots. Some
        Aspects of Florentine Diplomacy in the Fourteenth
        Century." *TRHS*, ser.5, 2 (1952): 21-46.

1360   ————. "Political Ideas in Sienese Art: The Frescoes
        by Ambrogio Lorenzetti and Taddeo di Bartolo in the
        Palazzo Pubblico." *JWCI*, 21 (1958): 179-207.

1361   ————. "Florentine Constitutionalism and Medici
        Ascendancy in the Fifteenth Century." *Florentine
        Studies*, ed. N. Rubinstein. London: Faber and Faber,
        1968, pp.442-62. On the fate of Bruni's ideas in the
        Medicean period.

1362   Seigel, Jerrold E. "'Civic Humanism' or Ciceronian
        Rhetoric? The Culture of Petrarch and Bruni." *Past
        and Present*, 34 (July 1966): 3-48.

1363   Soudek, Josef. "A Fifteenth-Century Humanistic Best-
        seller. The Manuscript Diffusion of Leonardo Bruni's
        Annotated Latin Version of the (Pseudo-) Aristotelian
        'Economics.'" *Philosophy and Humanism* (item 293),
        pp.129-43.

1364   ————. "The Genesis and Tradition of Leonardo Bruni's
        Annotated Latin Version of the (Pseudo-) Aristotelian
        Economics." *Scriptorium*, 12 (1958): 260-68.

1365   ————. "Leonardo Bruni and His Public: A Statistical
        and Interpretive Study of His Annotated Latin Version
        of the (Pseudo-) Aristotelian 'Economics.'" *SMRH*, 5
        (1968): 49-137.

1366   Toynbee, Paget. "Giannozzo Manetti, Leonardo Bruni,
        and Dante's 'Letter to the Florentines.'" *Modern
        Language Review*, 14 (1919): 111-12.

1367   Trexler, R.C. "Who Were the Eight Saints?" *Renais-
        sance News*, 16 (1963): 89-94.

1368   ————. "Ritual Behavior in Renaissance Florence: The
        Setting." *MH*, n.s. 4 (1973): 125-44.

1369   Ullman, B.L. "Leonardo Bruni and Humanistic Historiog-
        raphy." *MH*, 4 (1946): 45-61; repr. in his *Studies
        in the Italian Renaissance* (item 203).

1370   ————. "The Dedication Copy of Giovanni Dominici's
        Lucula Noctis--A Landmark in the History of the
        Renaissance." *MH*, 1 (1943): 109-23; repr. in his
        Studies in the Italian Renaissance (item 203).

1371   ————. *The Humanism of Coluccio Salutati*. Padua:
        Antenore, 1963.

1372   Vittorini, Domenico. "Leonardo Bruni Aretino and
        Humanism." *High Points in the History of Italian
        Literature*. New York: McKay, 1958, pp.90-100.

1373   ————. "Salutati's Letters to the Archbishop of
        Canterbury." *High Points in the History of Italian
        Literature*, pp.82-89.

1374   Witt, Ronald G. "Cino Rinuccini's *Responsiva alla
        Invettiva di Messer Antonio Lusco*." *RQ*, 23 (1970):
        133-50.

1375   ————. *Coluccio Salutati and His Public Letters*.
        Geneva: Droz, 1976.

1376   ————. "Coluccio Salutati and the Conception of the
        Poeta Theologus in the Fourteenth Century." *RQ*, 30
        (1977): 538-63.

1377   ————. "Coluccio Salutati and the Origins of Flor-
        ence." *Il Pensiero Politico*, 2 (1969): 161-72.

1378   ————. "Coluccio Salutati and the Political Life of
        the Commune of Buggiano (1351-1374)." *Rinascimento*,
        2d ser., 6 (1966): 27-56.

1379   ————. "Coluccio Salutati, Chancellor and Citizen of
        Lucca." *Traditio*, 25 (1969): 191-216.

1380   ————. "The 'De tyranno' and Coluccio Salutati's
        View of Politics and Roman History." *Nuova Rivista
        Storica*, 53 (1969): 434-74.

1381   ————. "Florentine Politics and the Ruling Class,
        1382-1407." *JMRS*, 6 (1976): 243-68.

1382   ————. *Hercules at the Crossroads*. *The Life, Works,
        and Thought of Coluccio Salutati*. Durham, N.C.:
        Duke University Press, 1983.

1383   ———. "The Rebirth of the Concept of Republican
        Liberty in Italy." *Renaissance Studies in Honor of
        Hans Baron* (item 296), pp.173-200.

1384   ———. "Salutati and Contemporary Physics." *JHI*,
        38 (1977): 667-72.

1385   ———. "Salutati and Plutarch." *Essays Presented to
        Myron P. Gilmore* (item 275), vol.1, pp.335-46.

1386   ———. "Toward a Biography of Coluccio Salutati."
        Rinascimento, 2d ser. 16 (1976): 19-34.

See also items 653, 705, 709, 881, 1210, 1786, 1824, 2745.

XIII. HUMANISM IN NORTHERN ITALY, 1375-1550

Humanism in northern Italy in the last decades of the fourteenth century was nurtured by the rich legacy of Petrarchan
humanism, with its concern for self-understanding and moral
improvement, best represented by Giovanni Conversini da Ravenna (1343-1408) and Pier Paolo Vergerio (1370-1444). By
the beginning of the fifteenth century, Venetian patricians,
such as Francesco Barbaro, were writing on such themes as
family life and good government, while absorbing Greek learning brought from Constantinople by Guarino da Verona and
George of Trebizond. Humanism also became firmly established
at the courts of the Visconti and Sforza in Milan, the Este
in Ferrara, and the Gonzaga in Mantua. By mid-century, Greek
literature was introduced in the universities, while at Padua
Aristotelian studies flourished in the work of Piero Pomponazzi. Such poets as Baptista Mantuanus and Marco Girolamo
Vida wrote in imitation of classical Latin verse, especially
the elegy. The political strain of Venetian humanism was
continued into the sixteenth century by the work of Gasparo
Contarini.

A. SOURCES

1387   Baccillieri, Tiberio. "Whether the Human Intellect Is
       One in Number in All Men," trans. L.A. Kennedy.
       Renaissance Philosophy (item 320), pp.55-66.

1388   Baptista Mantuanus. "Baptista Mantuanus--Amateur
       Physician," trans. Gordon W. Jones. *Bulletin of the
       History of Medicine*, 36 (1962): 148-62.

1389   ————. *The Bucolicks of Baptist Mantuan in Ten Ec-
       logues*, trans. Thomas Harvey. London: Humphrey
       Moseley, 1656.

1390   ————. *The Eclogs of the Poet B. Mantuan Carmelian*,
       trans. George Turberville. London: H. Bynneman,
       1567.

1391   Barbaro, Francesco. "On Wifely Duties (*De re uxoria*,
       preface and book 2)," trans. B.G. Kohl. *The Earthly
       Republic* (item 322), pp.189-228.

1392   Benedetti, Alessandro. *Diary of the Caroline War*, ed.
       and trans. Dorothy M. Schullian. New York: Ungar,
       1967.

1393   Buonaccorso da Montemagno. "A Declamation of Noble-
       ness," trans. John Tiptoft in R.J. Mitchell, *John
       Tiptoft (1427-1470)*. London: Longmans, Green, 1938,
       pp.213-41.

1394   Contarini, Gasparo. *The Commonwealth and Government
       of Venice*, trans. L. Lewkenor. London: John Windet
       for Edmund Mattes, 1599; repr. New York: Da Capo
       Press, 1969.

1395   ————. *The State of the Church of Rome ... as it
       appears by the Advices given to Paul III and Julius*

159

by Creatures of their Own, trans. William Clagett.
London: W. Rogers, 1688; *Somers Tract,* vol.3 (1751);
repr. vol.60 (1808).

1396   Dati, Leonardo.   "Leonardo Dati: *Hiensal Tragoedia.* A
       Critical Edition with Translation," J.R. Berrigan.
       HL, 25 (1976): 84-145.

1397   Dondi dall'Orologio, Giovanni.   "Letter to Fra Guglielmo
       da Cremona," trans. Neal W. Gilbert.   *Viator,* 8 (1977):
       339-46.   See item 1458.

1398   Fiera, Battista.   *De iusticia pingenda.   On the Paint-
       ing of Justice.   A Dialogue between Mantegna and
       Momus,* trans. James Wardrop.   London: Lion and Uni-
       corn Press, 1957.

1399   Flaminio, Marco Antonio.   *The Scholar's Vade Mecum,*
       trans. John Norton.   London: T. Sawbridge, 1674.

1400   Fracastoro, Girolamo.   *De Contagione et contagiosis
       morbis,* ed. and trans. Wilmer Cave Wright.   New York:
       Putnam, 1930.

1401   ————.   *Fracastoro Syphillis or the French Disease,*
       ed. and trans. Heneage Wynne-Finch.   London: W.
       Heinemann Medical Books, 1935.

1402   ————.   *Naugerius,* ed. with English translation by
       Ruth Kelso and introd. M.W. Bundy.   Illinois Studies
       in Language and Literature, vol.9, no.3.   Urbana,
       1924.

1403   Giovanni di Conversino da Ravenna.   *Dragmalogia de
       Eligibili Vite Genere,* ed. with trans. H.L. Eaker,
       with introd. and notes B.G. Kohl.   Lewisburg: Buck-
       nell University Press; London: Associated University
       Presses, 1980.

1404   Guarini, Battista.   "The Treatise of Battista Guarino
       De ordine docends et studendi."   W.H. Woodward,
       Vittorino de Feltre and Other Humanist Educators
       (item 338), pp.159-78.

1405   Loschi, Antonio.   *Achilles,* trans. J.R. Berrigan.
       Munich: W. Fink, 1975.   Latin text of A. da Schio's
       modern edition with Berrigan's translation on facing
       pages; see item 1017.

1406   Navagero, Andrea. *Lusus*, ed. and trans. Alice E.
        Wilson. Nieuwkoop: De Graaf, 1973.

1407   Palingenius, Marcellus. *The Zodiake of Life*, trans.
        Barnabe Googe. London: John Tisdale, 1560; London:
        John Tisdale, 1561; London: Henry Denham, 1565;
        London: H. Middleton, 1576; repr. New York: Scholars'
        Facsimiles and Reprints, 1947.

1408   Pomponazzi, Pietro. "On God's Foreknowledge and Human
        Freedom (De fato, de libero arbitrio et de prae-
        destinatione, Bk.4, complete)." *Renaissance Philos-
        ophy, Vol.1. The Italian Philosophers* (item 316),
        pp.231-80.

1409   ————. "On the Immortality of the Soul," trans.
        William Henry Hay, II. *The Renaissance Philosophy
        of Man* (item 311), pp.280-381.

1410   Sadoleto, Jacopo Cardinal. "Letter to the Genevans,"
        trans. John C. Olin. *A Reformation Debate: Sadoleto's
        Letter to the Genevans and Calvin's Reply.* New
        York: Harper and Row, 1966, pp.29-48.

1411   ————. *Sadoleto on Education (De pueris recte insti-
        tiendis)*, trans. E.T. Campagnac and K. Forbes. New
        York & London: Oxford University Press, 1966.

1412   Scaliger, J.C. *Select Translations from Scaliger's
        Poetics*, trans. F.M. Padelford. Yale Studies in
        English, 26. New York: Henry Holt, 1905.

1413   Telesio, Bernardino. "On the Nature of Things Accord-
        ing to Their Own Proper Principles (De rerum natura
        iusta propria principia, Bk.i, chaps. 1-16, complete)."
        *Renaissance Philosophy, Vol.1, The Italian Philos-
        ophers* (item 317), pp.301-37.

1414   Vergerio, Pier Paolo. "The Treatise *De ingenuis
        moribus* ..." W.H. Woodward, *Vittorino da Feltre and
        Other Humanist Educators* (item 338), pp.93-118.

1415   Vida, Marco Girolamo. *De arte poetica*, trans. Christ-
        opher Pitt. London: A. Bettesworth, 1725; 2nd ed.
        London: John Hughes, for Robert Dodsley, 1742; London:
        C. Hitch, 1743; repr. A.S. Cook, *The Art of Poetry.*
        Boston: Ginn, 1892, pp.39-156. Includes Latin text.

1416   ————. *The "De Arte Poetica" of Marco Girolamo Vida,*
          ed. and trans. Ralph G. Williams. New York: Columbia
          University Press, 1976.

1417   ————. *The Game of Chess. Marco Girolamo Vida's
          "Scachia Ludus,"* ed. and trans. Mario Di Cesare.
          Nieuwkoop: De Graaf, 1975.

                          B. *STUDIES*

1418   Adam, Rudol G. *Francesco Filelfo at the Court of
          Milan (1439-1481), A Contribution to the Study of
          Humanism in Northern Italy.* Bibliothek des Histor-
          ischen Instituts in Rom, 51. Tübingen: Max Niemeyer,
          1983.

1419   Ady, Cecilia Mary. "Humanism and Tyranny." *Umanesimo
          e scienza politica.* Roma-Firenze: Atti del Congresso
          Internazionale di Studi Umanistici, 1949. Ed. by
          E. Castelli. Milan: Marzorati, 1951, pp.43-49.

1420   Anderson, Marvin W. "Word and Spirit in Exile (1542-
          1561): The Biblical Writings of Peter Martyr Ver-
          migli." *Journal of Ecclesiastical History,* 21 (1970):
          193-201.

1421   Baron, Hans. "A Forgotten Chronicle of Early Fifteenth-
          Century Venice." *Essays in History and Literature
          Presented by Fellows of the Newberry Library to
          Stanley Pargellis,* ed. Heins Blum. Chicago: The
          Newberry Library, 1965, pp.19-36; repr. in *From
          Petrarch to Leonardo Bruni* (item 1133).

1422   Baumgartner, Leona, and J.F. Fulton. *A Bibliography of
          the Poem "Syphilus sive morbus gallicus."* New
          Haven: Yale University Press, 1935.

1423   Baxandall, Michael. "Guarino, Pisanello and Manuel
          Chrysoloras." *JWCI,* 28 (1965): 183-204.

1424   ————. "A Dialogue on Art from the Court of Leonello
          d'Este." *JWCI,* 26 (1963): 304-26.

1425   Berrigan, Joseph R. "The Latin Aesop of Ermolao Bar-
          baro." *Manuscripta,* 22 (1978): 141-48.

1426   ————. "The Libellus Fabellarum of Gregorio Correr."
        Manuscripta, 19 (1975): 131-38.

1427   Birnbaum, Marianna D. "Janus Pannonius, Bartolomeo
        Melzi, and the Sforzas." *RQ,* 30 (1977): 1-8.

1428   Bouwsma, William J. *Venice and the Defense of Republi-
        can Liberty, Renaissance Values in the Age of the
        Counter Reformation.* Berkeley and Los Angeles: Uni-
        versity of California Press, 1968.

1429   ————. "Changing Assumptions in Later Renaissance
        Culture." *Viator,* 7 (1976): 421-40.

1430   ————. "Venice and the Political Education of Europe."
        Renaissance Venice (item 284), pp.445-67.

1431   Branca, Vittore. "Ermolao Barbaro and Late Quattro-
        cento Venetian Humanism." *Renaissance Venice* (item
        284), pp.218-43.

1432   Breen, Quirinus. "Francesco Zambeccari: His Transla-
        tions and Fabricated Translations of Libanian Letters."
        Studies in the Renaissance, 11 (1964): 46-75.

1433   Bueno De Mesquita, D.M. "Niccolò Da Correggio at
        Milan." *Italian Studies,* 20 (1965): 42-54.

1434   Bundy, Murray W. "Fracastoro and the Imagination."
        Philological Quarterly, 20 (1941): 236-49.

1435   Chambers, D.S. *The Imperial Age of Venice, 1380-1580.*
        New York: Harcourt Brace Jovanovich, 1970. See
        especially chapter 3 on culture.

1436   Ciapponi, Lucia A. "Fragmentary Treatise on Epigraphic
        Alphabets by Fra Giocondo da Verona." *RQ,* 32 (1979):
        18-40.

1437   Connell, Susan. "Books and Their Owners in Venice
        1345-1480." *JWCI,* 35 (1972): 163-86.

1438   Curtius, E.R. "Sicco Polenton." *BHR,* 11 (1949): 219-
        22.

1439   Di Cesare, Mario A. *Bibliotheca Vidiana. A Bibliog-
        raphy of Marco Girolamo Vida.* Florence: Sansoni,
        1974.

1440   ————. *Vida's Christiad and Vergilian Epic*. New
        York: Columbia University Press, 1964.

1441   ————. "The *Ars Poetica* of Marco Girolamo Vida and
        the Manuscript Evidence." *Acta Conventus Neo-latini
        Lovaniensis* (item 288), pp.207-18.

1442   Diller, A. "The Library of Francesco and Ermolao Bar-
        baro." *IMU*, 6 (1963): 253-62.

1443   ————. "Three Greek Scribes Working for Bessarion:
        Trivizias, Callistus, Hermonymus." *IMU*, 10 (1967):
        403-10.

1444   ————. "The Greek Codices of Palla Strozzi and
        Guarino Veronese." *JWCI*, 15 (1952): 257-58.

1445   Dimsey, S.E. "Giacopo Castelvetro." *Modern Language
        Review*, 23 (1928): 424-31.

1446   Douglas, Andrew Halliday. *The Philosophy of Pietro
        Pomponazzi*. Cambridge: Cambridge University Press,
        1910; repr. Olm: Hildesheim, 1962.

1447   Douglas, Richard M. *Jacopo Sadoleto, 1477-1547*. *Hu-
        manist and Reformer*. Cambridge, Mass.: Harvard Uni-
        versity Press, 1959.

1448   Edwards, William F. "Niccolò Leoniceno and the Origins
        of Humanist Discussion of Method." *Philosophy and
        Humanism* (item 293), pp.283-305.

1449   Fahy, Conor. "Three Early Renaissance Treatises on
        Women." *Italian Studies*, 11 (1956): 30-55.

1450   Fenlon, Dermot. *Heresy and Obedience in Tridentine
        Italy: Cardinal Pole and the Counter Reformation*.
        Cambridge: Cambridge University Press, 1972.

1451   Gardner, Edmund G. *Dukes and Poets of Ferrara: A Study
        in the Religion and Politics of the Fifteenth and
        Early Sixteenth Century*. London: Constable; New
        York: Dutton, 1904.

1452   Geanakoplos, Deno J. "The Discourse of Demetrius Chal-
        condyles on the Inauguration of Greek Studies at the
        University of Padua in 1463." *Studies in the Renais-
        sance*, 21 (1974): 118-44.

1453   Gilbert, Felix. "Biondo, Sabellico, and the Begin-
       nings of Venetian Official Historiography." *Flor-
       ilegium Historiale* (item 302), pp.276-93.

1454   ————. "Religion and Politics in the Thought of
       Gasparo Contarini." *Action and Conviction in Early
       Modern Europe* (item 299); repr. in *History: Choice
       and Commitment* (item 693), pp.247-68.

1455   ————. "Humanism in Venice." *Florence and Venice*
       (item 276), vol.1, pp.13-26.

1456   ————. "The Date of the Composition of Contarini's
       and Giannotti's Books on Venice." *Studies in the
       Renaissance,* 14 (1967): 172-84.

1457   Gilbert, Neal W. "Francesco Vimercato of Milan: A
       Bio-Bibliography." *Studies in the Renaissance,* 12
       (1964): 188-217.

1458   ————. "A Letter of Giovanni Dondi dall'Orologio to
       Fra Guglielmo Centueri: A Fourteenth-Century Episode
       in the Quarrel of the Ancients and the Moderns."
       Viator, 8 (1977): 299-346. Includes edition of the
       Latin text and English translation of the letter.

1459   Gilmore, Myron P. "Myth and Reality in Venetian Poli-
       tical Theory." *Renaissance Venice* (item 284), pp.
       431-44.

1460   Gleason, Elisabeth Gregorich. "Sixteenth-Century
       Italian Interpretations of Luther." *ARG,* 60 (1969):
       160-73.

1461   ————. "On the Nature of Sixteenth-Century Italian
       Evangelism: Scholarship, 1953-1978." *The Sixteenth-
       Century Journal,* 9 (1978): 3-26.

1462   Grafton, Anthony, and Lisa Jardine. "Humanism and the
       School of Guarino: A Problem of Evaluation." *Past
       and Present,* 96 (1982): 51-80.

1463   Grant, Leonard W. "An Eclogue of Francesco Filelfo?"
       Manuscripta, 3 (1959): 171-72.

1464   Grierson, Philip. "Ercole D'Este and Leonardo Da
       Vinci's Equestrian." *Italian Studies,* 14 (1959):
       40-48.

1465   Grendler, Marcella. "A Greek Collection in Padua: The
       Library of Gian Vincenzo Pinelli (1535-1601)." *RQ,*
       33 (1980): 386-417.

1466   Grendler, Paul F. "The Concept of Humanism in Cinque-
       cento Italy." *Renaissance Studies in Honor of Hans
       Baron* (item 296), pp.445-64.

1467   Gundersheimer, Werner L. "Toward a Reinterpretation
       of the Renaissance in Ferrara." *BHR,* 30 (1968):
       267-81.

1468   ————. "Women, Learning, and Power: Eleonora of Ara-
       gon and the Court of Ferrara." *Beyond Their Sex*
       (item 291), pp.9-42.

1469   ————. "The Patronage of Ercole I d'Este." *JMRS,* 6
       (1976): 1-18.

1470   ————. *Ferrara, The Style of a Renaissance Despotism.*
       Princeton: Princeton University Press, 1973.

1471   ————. "Bartolomeo Goggio: A Feminist in Renaissance
       Ferrara." *RQ,* 33 (1980): 175-201.

1472   Hall, Vernon, Jr. *Life of Julius Caesar Scaliger
       (1484-1558).* Transactions of the American Philosoph-
       ical Society, n.s. 40, pt.2, pp.85-170. Philadelphia,
       1950.

1473   ————. "Scaliger's Defense of Poetry." *PMLA,* 63
       (1948): 1125-30.

1474   Hammer, William. "Balthazar Rasinus, Italian Humanist."
       Italica, 25 (1948): 15-27.

1475   ————. "Balthazar Rasinus and His Praise of Studies
       at the University of Pavia." *Studies in Philology,*
       37 (1940): 133-48. Edition of Latin oration of 1450
       with summary in English.

1476   Hicks, David L. "The Education of a Prince: Lodovico
       il Moro and the Rise of Pandolfo Petrucci." *Studies
       in the Renaissance,* 8 (1961): 88-102.

1477   Hobson, Anthony. "Manuscripts Captured at Vitoria."
       Cultural Aspects of the Italian Renaissance (item
       280), pp.485-98.

1478   Ianziti, Gary. "A Humanist Historian and His Docu-
        ments: Giovanni Simonetta, Secretary to the Sforzas."
        RQ, 34 (1981): 491-517.

1479   ———. "From Flavio Biondo to Lodrisio Crivelli: The
        Beginnings of Humanistic Historiography in Sforza
        Milan." *Rinascimento,* 20 (1980): 3-39.

1480   ———. "The First Edition of Giovanni Simonetta's
        De rebus gestis Francisci Sfortiae commentarii:
        Questions of Chronology and Interpretation." *BHR,*
        44 (1982): 137-47.

1481   Ilardi, Vincent. "'Italianità' among Some Italian
        Intellectuals of the Early Sixteenth Century."
        Traditio, 12 (1956): 339-67.

1482   James, Theodore E. "A Fragment of 'An Exposition of
        the First Letter of Seneca to Lucilius' Attributed
        to Peter of Mantua." *Philosophy and Humanism* (item
        293), pp.531-42.

1483   ———. "Peter Alboini of Mantua: Philosopher-
        Humanist." *Journal of the History of Philosophy,*
        12 (1974): 161-70.

1484   Kennedy, Leonard A. "The Philosophical Manuscripts of
        Cesare Cremonini." *Manuscripta,* 23 (1979): 79-87.

1485   King, Margaret L. "Book-Lined Cells: Women and Human-
        ism in the Early Italian Renaissance." *Beyond Their
        Sex* (item 291), pp.66-90.

1486   ———. "Caldiera and the Barbaros on Marriage and the
        Family: Humanist Reflections of Venetian Realities."
        JMRS, 6 (1976): 19-50.

1487   ———. "Goddess and Captive: Antonio Loschi's Poetic
        Tribute to Maddalena Scrovegni (1389), Study and
        Text." *MH,* n.s. 10 (1981): 103-27.

1488   ———. "The Patriciate and the Intellectuals: Powers
        and Ideas in Quattrocento Venice." *Societas,* 5
        (1975): 295-312.

1489   ———. "Personal, Domestic and Republican Values in
        the Moral Philosophy of Giovanni Caldiera." *RQ,* 28
        (1975): 535-75.

1490   ————. "The Religious Retreat of Isotta Nogarola
          (1418-1466): Sexism and Its Consequences in the
          Fifteenth Century." *Signs,* 3 (1978): 807-22.

1491   ————. "A Study in Venetian Humanism at Mid-Quattro-
          cento: Filippo da Rimini and his 'Symposium de
          Paupertate.'" *Studi Veneziani,* n.s. 2 (1978): 75-
          96; n.s. 3 (1979): 141-86.

1492   ————. "Thwarted Ambitions: Six Learned Women of the
          Italian Renaissance." *Soundings,* 59 (1976): 280-304.

1493   Kohl, B.G. "The Manuscript Tradition of Some Works of
          Giovanni da Ravenna." *Acta Conventus Neo-Latini
          Amstelodamensis* (item 305), pp.610-19.

1494   ————. "Political Attitudes of North Italian Human-
          ists in the Late Trecento." *Studies in Medieval
          Culture,* 4 (1974): 418-27.

1495————. "The Works of Giovanni di Conversino da Ravenna:
          A Catalogue of Manuscripts and Editions." *Traditio,*
          31 (1975): 349-67.

1496   ————, and James Day. "Giovanni Conversini's *Consola-
          tio ad Donatum* on the Death of Petrarch." *Studies
          in the Renaissance,* 21 (1974): 9-30.

1497   Kraye, Jill. "Francesco Filelfo's Lost Letter *De
          Ideis.*" JWCI, 42 (1979): 236-49.

1498   Kristeller, Paul Oskar. "Some New Additions to the
          Correspondence of Guarino da Verona, 2. An Unknown
          Letter of Giovanni Barbo to Guarino." *IMU,* 8 (1965):
          243-48.

1499   ————. "Pier Candido Decembrio and His Unpublished
          Treatise on the Immortality of the Soul." *The Clas-
          sical Tradition* (item 306), pp.536-58.

1500   ————. "Two Unpublished Questions on the Soul of
          Pietro Pomponazzi." *MH,* 9 (1955): 76-101; 10 (1956):
          151.

1501   Labalme, Patricia H. *Bernardo Giustiniani: A Venetian
          of the Quattrocento.* Rome: Storia e Letteratura,
          1969.

1502   ————. "Identification and Translation of a Letter
        of Guarino Guarini of Verona." *JWCI*, 18 (1955): 142-
        43.

1503   ————. "The Last Will of a Venetian Patrician (1498)."
        Philosophy and Humanism (item 293), pp.483-501.

1504   ————. "Women's Roles in Early Modern Venice: An Ex-
        ceptional Case." *Beyond Their Sex* (item 291), pp.
        129-52.

1505   Labowsky, L. *Bessarion's Library and the Bibliotheca
        Marciana*. Rome: Storia e Letteratura, 1979.

1506   ————. "Manuscripts from Bessarion's Library Found
        in Milan." *Medieval and Renaissance Studies*, 5
        (1961): 117-26.

1507   ————. "An Unnoticed Letter from Bessarion to Lorenzo
        Valla." *Medieval Learning and Literature. Essays
        Presented to Richard William Hunt,* ed. J.J.G. Alex-
        ander and M.T. Gibson. Oxford: Clarendon Press,
        1976, pp.366-75.

1508   McLelland, J.C., ed. *Peter Martyr and Italian Reform*.
        Waterloo, Ont.: Wilfred Laurier University Press,
        1980.

1509   McManamon, John M., S.J. "Innovation in Early Humanist
        Rhetoric: The Oratory of Pier Paolo Vergerio the
        Elder." *Rinascimento*, 2nd ser., 22 (1982): 3-32.

1510   McNair, Philip M.J. "The Reformation of the Sixteenth
        Century in Renaissance Italy." *Religion and Human-
        ism* (item 293), pp.149-66.

1511   Maddison, Carol. *Marcantonio Flaminio: Poet, Humanist,
        and Reformer*. Chapel Hill: University of North
        Carolina Press, 1965.

1512   Mahoney, Edward P. "Nicoletto Vernia on the Soul and
        Immortality." *Philosophy and Humanism* (item 293),
        pp.144-63.

1513   Mallett, M.E. "Some Notes on a Fifteenth-Century
        'condottiere' and His Library: Count Antonio da
        Marsciano." *Cultural Aspects of the Italian Renais-
        sance* (item 280), pp.202-15.

1514   Marti, Berthe. "Gomez *versus* the Spanish College at
        Bologna." *Didascaliae: Studies in Honor of Anselm
        M. Albareda,* ed. Sesto Prete. New York: Bernard M.
        Rosenthal, 1961, pp.293-319.

1515   Matsen, Herbert S. "Alessandro Achillini (1463-1512)
        and 'Ockhamism' at Bologna (1490-1500)." *Journal of
        the History of Philosophy,* 13 (1975): 437-51.

1516   ———. "Students' 'Ars' Disputations at Bologna
        around 1500, Illustrated from the Career of Ales-
        sandro Achillini, 1463-1512." *History of Education,*
        6 (1977): 169-81.

1517   ———. *Alessandro Achillini (1463-1512) and His Doc-
        trine of 'Universals' and 'Transcendentals': A Study
        in Renaissance 'Ockhamism.'* Lewisburg, Pa.: Bucknell
        University Press, 1974.

1518   ———. "Giovanni Garzoni (1419-1505) to Alessandro
        Achillini (1463-1512): An Unpublished Letter and
        Defense." *Philosophy and Humanism* (item 293), pp.
        518-30.

1519   Mercer, R.G.G. *The Teaching of Gasparino Barzizza with
        Special Reference to His Place in Paduan Humanism.*
        London: Modern Humanities Research Association, 1979.

1520   Miller, Clement. "Francesco Zambeccari and a Musical
        Friend." *RQ,* 25 (1972): 426-28.

1521   Monfasani, John. "Bessarion Latinus." *Rinascimento,*
        21 (1981): 165-209. Includes editions of short
        Latin texts by Bessarion.

1522   ———. *George of Trebizond. A Biography and a Study
        of His Rhetoric and Logic.* Leiden: Brill, 1976.

1523   Muir, Edward. "Images of Power: Art and Pageantry in
        Renaissance Venice." *American Historical Review,* 84
        (1979): 16-53.

1524   Oliver, R.P. "The Satires of Filelfo." *Italica,* 26
        (1949): 23-46.

1525   Panizza, Letizia A. "Gasparino Barzizza's Commentaries
        on Seneca's Letters." *Traditio,* 33 (1977): 297-358.
        With edition of texts.

1526   Pascal, Louis B.   "The Council of Trent and Bible
         Study: Humanism and Scripture." *Catholic Historical
         Review,* 52 (1966): 18-38.

1527   Pascal, Paul. "The 'Scriptorum illustrium linquae
         Latinae' of Sicco Polenton." Acta Conventus Neo-Latini
         Amstelodamensis (item 305), pp.851-58.

1528   Peebles, B.M. "Studies in Pietro Donato Avogaro of
         Verona, 1. A Displaced Manuscript Located, the Writ-
         ings Surveyed." *IMU,* 5 (1962): 1-49.

1529   Percival, W. Keith. "Textual Problems in the Latin
         Grammar of Guarino Veronese." *Res Publica Litterarum,*
         1 (1978): 241-54.

1530   Pigman, G.W., III. "Barzizza's Treatise on Imitation."
         BHR, 44 (1982): 341-52.

1531   ————. "Barzizza's Studies of Cicero." *Rinascimento,*
         21 (1981): 123-63. Includes Latin edition of Bar-
         zizza's life of Cicero.

1532   Pine, Martin. "Pietro Pomponazzi and the Medieval
         Tradition of God's Foreknowledge." *Philosophy and
         Humanism* (item 293), pp.100-15.

1533   ————. "Pomponazzi and the Problem of 'Double Truth.'"
         JHI, 29 (1968): 163-76.

1534   Rabil, Albert, Jr. *Laura Cereta, Quattrocento Humanist.*
         Binghamton, N.Y.: Center for Medieval and Early
         Renaissance Studies, 1981.

1535   Richards, J.P.C. "The 'Elysium' of Julius Caesar Bor-
         donius." *Studies in the Renaissance,* 9 (1962): 195-
         217. On J.C. Scaliger's work.

1536   ————. "The Poems of Galeatius Ponticus Facinus."
         Studies in the Renaissance, 6 (1959): 94-128.

1537   Robathan, Dorothy M. "A Fifteenth-Century History of
         Latin Literature." *Speculum,* 7 (1932): 239-48. On
         Sicco Polenton.

1538   Robey, D. "Humanism and Education in the Early Quattro-
         cento: The *De Ingenuis Moribus* of P.P. Vergerio."
         BHR, 42 (1980): 27-58.

1539   ————. "P.P. Vergerio the Elder: Republicanism and
         Civic Values in the Work of an Early Humanist."
         Past and Present, 58 (1973): 3-37.

1540   ————. "Virgil's Statue at Mantua and the Defense of
         Poetry: An Unpublished Letter of 1397." *Rinascimento*,
         2d ser., 9 (1969): 183-204.

1541   ————, and John Law. "The Venetian Myth and the 'De
         Republica Veneta' of Pier Paolo Vergerio." *Rinasci-
         mento*, 2d ser., 15 (1975): 3-59.

1542   Robin, Diana. "A Reassessment of the Character of
         Francesco Filelfo (1398-1481)." *RQ*, 36 (1983): 202-
         24.

1543   Rose, Paul Lawrence. "The Accademia Venetiana, Science
         and Culture in Renaissance Venice." *Studi Veneziani*,
         11 (1969): 191-242.

1544   ————. "Bartolomeo Zamberti's Funeral Oration for the
         Humanist Encyclopaedist Giorgio Valla." *Cultural
         Aspects of the Italian Renaissance* (item 280), pp.
         299-310.

1545   Ross, James Bruce. "The Emergence of Gasparo Contarini:
         A Bibliographical Essay." *Church History*, 41 (1972):
         22-45.

1546   ————. "Gasparo Contarini and His Friends." *Studies
         in the Renaissance*, 17 (1970): 192-232.

1547   ————. "Venetian Schools and Teachers, Fourteenth to
         Early Sixteenth Century: A Survey and a Study of
         Giovanni Battista Egnazio." *RQ*, 29 (1976): 521-66.

1548   Sanford, Eva M. "Gaspare Veronese, Humanist and
         Teacher." *TAPA*, 84 (1953): 190-209. On texts
         taught and methods used in Italian schools of the
         mid-fifteenth century.

1549   Schmitt, Charles B. "Alberto Pio and the Aristotelian
         Studies of His Time." *Società, politica e cultura a
         Carpi ai tempi di Alberto III Pio*, 2 vols. Padua:
         Antenore, 1981, vol.1, pp.43-64.

1550   Sheppard, L.A. "A Fifteenth-Century Humanist, Fran-
         cesco Filelfo." *The Library*, ser.4, 16 (1935-1936):
         1-27.

1551   Skulsky, Harold. "Paduan Epistemology and the Doc-
        trine of the One Mind." *Journal of the History of
        Philosophy*, 6 (1968): 341-62.

1552   Smith, Leonard. "P.P. Vergerio: 'De situ veteris et
        inclitae Urbis Romae.'" *EHR*, 41 (1926): 571-77.

1553   Soons, A. "The Celebration of Rustic Virtues in the
        Works of Titus Livius de Frulovisiis." *JMRS*, 1
        (1971): 119-29.

1554   Stormon, E.J. "Bessarion before the Council of Flor-
        ence: A Survey of His Early Writings (1423-1437)."
        Byzantina Australiensia, 1 (1980): 128-56.

1555   Tedeschi, John. "Italian Reformers and the Diffusion
        of Renaissance Culture." *The Sixteenth-Century
        Journal*, 5 (1974): 79-94.

1556   ————. "A Sixteenth-Century Italian Erasmian and the
        Index." *Essays Presented to Myron P. Gilmore* (item
        275), vol.1, pp.305-16.

1557   Tenenti, Alberto. "The Sense of Space and Time in the
        Venetian World of the Fifteenth and Sixteenth Cen-
        turies." *Renaissance Venice* (item 284), pp.17-46.

1558   Thomson, Ian. "Manuel Chrysoloras and the Early Ital-
        ian Renaissance." *Greek, Roman and Byzantine Studies*,
        7 (1966): 63-82.

1559   ————. "Some Notes on the Contents of Guarino's
        Library." *RQ*, 29 (1976): 169-77.

1560   ————. "A Textual Problem in the Epistolary of
        Guarino." *RQ*, 24 (1971): 485-86.

1561   Tournoy, Gilbert. "Francesco Diedo, Venetian Humanist
        and Politician of the Quattrocento." *HL*, (1970):
        201-34.

1562   Webb, Diana M. "Andrea Biglia at Bologna, 1424-7: A
        Humanist Friar and the Troubles of the Church."
        BIHR, 49 (1976): 41-59.

1563   Weiss, R. "Two Unnoticed 'Portraits' of Cardinal
        Bessarion." *Italian Studies*, 22 (1967): 1-5.

1564   ————. "Giovanni Aurelio Augurello, Girolamo
        Avogadro, and Isabella D'Este." *Italian Studies,*
        17 (1962): 1-11.

1565   ————. "Some Unpublished Correspondence of Guarino
        da Verona." *Italian Studies,* 2 (1938-39): 110-17.

1566   Wilson, Harold S. "George of Trebizond and Early
        Humanist Rhetoric." *Studies in Philology,* 40 (1943):
        367-79.

1567   Zimmermann, T.C. Price. "Confession and Autobiography
        in the Early Renaissance." *Renaissance Studies in
        Honor of Hans Baron* (item 296), pp.119-40. Dis-
        cusses autobiography of Giovanni Conversini da
        Ravenna.

See also items 442, 468, 581, 750-51, 2051, 2078-79, 2389,
        2542, 2557, 2618, 2661, 2743, 3059.

XIV. HUMANISM IN TUSCANY, ROME AND NAPLES, 1440-1550

In the second half of the fifteenth century, Florentine
humanism took a turn toward Greek studies and philosophical
speculation with the founding of the Platonic Academy and
major works in the Platonic tradition by Marsilio Ficino,
Greek translations by Angelo Poliziano, and the syncretistic
philosophizing of Giovanni Pico della Mirandola. Paul Oskar
Kristeller is the leading scholar of Florentine Platonism and
his many works provide an authoritative guide to that tradition. Other major humanists include the book-hunter and
social critic, Poggio Bracciolini, the great Latin philolo-
gist and student of ancient philosophies, Lorenzo Valla, and
the scholar-historian-humanist, Pope Pius II (Aeneas Sylvius
Piccolomini). For the model of the universal man of the
Renaissance see the studies on Leon Battista Alberti by Cecil
Grayson and Joan Kelly-Gadol, while Rome in the Renaissance
is well described by historians John O'Malley and John D'Amico.

A. SOURCES

1568   Alberti, Leon Battista. "The Conspiracy of Stefano
        Porcari (De Porcaria Conjuratione)." *Humanism and
        Liberty* (item 336), pp.107-15.

1569   ————. "Happiness (*De felicitate*)." *Humanism and
        Liberty* (item 336), pp.103-06.

1570   ————. *The Family in Renaissance Florence (I Libri
        della famiglia),* trans. Renée Neu Watkins. Columbia:
        University of South Carolina Press, 1969.

1571   ————. *The Albertis of Florence: Leon Battista
        Alberti's Della famiglia,* trans. Guido A. Guarino.
        Lewisburg, Pa.: Bucknell University Press, 1971.

1572   ————. "Three Dialogues (Intercoenales)," complete.
        *Renaissance Philosophy, Vol.1, The Italian Philos-
        ophers* (item 316), pp.27-39.

1573   ————. *On Painting and On Sculpture, The Latin Texts
        of De pictura et De statua,* ed. and trans. Cecil
        Grayson. London: Phaidon, 1972.

1574   ————. *On Painting,* trans. John R. Spencer. New
        Haven: Yale University Press, 1956.

1575   Bertrand de Mignanelli. "Ascensus Barcoch, a Latin
        Biography of the Malmūk Sultan Barqūq of Egypt,"
        trans. Walter J. Fischel. *Arabica,* 6 (1959): 64-74,
        152-72.

1576   ————. "A New Latin Source of Tamerlane's Conquest of
        Damascus, (1400-1401)," trans. Walter J. Fischel.
        Öriens, (1956): 201-32.

1577   Bracciolini, Poggio. *The Facetiae or Jocose Tales of
        Poggio,* anon. English trans. Paris: I. Liseux, 1879.

1578   ———. *The Facetiae, Unexpurgated Translation,* ed.
        Bernhardt J. Hurwood. New York: Award Books, 1968.

1579   ———. "On Nobility (*De nobilitate*)." *Humanism and
        Liberty* (item 336), pp.121-48.

1580   ———. "On Avarice (*De avaritia*)," trans. B.G. Kohl
        and E.B. Welles. *The Earthly Republic* (item 322),
        pp.241-89.

1581   ———. "Trial and Martyrdom of Jerome of Prague: A
        Letter from Poggio Bracciolini to His Friend Leonardo
        Aretino, Giving an Account of the Trial and Martyr-
        dom of Jerome of Prague," trans. Rev. Oliver A.
        Taylor. *Bibliotheca Sacra and Theological Review,*
        2 (1845): 636-49.

1582   ———. *Two Renaissance Book Hunters: The Letters of
        Poggius Bracciolini to Nicolaus de Niccolis,* trans.
        Phyllis W.G. Gordan. New York: Columbia University
        Press, 1974.

1583   Burchard, Johann. *At the Court of Borgia, Being an
        Account of the Reign of Pope Alexander VI,* trans.
        Geoffrey Parker. London: Folio Society, 1963.

1584   ———. *The Diary of John Burchard of Strasburg, Pon-
        tifical Master of Ceremonies, A.D. 1438-1506,* trans.
        Arnold Harris Mathew. London: Francis Griffiths,
        1910.

1585   Cajetan de Vio, Thomas. *Aristotle on Interpretation,
        Commentary by St. Thomas and Cajetan,* trans. Jean T.
        Oesterle. Milwaukee, Wis.: Marquette University
        Press, 1962.

1586   ———. *Commentary on St. Thomas Aquinas, On Being
        and Essence,* trans. Lottie H. Kendzierski and Francis
        C. Wade, S.J. Milwaukee, Wis.: Marquette University
        Press, 1965.

1587   ———. "On the Immortality of Minds," trans. James K.
        Sheridan. *Renaissance Philosophy* (item 320), pp.41-
        54.

1588   ———. *The Analogy of Names and the Concept of Being,*
        trans. Edward A. Bushinski and Henry J. Koren. Pitts-
        burgh: Duquesne University Press, 1953.

1589   Colonna, Francesco. *Hypnerotomachia. The Strife of
        Love in a Dreame,* trans. Sir Robert Dallington.
        London: William Holme, 1592; repr. New York: Da Capo,
        1969.

1590   ———. *Hypnerotomachia, The Strife of Love in a
        Dreame,* trans. Sir Robert Dallington. London, 1592;
        repr. with introd. by L. Gent. Delmar, N.Y.: Scholars'
        Facsimiles and Reprints, 1973.

1591   Cortese, Paolo. "Introduction to the First Book of the
        'Sentences,'" trans. W. Felver. *Renaissance Philos-
        ophy* (item 320), pp.29-37.

1592   *The Council of Constance: The Unification of the Church,*
        trans. Louise R. Loomis; ed. John H. Mundy and
        Kennerly M. Woody. New York: Columbia University
        Press, 1961.

1593   Ficino, Marsilio. *Commentary on Plato's Symposium,*
        trans. Sears R. Jayne. Columbia: University of Mis-
        souri Press, 1944.

1594   ———. "Concerning the Sun (*De sole,* abridged)."
        *Renaissance Philosophy, Vol.1, The Italian Philos-
        ophers* (item 316), pp.118-40.

1595   ———. "Ficino's *Platonic Theology,*" trans. Josephine
        Burroughs. *JHI,* 5 (1944): 227-42.

1596   ———. "Five Questions Concerning the Mind," trans.
        Josephine Burroughs. *The Renaissance Philosophy of
        Man* (item 311), pp.193-212.

1597   ———. *Marsilio Ficino: The Philebus Commentary. A
        Critical Edition and Translation,* ed. and trans.
        Michael J.B. Allen. Berkeley and Los Angeles: Uni-
        versity of California Press, 1975.

1598   ———. *Marsilio Ficino and the Phaedran Charioteer*
        (Ficino's Commentary on Plato's *Phaedra*), ed. and
        trans. Michael J.B. Allen. Berkeley and Los Angeles:
        University of California Press, 1981.

1599   ———. *The Book of Life* (De vita), trans. C. Boer.
        Irving, Tex.: Spring Publications, 1980.

1600   ————. *The Letters of Marsilio Ficino,* 2 vols.,
        trans. members of the Language Department of the
        School of Economic Science, London, preface by
        Paul Oskar Kristeller. London: Shepheard-Walwyn,
        1975-1978. The first two volumes contain a transla-
        tion of Books 1-3 of Ficino's *Epistulae.*

1601   Giovio, Paolo. *An Italian Portrait Gallery: Being the
        Elogia of Paolo Giovio,* trans. Florence Alden Gragg.
        Boston: Chapman and Grimes, 1935.

1602   ————. *The Historie* ... *of the Legation or Ambassade
        of* ... *Moscovia to Pope Clement the VII,* trans.
        Richard Eden. In Peter Martyr Anglerius, *The Dec-
        ades of the Newe World.* London: Rycharde Zug, 1555;
        repr. Edward Arber, *The First Three English Books on
        America.* Westminster: Constable, 1895.

1603   Mancini, Domenico. *The Mirrour of Good Manners (De
        quatuor virtutibus),* trans. Alexander Barclay.
        London: Pynson, c.1523; repr. 1570; repr. Spencer
        Society 38, Manchester, 1885.

1604   ————. *The Mirrour of Good Manners (De quatuor vir-
        tutibus),* trans. George Turberville. London:
        Bynneman, 1568.

1605   ————. *The Usurpation of Richard the Third,* ed. and
        trans. C.A.J. Armstrong. London: Oxford University
        Press, 1936.

1606   Manetti, Giannozzo. "On the Dignity of Man." *Two
        Views of Man,* trans. B. Murchland. New York: Ungar,
        1966, pp.63-101.

1607   ————. "On the Dignity and Excellence of Man (*De
        Dignitate et excellentia hominis,* Preface and Book
        4)." *Renaissance Philosophy, Vol.1, The Italian
        Philosophers* (item 316), pp.65-101.

1608   Patrizi, Francesco. *A Moral Methode of Civil Policie* ...
        *the Institution, State, and Government of a Common
        Weale,* trans. Ralph Robinson. London, 1576.

1609   ————. *The True Order and Methode of Writing and
        Reading Histories,* trans. Thomas Blundeville. Lon-
        don: W. Seres, 1574; repr. Hugh G. Dick, *Huntington
        Library Quarterly,* 3 (1940): 149-70.

1610   Pico della Mirandola, Giovanni. *A Platonick Discourse*
        upon Love, trans. Thomas Stanley, ed. Edmund G.
        Gardner. Boston: Merrymount Press, 1914.

1611   ———. *Giovanni Pico della Mirandola: His Life by His*
        Nephew Giovanni Francesco Pico, also Three of His
        Letters, His Interpretation of Psalm 16, His Twelve
        Rules of a Christian Life, His Twelve Points of a
        Perfect Lover, and His Deprecatory Hymn to God, ed.
        J.M. Rigg, with trans. Sir Thomas More. London:
        D. Nutt, 1890.

1612   ———. "Letter to Ermolao Barbaro." *Renaissance*
        Philosophy, Vol.1, The Italian Philosophers (item
        316), pp.106-17.

1613   ———. *Of Being and Unity (De ente et uno),* trans.
        Victor Michael Hamm. Milwaukee: Marquette University
        Press, 1943.

1614   ———. *On the Dignity of Man, On Being and the One,*
        Heptaplus, introd. Paul J.W. Miller. Indianapolis:
        Bobbs-Merrill, 1965.

1615   ———. *On the Dignity of Man,* trans. Charles Glenn
        Wallis. Annapolis, Md.: St. John's Book Store, 1940.

1616   ———. *On the Imagination, Latin Text with English*
        Translation, trans. Harry Caplin. Cornell Studies
        in English, 16. New Haven: Yale University Press,
        1930; repr. Westport, Conn.: Greenwood Press, 1971.

1617   ———. "Oration on the Dignity of Man," trans. E.L.
        Forbes. *The Renaissance Philosophy of Man* (item
        311), pp.223-54.

1618   ———. "Oration on the Dignity of Man, complete."
        Renaissance Philosophy, Vol.1, The Italian Philos-
        ophers (item 316), pp.141-71.

1619   ———. "Translation of 'On the Dignity of Man,' Ora-
        tion of Giovanni Pico della Mirandola," trans. E.L.
        Forbes. *JHI,* 3 (1942): 347-54.

1620   Pius II. *Aeneae Silvii De liberorum educatione,* trans.
        Brother Joel Stanislaus Nelson. Washington, D.C.:
        Catholic University of America Press, 1940.

1621   ————. *De gestis Concilii Basiliensis,* ed. and trans.
        D. Hay and W.K. Smith. Oxford: Clarendon Press, 1967.

1622   ————. *The Commentaries of Pius II,* trans. F.A. Gragg
        with introd. and notes L.C. Gabel. Smith College
        Studies in History, 22, 25, 30, 35, 43. Northampton,
        Mass.: Department of History of Smith College, 1937-
        1957. Abridged one-vol. ed. as *Memoirs of a Renais-
        sance Pope.* New York: Capricorn Books, 1959.

1623   ————. *The Tale of the Two Loves, translation of De
        duobus Amantibus,* trans. Flora Grierson. London:
        Constable, 1929; repr. Westport, Ct.: Hyperion Press,
        1979.

1624   ————. "The Treatise of Aeneas Sylvius Piccolomini,
        Afterwards Pius II, *De Liberorum Educatione.*"
        William Harrison Woodward, *Vittorino da Feltre and
        Other Humanist Educators* (item 338), pp.134-58.

1625   Platina, i.e. Bartolomeo de'Sacchi di Piadena. *The
        Lives of the Popes from the Time of Our Saviour
        Jesus Christ to the Reign of Sixtus IV.* London:
        C. Wilkinson, 1685; repr. 2 vols., ed. W. Benham.
        London: Griffith, Farran, Okedan and Welsh, 1888.

1626   Poliziano, Angelo. "The Pazzi Conspiracy (*Coniura-
        tionis Commentarium*)," trans. E.B. Welles. *The
        Earthly Republic* (item 322), pp.305-22.

1627   ————. "The Pazzi Conspiracy (*Coniurationis Commen-
        tarium*)." *Humanism and Liberty* (item 336), pp.171-
        83.

1628   Rinuccini, Alamanno. "Liberty (*De libertate*)." *Human-
        ism and Liberty* (item 336), pp.193-224.

1629   Item deleted.

1630   Sannazaro, Jacopo. *Arcadia Piscatory Eclogues,* trans.
        Ralph Nash. Detroit: Wayne State University Press,
        1966.

1631   Valla, Lorenzo. "Dialogue on Free Will," trans. C.E.
        Trinkaus. *The Renaissance Philosophy of Man* (item
        311), pp.155-84.

1632   ———. "In Praise of Saint Thomas Aquinas (Encomium
        Sancti Thomae Aquinatis, 1475)," trans. M. Esther
        Hanley. *Renaissance Philosophy* (item 320), pp.12-27.

1633   ———. "On Free Will, De libero arbitrio, complete."
        *Renaissance Philosophy, Vol.1, The Italian Philos-
        ophers* (item 316), pp.40-64.

1634   ———. *On Pleasure, De voluptate,* trans. A. Kent
        Hieatt and Maristella Lorch. Janus Series 1. New
        York: Abaris Books, 1977. Literal translation with
        introd. and some notes on Lorch's critical edition
        of *De Vero Falsoque Bono* of 1970.

1635   ———. *The Treatise of Lorenzo Valla on the Donation
        of Constantine,* trans. Christopher B. Coleman. New
        Haven: Yale University Press, 1922; repr. New York:
        Octagon, 1971.

1636   Vegio, Maffeo. *Mapheus Vegius and His Thirteenth Book
        of the Aeneid; a Chapter on Vergil in the Renaissance,*
        ed. Ana Cox Brinton. Stanford: California University
        Press, 1930.

1637   Vespasiano da Bisticci. *The Vespasiano Memoirs, Lives
        of Illustrious Men of the Fifteenth Century,* trans.
        Emily Waters and William George. London: G. Rout-
        ledge and Sons, 1926.

B. STUDIES

1638   Allen, Michael J.B. "The Absent Angel in Ficino's
        Philosophy." *JHI,* 36 (1975): 219-40.

1639   ———. "Cosmogony and Love: The Role of *Phaedrus* in
        Ficino's *Symposium* Commentary." *JMRS,* 10 (1980):
        131-53.

1640   ———. "Ficino's Lecture on the Good." *RQ,* 30
        (1977): 160-71.

1641   ———. "Ficino's Theory of the Five Substances and
        the Neoplatonists' *Parmenides*." *JMRS,* 12 (1982):
        19-44.

1642   ————. "Two Commentaries on the *Phaedrus*: Ficino's
        Indebtedness to Hermias." *JWCI*, 43 (1980): 110-29.

1643   ————, and Roger A. White. "Ficino's Hermias Trans-
        lation and a New Apologue." *Scriptorium*, 35 (1981):
        39-47.

1644   Anderson, William S. "Valla, Juvenal, and Probus."
        Traditio, 21 (1965): 383-424.

1645   Andrews, Avery. "The 'Lost' Fifth Book of the Life of
        Pope Paul II." *Studies in the Renaissance*, 17 (1970):
        7-45.

1646   Antonovics, A.V. "The Library of Cardinal Domenico
        Caprancia." *Cultural Aspects of the Italian Renais-
        sance* (item 280), pp.141-59.

1647   Ashmole, Bernard. "Cyriac of Ancona." *Proceedings of
        the British Academy*, 45 (1959): 25-41.

1648   Babinger, Franz. "Notes on Cyriac of Ancona and Some
        of His Friends." *JWCI*, 25 (1962): 321-23.

1649   Baca, Albert R. "Vis Sententiarum: J.C. Scaliger's
        Verdict Concerning Ovid." *Acta Conventus Neo-latini
        Amstelodamensis* (item 305), pp.48-57.

1650   Baron, Hans. "Franciscan Poverty and Civic Wealth in
        Humanistic Thought." *Speculum*, 13 (1938): 1-37.

1651   Belladonna, Rita. "Pontanus, Machiavelli and a Case
        of Religious Dissimulation in Early Sixteenth-Century
        Siena. Carli's Trattati nove della prudenza." *BHR*,
        37 (1975): 377-85.

1652   ————. "Sperone Speroni and Alessandro Piccolomini
        on Justification." *RQ*, 25 (1972): 161-73.

1653   Bentley, Jerry H. "Biblical Philology and Christian
        Humanism: Lorenzo Valla and Erasmus as Scholars of
        the Gospels." *The Sixteenth-Century Journal*, 8
        (1977): 9-28.

1654   Black, R. "Ancients and Moderns in the Renaissance:
        Rhetoric and History in Accolti's *Dialogue on the
        Preeminence of Men of His Own Time*." *JHI*, 43 (1982):
        1-32.

1655   Blau, Joseph L. *The Christian Interpretation of the Cabala in the Renaissance.* New York: Columbia University Press, 1944; repr. Port Washington, N.Y.: Kennikat Press, 1965.

1656   Boas, George. "Philosophies of Science in Florentine Platonism." *Art, Science, and History in the Renaissance*, ed. Charles S. Singleton. Baltimore: Johns Hopkins Press, 1967, pp.239-54.

1657   Bodnar, E.W. *Cyriacus of Ancona and Athens.* Bruxelles-Bercham: Latomus, 1960.

1658   Boulting, William. *Aeneas Silvius (Enea Silvio de' Piccolomini--Pius II) Orator, Man of Letters, Statesman, and Pope.* London: Constable, 1908.

1659   Breen, Quirinus. "Giovanni Pico della Mirandola on the Conflict of Philosophy and Rhetoric." *JHI*, 13 (1952): 384-412; repr. *Christianity and Humanism* (item 218).

1660   ———. "Melanchthon's Reply to Giovanni Pico della Mirandola." *JHI*, 13 (1952): 413-26; repr. *Christianity and Humanism* (item 218).

1661   Brown, Alison M. *Bartolomeo Scala, 1430-1497. Chancellor of Florence, The Humanist as Bureaucrat.* Princeton: Princeton University Press, 1979.

1662   ———. "The Guelf Party in 15th Century Florence: The Transition from Communal to Medicean State." *Rinascimento,* 20 (1980): 41-86.

1663   ———. "The Humanist Portrait of Cosimo de' Medici, Pater Patriae." *JWCI*, 24 (1961): 186-221.

1664   ———, and A.C. De la Mare. "Bartolomeo Scala's Dealings with Booksellers, Scribes and Illuminators, 1459-1463." *JWCI*, 39 (1976): 237-45.

1665   Brown, Peter. "Pietro degli Angeli da Barga: 'Humanista dello Studio di Pisa.'" *Italica,* 47 (1970): 285-95.

1666   Bullock, Alan. "A Hitherto Unexplored Manuscript of 100 Poems by Vittoria Colonna in the Biblioteca Nazionale." *Italian Studies,* 21 (1966): 42-56.

1667   ———. "Three New Poems by Vittoria Colonna."
        Italian Studies, 24 (1969): 44-54.

1668   Burroughs, Charles. "A Planned Myth and Myth of Plan-
        ning: Nicholas V and Rome." *Rome in the Renaissance*
        (item 300), pp.197-207.

1669   Butrica, J.L. "Pontanus, Puccius, Pocchus, Petreius,
        and Propertius." *Res Publica Litterarum,* 3 (1980):
        5-9.

1670   Cassirer, Ernst. "Ficino's Place in Intellectual His-
        tory. Review of Paul O. Kristeller's 'The Philosophy
        of Marsilio Ficino.'" *JHI,* 4 (1943): 483-501.

1671   ———. "Giovanni Pico della Mirandola." *JHI,* 3
        (1942): 123-44; repr. *Renaissance Essays* (item 290),
        pp.11-60.

1672   Casson, L.F. "A Manuscript of Landino's 'Xandra' in
        South Africa." *Studies in the Renaissance,* 10
        (1963): 44-59.

1673   Cerreta, Florindo V. "An Account of the Early Life of
        the Accademia degli Infiammati in the Letters of
        Alessandro Piccolomini to Benedetto Varchi." *The
        Romanic Review,* 48 (1957): 249-64.

1674   Chambers, D.S. "Studium Urbis and 'gabella studii':
        The University of Rome in the Fifteenth Century."
        Cultural Aspects of the Italian Renaissance (item
        280), pp.68-110.

1675   Clark, A.C. "The Literary Discoveries of Poggio."
        The Classical Review, 13 (1899): 119-30.

1676   Clough, Cecil H. "Cardinal Bessarion and Greek at the
        Court of Urbino." *Manuscripta,* 8 (1964): 160-71.

1677   ———. "Federigo di Montefeltro's Patronage of the
        Arts, 1468-1482." *JWCI,* 36 (1973): 129-44.

1678   ———. "Sources for the History of the Duchy of
        Urbino in Pope Clement XI's Library: A Miscellany in
        Seventeen Volumes." *BJRL,* 14 (1970): 34-56, 88-107,
        161-75.

1679   Cochrane, Eric, ed. *The Late Italian Renaissance,*
        1525-1630. New York: Harper and Row, 1970.

1680   ———. "The End of the Renaissance in Florence."
        BHR, 27 (1965): 7-29.

1681   Costa, Dennis. "Struck Sow or Broken Heart: Pico's
        Oratio as Ritual Sacrifice." *JMRS,* 12 (1982): 221-
        35.

1682   Craven, William G. *Giovanni Pico della Mirandola:*
        Symbol of His Age. Modern Interpretations of a
        Renaissance Philosopher. Geneva: Droz, 1981.

1683   Creighton, Mandell. *A History of the Papacy from the*
        Great Schism to the Sack of Rome, 6 vols. London:
        Longmans, Green, 1897.

1684   D'Amico, John F. "A Humanist Response to Martin
        Luther: Raffaele Maffei's Apologeticus." *Sixteenth-*
        Century Journal, 6 (1975): 37-56.

1685   ———. "Beatus Rhenanus and Italian Humanism." *JMRS,*
        9 (1979): 237-60.

1686   ———. "Beatus Rhenanus, Tertullian, and the Refor-
        mation: A Humanist's Critique of Scholasticism."
        ARG, 71 (1980): 37-63.

1687   ———. "Paolo Cortesi's Rehabilitation of Giovanni
        Pico della Mirandola." *BHR,* 44 (1982): 37-51.

1688   ———. *Renaissance Humanism in Papal Rome, Humanists*
        and Churchmen on the Eve of the Reformation. Balti-
        more: Johns Hopkins University Press, 1983. A major
        study of humanism in Rome in the late fifteenth and
        early sixteenth centuries.

1689   D'Andrea, Antonio. "The Last Years of Innocent Gen-
        tillet: 'Princeps Adversariorum Machiavelli.'" *RQ,*
        20 (1967): 12-16.

1690   ———. "The Political and Ideological Context of
        Innocent Gentillet's *Anti-Machiavel.*" *RQ,* 23
        (1970): 397-411.

1691   Dannenfeldt, Karl H.   "The Pseudo-Zoroastrian Oracles
        in the Renaissance." *Studies in the Renaissance,* 4
        (1957): 7-30.

1692   Davies, M.C.   "Poggio Bracciolini as Rhetorician and
        Historian: Unpublished Pieces." *Rinascimento,* 2nd
        ser. 22 (1982): 153-82.

1693   De Gaetano, Armand L.   "Gelli's Eclecticism on the
        Question of Immortality and the Italian Version of
        Porzio's *De Humana mente.*" *Philological Quarterly,*
        47 (1968): 532-46.

1694   ————. *Gianbattista Gelli and the Florentine Academy:
        The Rebellion against Latin.* Florence: Olschki,
        1976.

1695   ————. "The Florentine Academy and the Advancement
        of Learning through the Vernacular: The Orti Ori-
        cellari and the Sacra Accademia." *BHR,* 30 (1968):
        19-52.

1696   De la Mare, Albinia.   "The Library of Francesco Sas-
        setti (1421-1490)." *Cultural Aspects of the Italian
        Renaissance* (item 280), pp.160-201.

1697   De Petris, A.   "Giannozzo Manetti and His *Consola-
        toria.*" *BHR,* 41 (1979): 493-521.

1698   Devereux, James A., S.J.   "The Textual History of
        Ficino's *De Amore.*" *RQ,* 28 (1965): 173-82.

1699   Di Tommaso, Andrea.   "Nature and the Aesthetic Social
        Theory of Leon Battista Alberti." *MH,* n.s. 3 (1972):
        31-50.

1700   Item deleted.

1701   Item deleted.

1702   Donnelly, John Patrick, S.J.   "Three Disputed Vermigli
        Tracts." *Essays Presented to Myron P. Gilmore* (item
        275), vol.1, pp.37-46.

1703   Dulles, Avery. *Princeps Concordiae: Pico della
        Mirandola and the Scholastic Tradition.* Cambridge,
        Mass.: Harvard University Press, 1941.

1704   Dunston, A.J.   "Two Gentlemen of Florence: Amerigus
        and Philippus Corsinus." *Scriptorium,* 22 (1968):
        46-50.

1705   Finch, Chauncey E.   "The Alphabetical Notes in
        Rinuccio's Translation of Aesop's Fables." *MH,* 11
        (1957): 90-93.

1706   Gabel, Leona C.   "The First Revival of Rome, 1420-
        1484." *The Renaissance Reconsidered* (item 282),
        pp.13-26.

1707   Gadol, Joan. *Leon Battista Alberti, Universal Man of
        the Early Renaissance.* Chicago: University of
        Chicago Press, 1969.

See also Kelly-Gadol, Joan.

1708   Gardiner, Linda Janik.   "Lorenzo Valla: The Primacy of
        Rhetoric and the De-moralization of History."
        History and Theory, 12 (1973): 389-404.

1709   Gilbert, Allan H. *Machiavelli's 'Prince' and Its
        Forerunners: The Prince as a Typical Book "De
        Regimine Principum."* Durham, N.C.: Duke University
        Press, 1938; repr. New York: Barnes and Noble, 1968.

1710   Gilbert, Felix.   "Florentine Political Assumptions in
        the Period of Savonarola and Soderini." *JWCI,* 20
        (1957): 187-214.

1711   ————.   "The Humanist Concept of the Prince and *The
        Prince* of Machiavelli." *Journal of Modern History,*
        11 (1939): 449-83; repr. *History: Choice and Com-
        mitment* (item 693), pp.91-114.

1712   Gilbert, Neal W.   "The Early Italian Humanists and
        Disputation." *Renaissance Studies in Honor of Hans
        Baron* (item 296), pp.201-26.

1713   Gill, Joseph, S.J.   "A Tractate about the Council of
        Florence Attributed to George Amiroutzes." *Journal
        of Ecclesiastical History,* 9 (1958): 30-37.

1714   ————. *Personalities of the Council of Florence.*
        New York: Barnes and Noble, 1964.

1715   Gombrich, Ernst H. "Alberto Avogadro's Descriptions
        of the Badia of Fiesole and the Villa of Careggi."
        IMU, 5 (1962): 217-30.

1716   ————. "Botticelli's Mythologies: A Study in the
        Neo-Platonic Symbolism of His Circle." *JWCI,* 8
        (1946): 7-60.

1717   Grafton, Anthony. "On the Scholarship of Politian and
        Its Context." *JWCI,* 40 (1977): 159-88.

1718   Grant, W. Leonard. "An Eclogue of Giovanni Pontano."
        Philological Quarterly, 36 (1957): 76-83.

1719   ————. "An Eclogue of Giovanni Quatrario." *Studies
        in the Renaissance,* 5 (1958): 7-14.

1720   ————. "Giovanni Pico and 'Malius' Again." *Philo-
        logical Quarterly,* 32 (1953): 223-24.

1721   ————. "The Life of Naldo Naldi." *Studies in Phil-
        ology,* 60 (1963): 606-17.

1722   ————. "Pico and Malius." *Philological Quarterly,*
        31 (1952): 95-96.

1723   Gravelle, Sarah Stever. "Lorenzo Valla's Comparison
        of Latin and Greek and the Humanist Background."
        BHR, 44 (1982): 269-89.

1724   Gray, Hanna H. "Valla's *Encomium of St. Thomas
        Aquinas* and the Humanist Conception of Christian
        Antiquity." *Essays in History and Literature Pre-
        sented by Fellows of the Newberry Library to Stanley
        Pargellis,* ed. Heinz Blum. Chicago: Newberry
        Library, 1965, pp.37-51.

1725   Grayson, Cecil. "Alberti and the Vernacular Eclogue
        in the Quattrocento." *Italian Studies,* 11 (1956):
        16-30.

1726   ————. "Leone Battista and the Beginnings of Italian
        Grammar." *Proceedings of the British Academy,* 49
        (1963): 291-311.

1727   ————. "The Humanism of Alberti." *Italian Studies,*
        12 (1957): 37-56.

1728   Greene, Thomas M.   "Resurrecting Rome: The Double Task
       of the Humanist Imagination."   *Rome in the Renais-
       sance* (item 300), pp.41-54.

1729   Gregorovius, Ferdinand.   *History of the City of Rome
       in the Middle Ages,* trans. from 4th German edition
       Anne Hamilton.   2nd ed., 8 vols.   London: G. Bell,
       1906.   Volumes 6-8 treat Rome during the Renaissance.

1730   Grimm, Harold J.   "Lorenzo Valla's Christianity."
       Church History, 18 (1949): 75-88.

1731   Gutkind, Curt.   *Cosimo de' Medici.   Pater Patriae,
       1389-1464.*   Oxford: Clarendon Press, 1938.

1732   Hale, J.R.   *Florence and the Medici.*   London: Thames
       and Hudson, 1977.

1733   Hathaway, Baxter.   *The Age of Criticism: The Late
       Renaissance in Italy.*   Ithaca, N.Y.: Cornell Univer-
       sity Press, 1962.

1734   Hausmann, F.R.   "Demetrio Calcondilla--Demetrio
       Castrano--Pietro Dementrio--Demetrio Guazzelli?"
       BHR, 32 (1970): 607-11.

1735   Hay, Denys.   "Flavio Biondo and the Middle Ages."
       Proceedings of the British Academy, 45 (1959): 97-
       127.

1736   Heath, Michael J.   "Renaissance Scholars and the Origins
       of the Turks."   *BHR,* 41 (1979): 453-71.

1737   Hill, Julia Cotton.   "Death and Politian."   *Durham
       University Journal,* 46 (1953-54): 96-103.

1738   ———.   "Politian, Humanist Poet."   *Italica,* 46 (1969):
       176-90.   A review essay on Ida Maier's studies.

1739   Horkan, Vincent J.   *Educational Theories and Principles
       of Maffeo Vegio.*   Washington, D.C.: The Catholic Uni-
       versity of America Press, 1953.

1740   Hough, Samuel Jones.   "An Early Record of Marsilio
       Ficino."   *RQ,* 30 (1977): 301-04.

1741   Hughes, Phillip Edgcumbe. "Pico della Mirandola: A
        Study of an Intellectual Pilgrimage." *Philosophia
        Reformata,* 23 (1958): 108-35, 164-81; 24 (1959):
        17-44, 65-73.

1742   Jacob, E.F. "Giuliano Cesarini." *BJRL,* 51 (1968-69):
        104-21.

1743   Jardine, Lisa. "Lorenzo Valla and the Intellectual
        Origins of Humanistic Dialectic." *Journal of the
        History of Philosophy,* 15 (1977): 143-64.

1744   Kaminsky, H. "Pius Aeneas among the Taborites."
        Church History, 28 (1959): 282-309.

1745   Kaske, Carol V. "Marsilio Ficino and the Twelve Gods
        of the Zodiac." *JWCI,* 45 (1982): 195-202.

1746   Kelly-Gadol, Joan. "Tommaso Campanella: The Agony of
        Political Theory on the Counter-Reformation." *Phil-
        osophy and Humanism* (item 293), pp.164-89.

1747   Kennedy, Ruth W. "The Contribution of Martin V to the
        Rebuilding of Rome, 1420-1431." *The Renaissance Re-
        considered* (item 282), pp.27-52.

1748   Kibre, Pearl. "The Intellectual Interests Reflected
        in Libraries of the Fourteenth and Fifteenth Cen-
        turies." *JHI,* 7 (1946): 257-97.

1749   ————. *The Library of Pico della Mirandola.* New
        York: Columbia University Press, 1936.

1750   Kirk, Russell. "Pico della Mirandola and Human Dignity."
        Month, 15 (1956): 74-78.

1751   Kristeller, Paul Oskar. "The European Diffusion of
        Italian Humanism." *Italica,* 39 (1962): 1-20; repr.
        Renaissance Thought II (item 193), pp.69-88.

1752   ————. "The European Significance of Florentine
        Platonism." *Medieval and Renaissance Studies, 1967,*
        ed. John M. Headley. Chapel Hill: University of
        North Carolina Press, 1968, pp.206-29.

1753   ————. "Ficino and Pomponazzi on the Place of Man in
        the Universe." *JHI,* 5 (1944): 220-26; repr. *Studies
        in Renaissance Thought and Letters* (item 194), chap.
        14.

1754 ———. "Ficino and Renaissance Platonism." *The Personalist,* 36 (1955): 238-49.

1755 ———. "Florentine Platonism and Its Relation with Humanism and Scholasticism." *Church History,* 8 (1939): 201-11.

1756 ———. "Francesco da Diacceto and Florentine Platonism in the Sixteenth Century." *Miscellanea Giovanni Mercati* (item 295), pp.260-304; repr. *Studies in Renaissance Thought and Letters* (item 194), chap.15.

1757 ———. "Giovanni Pico della Mirandola and His Latin Poems: A New Manuscript." *Manuscripta,* 20 (1976): 154-62.

1758 ———. "Giovanni Pico della Mirandola and His Sources." *L'opera e il pensiero di Giovanni Pico della Mirandola.* Florence: Istituto Nazionale di Studi sul Rinascimento, 1965, vol.1, pp.35-133.

1759 ———. "The Humanist Bartolomeo Facio and His Unknown Correspondence." *Renaissance to Counter Reformation* (item 279), pp.56-74.

1760 ———. "The Latin Poems of Giovanni Pico della Mirandola: Supplementary Note." *Poetry and Poetics from Ancient Greece to the Renaissance: Studies in Honor of James Hutton,* ed. G.M. Kirkwood. Ithaca: Cornell University Press, 1975, pp.185-206.

1761 ———. "Marsilio Ficino as a Beginning Student of Plato." *Scriptorium,* 20 (1966): 41-54.

1762 ———. "Marsilio Ficino as a Man of Letters and the Glosses Attributed to Him in the Caetani Codex of Dante." *RQ,* 36 (1983): 1-47. Traces the history of the codex and shows the glosses belong to a member of the circle of Salutati in the early fifteenth century.

1763 ———. "The Philosophy of Man in the Italian Renaissance." *Italica,* 24 (1947): 93-112; repr. *Studies in Renaissance Thought and Letters* (item 194), chap. 13, and *Renaissance Thought* (item 192), pp.120-39.

1764   ————. *The Philosophy of Marsilio Ficino,* trans.
        Virginia Conant. New York: Columbia University
        Press, 1943; repr. Gloucester, Mass.: Peter Smith,
        1964.

1765   ————. "The Platonic Academy of Florence." *Renais-
        sance News,* 14 (1961): 147-59; repr. *Renaissance
        Thought II* (item 193), pp.89-101.

1766   ————. "The Scholastic Background of Marsilio Ficino,
        with an Edition of Unpublished Texts." *Traditio,* 2
        (1944): 257-318; repr. *Studies in Renaissance
        Thought and Letters* (item 194), chap.4.

1767   ————. "Sebastiano Salvini, a Florentine Humanist
        and Theologian, and a Member of Marsilio's Platonic
        Academy." *Didascaliae: Studies in Honor of Anselm
        M. Albareda,* ed. S. Prete. New York: Bernard M.
        Rosenthal, 1961, pp.207-43.

1768   ————. "The Theory of Immortality in Marsilio Ficino."
        JHI, 1 (1940): 299-319.

1769   ————. "An Unknown Correspondence of Alessandro
        Braccessi with Niccolò Michelozzi, Naldo Naldi,
        Bartolomeo Scala, and Other Humanists (1470-1472) in
        MS. Bold. Auct. F.2.17." *Classical, Mediaeval and
        Renaissance Studies in Honor of Berthold Louis
        Ullman* (item 287), vol.2, pp.311-63.

1770   ————. "An Unpublished Description of Naples by
        Francesco Bandino." *Romanic Review,* 33 (1942): 290-
        306; repr. *Studies in Renaissance Thought and
        Letters* (item 194), chap.19.

1771   Langdale, Maria. "A Bilingual Work of the Fifteenth
        Century: Giannozzo Manetti's 'Dialogus Consolator-
        ius.'" *Italian Studies,* 31 (1976): 1-16.

1772   Lebano, Edoardo A. "Luigi Pulci and Late Fifteenth-
        Century Humanism in Florence." *RQ,* 27 (1974): 489-99.

1773   Lee, Egmont. *Sixtus IV and Men of Letters.* Rome:
        Storia e Letteratura, 1978. Treats humanists at the
        papal court and the University of Rome with full
        bibliography and appendix of documents.

1774   Lehmann, Phyllis L. *Cyriacus of Ancona's Egyptian Visit and Its Reflection in Gentile Bellini and Hieronymous Bosch.* Locust Valley, N.Y.: Augustin, 1977.

1775   ———. *Samothracian Reflections, Aspects of the Revival of the Antique.* Princeton: Princeton University Press, 1973.

1776   Lockwood, Dean P. "In Domo Rinucii." *Classical and Mediaeval Studies in Honor of Edward Kennard Rand, Presented upon the Completion of His Fortieth Year of Teaching,* ed. L.W. Jones. New York: Published by the Editor, 1938, pp.177-90. Study of interests and handwriting of Rinucci, fifteenth-century Florentine humanist.

1777   Loomis, Louise Ropes. "The Greek Renaissance in Italy." *American Historical Review,* 13 (1907/1908): 246-58.

1778   ———. "The Greek Studies of Poggio Bracciolini." *Studies in Memory of Gertrude Schoepperle Loomis,* ed. R.S. Loomis. New York: Columbia University Press, 1927, pp.489-512.

1779   Lorch, Maristella de Panizza. "'Voluptas, molle quodam et non invidiosum nomen': Lorenzo Valla's Defense of 'voluptas' in the Preface to His 'De voluptate.'" *Philosophy and Humanism* (item 293), pp.214-28.

1780   Luck, George. "Vir Facetus: A Renaissance Ideal." *Studies in Philology,* 55 (1958): 107-21. Treats Pontano's *De Sermone.*

1781   Ludwig, Walther. "Lorenzo Strozzi's Epigrams on Borso and Ercole d'Este." *Res Publica Litterarum,* 1 (1978): 171-76.

1782   McGann, M.J. "The Medicean Dedications of Books 1-3 of the *Hymni Naturales* of Michael Marullus." *Res Publica Litterarum,* 3 (1980): 87-90.

1783   McGinnes, Frederick J. "The Rhetoric of Praise and the New Rome of the Counter Reformation." *Rome in the Renaissance* (item 300), pp.355-70.

1784   McManamon, John M. "Renaissance Preaching. Theory
        and Practice. A Holy Thursday Sermon of Aurelio
        Brandolini." *Viator,* 10 (1979): 355-73. Includes
        a study of the fifteenth-century humanist and edi-
        tion of the Latin text of the sermon.

1785   McNair, Philip. "Poliziano's Horoscope." *Cultural
        Aspects of the Italian Renaissance* (item 280),
        pp. 244-61.

1786   Marsh, David. *The Quattrocento Dialogue, Classical
        Tradition and Humanist Innovation.* Cambridge, Mass.:
        Harvard University Press, 1980. Analyses of works
        by Bruni, Poggio, Valla, Alberti and Pontano against
        the background of the Ciceronian model.

1787   ———. "Boccaccio in the Quattrocento: Manetti's
        Dialogus in symposio." *RQ,* 33 (1980): 337-50.

1788   ———. "Grammar, Method, and Polemic in Lorenzo
        Valla's 'Elegantiae.'" *Rinascimento,* 19 (1979): 91-
        116.

1789   Mazzocco, Angelo. "Rome and the Humanists: The Case
        of Biondo Flavio." *Rome in the Renaissance* (item
        300), pp.185-95.

1790   ———. "Some Philological Aspects of Biondo Flavio's
        Roma Triumphans." *HL,* 28 (1979): 1-26.

1791   Milham, Mary Ella. "The Manuscripts of Platina 'De
        Honesta Voluptate ... ' and Its Source, Martino."
        Scriptorium, 26 (1972): 127-28.

1792   Minor, Andrew G., and Bonner Mitchell. *A Renaissance
        Entertainment: Festivities for the Marriage of Cosimo
        I, Duke of Florence, in 1539.* Columbia: University
        of Missouri Press, 1968.

1793   Mitchell, Bonner. *Rome in the High Renaissance, The
        Age of Leo X.* Norman: University of Oklahoma Press,
        1973.

1794   Mitchell, Charles. "Archaeology and Romance in Renais-
        sance Italy." *Italian Renaissance Studies* (item
        289), pp.455-83.

1795   ————. "Ex libris Kiriaci Anconitani." *IMU*, 5
        (1962): 283-300.

1796   ————. "Felice Feliciano Antiquarius." *Proceedings
        of the British Academy*, 47 (1961): 197-221.

1797   Mitchell, R.J. *The Laurels and the Tiara: Pope Pius
        II, 1458-1464*. Garden City, N.Y.: Doubleday, 1963.

1798   Nachod, Hans. "The Inscription in Federigo da Monte-
        feltro's Studio in the Metropolitan Museum: Distichs
        by His Librarian Federigo Veterano." *MH*, 2 (1944):
        98-105.

1799   Nelson, John Charles. *Renaissance Theory of Love, The
        Context of Giordano Bruno's Eroici furori*. New York:
        Columbia University Press, 1955. Mainly on the
        vernacular tradition.

1800   Novak, C.C. "Giovanni Pico della Mirandola and
        Jochanan Alemanno." *JWCI*, 45 (1982): 125-47.

1801   Oechslin, W. "Leon Battista Alberti." *BHR*, 34 (1972):
        529-34.

1802   Oliver, R.P. "'New Fragments' of Latin Authors in
        Perotti's *Cornucopiae*." *TAPA*, 78 (1947): 376-424.

1803   ————. *Niccolò Perotti's Version of the Enchiridion
        of Epictetus*. Urbana: University of Illinois Press,
        1954.

1804   ————. "Politian's Translation of the *Enchiridion*."
        TAPA, 89 (1958): 185-217. On the first Latin version
        of Epictetus' famed Greek Stoic work.

1805   O'Malley, John. "An Ash Wednesday Sermon on the Dig-
        nity of Man for Pope Julius II, 1513." *Essays Pre-
        sented to Myron P. Gilmore* (item 275), vol.1, pp.
        193-208.

1806   ————. "Giles of Viterbo: A Reformer's Thought on
        Renaissance Rome." *RQ*, 20 (1967): 1-11.

1807   ————. *Giles of Viterbo on Church and Reform: A
        Study in Renaissance Thought*. Leiden: Brill, 1968.

1808   ———. "Man's Dignity, God's Love, and the Destiny
         of Rome: A Text of Giles of Viterbo." *Viator,* 3
         (1972): 389-416.

1809   ———. *Praise and Blame in Renaissance Rome.* Durham,
         N.C.: Duke University Press, 1979.

1810   ———. "Preaching for the Popes." *Pursuit of Holi-
         ness* (item 304), pp.408-39.

1811   ———. *Rome and the Renaissance: Studies in Culture
         and Religion.* London: Variorum Reprints, 1982.

1812   ———. "Some Renaissance Panegyrics of Aquinas." *RQ,*
         27 (1974): 174-93.

1813   ———. "The Vatican Library and the Schools of
         Athens: A Text of Battista Casali, 1508." *JMRS,* 7
         (1977): 271-88.

1814   Oppel, John W. "Peace vs. Liberty in the Quattrocento:
         Poggio, Guarino, and the Scipio-Caesar Controversy."
         JMRS, 4 (1974): 221-66.

1815   ———. "Poggio, San Bernardino of Siena, and the
         Dialogue *On Avarice.*" *RQ,* 30 (1977): 564-87.

1816   Origo, Iris. *The World of San Bernardino.* New York:
         Harcourt Brace and World, 1962.

1817   Palmerino, Richard J. "Palmieri's *Città di Vita:*
         More Evidence of Renaissance Platonism." *BHR,* 44
         (1982): 601-04.

1818   Panizza, Letizia A. "Lorenzo Valla's *De Vero Falsoque
         Bono.* Lactantius and Oratorial Scepticism." *JWCI,*
         41 (1978): 76-107.

1819   Partner, Peter. *Renaissance Rome, 1500-1559.* Berkeley
         and Los Angeles: University of California Press,
         1976.

1820   ———. *The Papal State Under Martin V.* London:
         British School at Rome, 1958.

1821   Pepin, H.J., Jr. "Lorenzo Valla and Isidore of
         Seville." *Traditio,* 31 (1975): 343-48.

1822   Perosa, Alessandro. "Febris: A Poetic Myth Created by
       Poliziano." *JWCI*, 9 (1946): 74-95.

1823   Phillips, Oliver C. "Francesco Patrizi's Two Epigrams
       on the Epigram." *Res Publica Litterarum*, 3 (1980):
       139-41.

1824   Pocock, J.G.A. *The Machiavellian Moment: Florentine
       Political Thought and the Atlantic Republican Tradi-
       tion.* Princeton: Princeton University Press, 1975.

1825   Prete, Sesto. *Some Unknown Poems by Tito Vespasiano
       Strozzi.* Fano: Typis Paulinis, 1968.

1826   Purnell, Frederick, Jr. "Francesco Patrizi and the
       Critics of Hermes Trismegistus." *JMRS*, 6 (1976):
       155-78.

1827   Raby, Julian. "Cyriacus of Ancona and the Ottoman
       Sultan Mehmed II." *JWCI*, 43 (1980): 242-46.

1828   Ravenscroft, Judith. "The Third Book of Alberti's
       'Della Famiglia' and Its Two 'Rifacimenti.'" *Italian
       Studies*, 29 (1974): 45-53.

1829   Richards, J.F.C. "Some Early Poems of Antonio Gerald-
       ini." *Studies in the Renaissance*, 13 (1966): 123-
       46.

1830   ————. "The Poems of C. Aurelius Cambinius." *Stud-
       ies in the Renaissance*, 12 (1965): 73-109.

1831   Richardson, B. "A Manuscript of Biagio Buonaccorsi."
       BHR, 36 (1974): 589-601.

1832   ————. "Pontano's 'De prudentiia' and Machiavelli's
       'Discorsi.'" *BHR*, 33 (1971): 353-57.

1833   Robathan, Dorothy M. "A Postscript on Martino Filet-
       ico." *MH*, 8 (1954): 56-61.

1834   Robb, Nesca A. *Neoplatonism of the Italian Renais-
       sance.* London: George Allen and Unwin, 1935.

1835   Rowe, John Gordon. "The Tragedy of Aeneas Sylvius
       Piccolomini (Pope Pius II): An Interpretation."
       Church History, 30 (1961): 288-313.

1836   Rubinstein, Nicolai. "An Unknown Letter by Jacopo di
       Poggio Bracciolini on Discoveries of Classical
       Texts." *IMU,* 1 (1958): 383-400.

1837   Ryder, A.F.C. "Antonio Beccadelli: A Humanist in
       Government." *Cultural Aspects of the Italian Renais-
       sance* (item 280), pp.123-40.

1838   ————. *The Kingdom of Naples under Alfonso the Mag-
       nanimous.* Oxford: Oxford University Press, 1976.

1839   Salomon, Richard G. "Poggio Bracciolini and Johannes
       Hus." *JWCI,* 19 (1956): 174-77.

1840   Salvadori, Max. "The End of the Renaissance in Italy,
       1530-1559." *The Renaissance Reconsidered* (item 282),
       pp.53-78.

1841   Samuels, Richard S. "Benedetto Varchi, the *Academia
       degli Infiammati,* and the Origins of the Italian
       Academic Movement." *RQ,* 29 (1976): 599-635.

1842   Santayana, S.G. *Two Renaissance Educators: Alberti
       and Piccolomini.* Boston: Meador, 1930.

1843   Santosuosso, A. "Books, Readers and Critics. The
       Case of Giovanni della Casa, 1537-1975." *La Biblio-
       filia,* 77 (1977): 101-86. A bibliography of Casa's
       works and their translations, e.g. the Latin
       Galatheus.

1844   ————. "On the Authorship of Della Casa's Biography
       of Cardinal Gasparo Contarini." *RQ,* 28 (1975):
       183-90.

1845   Scaglione, Aldo. "The Humanist as Scholar and Poli-
       tian's Conception of the 'Grammaticus.'" *Studies in
       the Renaissance,* 8 (1961): 49-70.

1846   Schevill, Ferdinand. *A History of Florence.* New York:
       Harcourt Brace, 1936, chaps. 18-19, 24-25.

1847   Schmitt, Charles B. "A Fifteenth-Century Translation
       of Poggio's Letter on Jerome of Prague." *ARG,* 58
       (1967): 5-15.

1848   ————. *Gianfrancesco Pico della Mirandola (1469-
       1533) and His Critique of Aristotle.* The Hague:
       Mouton, 1967.

1849   ————. "Gianfrancesco Pico della Mirandola and the
        Fifth Lateran Council." *ARG,* 61 (1970): 161-78.

1850   ————. "Girolamo Borro's 'Multae sunt nostrarum
        ignorationum causae' (MS. Vat. Ross. 1009)." *Phil-
        osophy and Humanism* (item 293), pp.462-76.

1851   ————. "Henry of Ghent, Duns Scotus and Gianfrancesco
        Pico on Illumination." *Mediaeval Studies,* 25 (1963):
        231-58.

1852   ————. "Perennial Philosophy: From Agostino Steuco
        to Leibniz." *JHI,* 27 (1966): 505-32.

1853   ————. "Who Reads Gianfrancesco Pico della Miran-
        dola?" *Studies in the Renaissance,* 11 (1964): 105-
        32.

1854   Schoell, Frank L. "George Chapman and the Italian
        Neo-Latinists of the Quattrocento." *Modern Philology,*
        13 (1915-16): 215-40.

1855   Schofield, Richard. "Giovanni da Tolentin Goes to
        Rome: A Description of the Antiquities of Rome in
        1490." *JWCI,* 43 (1980): 246-56.

1856   Scott, W.O. "Perotti, Ficino and Furor Poeticus."
        Res Publica Litterarum, 4 (1981): 273-84.

1857   Seigel, Jerrold. "The Teaching of Argyropulos and the
        Rhetoric of the First Humanists." *Action and Con-
        viction in Early Modern Europe* (item 299), pp.220-36.

1858   Seppard, Anne. "The Influence of Hermias on Marsilio
        Ficino's Doctrine of Inspiration." *JWCI,* 43 (1980):
        97-109.

1859   Shepherd, William. *The Life of Poggio Bracciolini.*
        Liverpool: T. Cadell, Jun. & W. Daires, 1802; 2nd ed.
        Liverpool: Longmans, Rees, 1837.

1860   Smith, Leslie F. "A Notice of the 'Epigrammata' of
        Francesco Patrizi, Bishop of Gaeta." *Studies in the
        Renaissance,* 15 (1968): 92-143.

1861   ————. "Lodrisio Crivelli of Milan and Aeneas Sylvius,
        1457-1464." *Studies in the Renaissance,* 9 (1962):
        31-63.

1862   ————. "The Poems of Franciscus Patricius." *Manu-
         scripta,* 10 (1966): 94-102, 145-59; 11 (1967): 141-
         43; 12 (1968): 10-21.

1863   Sonkowsky, Robert P. "A Fifteenth-Century Rhetorical
         Opusculum." *Classical Mediaeval and Renaissance
         Studies in Honor of Berthold Louis Ullman* (item 287),
         vol.2, pp.259-81.

1864   Starn, Randolph. "Additions to the Correspondence of
         Donato Giannotti: A List and Sampling of Fifty-Four
         Unpublished Letters." *Rinascimento,* n.s. 4 (1964):
         101-24.

1865   ————. *Donato Giannotti and His 'Epistolae.'* Geneva:
         Droz, 1968.

1866   Stephens, John. "Giovanbattista Cibo's Confession."
         Essays Presented to Myron P. Gilmore (item 275),
         vol.1, pp.255-70.

1867   Stinger, Charles. "Ambrogio Traversari and the 'Tempio
         degli Scolari' at S. Maria degli Angeli in Florence."
         Essays Presented to Myron P. Gilmore (item 275), vol.1,
         pp.272-86.

1868   ————. "Greek Patristics and Christian Antiquity in
         Renaissance Rome." *Rome in the Renaissance* (item
         300), pp.153-69.

1869   ————. *Humanism and the Church Fathers: Ambrogio
         Traversari (1386-1439) and Christian Antiquity in
         the Italian Renaissance.* Albany, N.Y.: State Uni-
         versity of New York Press, 1977.

1870   ————. "*Roma Triumphans:* Triumphs in the Thought and
         Ceremonies of Renaissance Rome." *MH,* n.s. 10 (1981):
         189-201.

1871   Stokes, Adrian D. *Art and Science: A Study of Alberti,
         Piero della Francesca, and Giorgione.* London: Faber
         and Faber, 1949.

1872   Sturm, Sara. *Lorenzo de' Medici.* New York: Twayne,
         1974.

1873 Terpening, Ronnie H. "Poliziano's Treatment of a
      Classical Topos: *Ekphrasis*, Portal to the *Stanze*."
      Italian Quarterly, 17, 65 (1973): 39-71.

1874 Tigerstedt, E.N. "The Poet as Creator: Origins of a
      Metaphor." *Comparative Literature Studies*, 5 (1968):
      455-88. On Ficino's and Landino's development of
      the metaphor.

1875 Toews, John B. "The View of Empire in Aeneas Sylvius
      Piccolomini." *Traditio*, 24 (1968): 471-87.

1876 Trinkaus, Charles. "A Humanist's Image of Humanism:
      The Inaugural Orations of Bartolomeo della Fonte."
      Studies in the Renaissance, 7 (1960): 90-147.

1877 ———. "The Unknown 'Quattrocento' Poetics of Bar-
      tolommeo della Fonte." *Studies in the Renaissance*,
      13 (1966): 40-122.

1878 Tuttle, E.F. "Analogy and Language Change in the
      Notes of a Renaissance Florentine." *BHR*, 39 (1977):
      239-52.

1879 Waddington, Raymond B. "The Sun at the Center: Struc-
      ture as Meaning in Pico della Mirandola's 'Heptaplus.'"
      JMRS, 3 (1973): 69-86.

1880 Wadsworth, James B. "Lorenzo de' Medici and Marsilio
      Ficino: An Experiment in Platonic Friendship." *The
      Romanic Review*, 46 (1955): 90-100.

1881 Walker, D.P. "Niccolò Perotti's Version of the
      Enchiridion of Epictetus." *BHR*, 17 (1955): 336-37.

1882 ———. *Spiritual and Demonic Magic from Ficino to
      Campanella*. Studies of the Warburg Institute, vol.
      22. London: Warburg Institute, 1958; 2nd ed. Notre
      Dame: University of Notre Dame Press, 1975.

1883 Wasserstein, A. "Politian's Commentary on the *Silvae*
      of Statius." *Scriptorium*, 10 (1956): 83-89.

1884 Waswo, Richard. "The 'Ordinary Language Philosophy'
      of Lorenzo Valla." *BHR*, 41 (1979): 255-71.

1885   Watanabe, Marmichi. "Authority and Consent in Church
       Government: Panormitanus, Aeneas Sylvius, Cusanus."
       JHI, 33 (1972): 217-36.

1886   Watkins, Renée Neu. "The Authorship of the 'Vita
       Anonyma' of Leon Battista Alberti." *Studies in the
       Renaissance,* 4 (1957): 101-12.

1887   ————. "The Death of Jerome of Prague: Divergent
       Views." *Speculum,* 42 (1967): 104-29.

1888   Weinstein, Donald. *Savonarola and Florence: Prophecy
       and Patriotism in the Renaissance.* Princeton:
       Princeton University Press, 1970.

1889   ————. "The Apocalypse in Sixteenth-Century Florence:
       The Vision of Albert of Trent." *Renaissance Studies
       in Honor of Hans Baron* (item 296), pp.311-32.

1890   Weiss, Rainer. "The Humanist Rediscovery of Rhetoric
       as Philosophy: Giovanni Pontano's *Aegidius*." *Phil-
       osophy and Rhetoric,* 13 (1980): 25-42.

1891   Weiss, Roberto. "A New Francesco Colonna." *Italian
       Studies,* 16 (1961): 78-83.

1892   ————. "In obitu Ursini Lanfredini, A Footnote to
       the Literary History of Rome under Pope Innocent
       VIII." *IMU,* 2 (1959): 355-66.

1893   Welliver, Warman. *Lorenzo and Florence.* Indianapolis:
       Clio Press, 1961.

1894   Westfall, Carroll William. "Biblical Typology in the
       Vita Nicolai V by Giannozzo Manetti." *Acta Conven-
       tus Neo-Latini Lovaniensis* (item 288), pp.701-09.

1895   Whitfield, J.H. "Leon Battista Alberti, Ariosto, and
       Dosso Dossi." *Italian Studies,* 21 (1966): 16-30.

1896   ————. "*Momus* and the Nature of Humanism." *Classi-
       cal Influences on European Culture A.D. 500-1500*
       (item 277), pp.177-81. On Alberti's work.

1897   Whittaker, John. "Greek Manuscripts from the Library
       of Giles of Viterbo, at the Biblioteca Angelica in
       Rome." *Scriptorium,* 31 (1977): 212-39.

1898 Wieruszowski, Helene. "Jacob Burckhardt (1818-1897)
and Vespasiano da Bisticci (1422-1498)." *Philosophy
and Humanism* (item 293), pp.387-405.

1899 Wilcox, Donald. "Matteo Palmieri and the 'De captivi-
tate Pisarum liber.'" *Renaissance Studies in Honor
of Hans Baron* (item 296), pp.265-82.

1900 Wilson, Robert H. "The Poggiana in Caxton's *Esope*."
Philological Quarterly, 30 (1951): 348-52.

1901 Wirszubski, Chaim. "Francesco Giorgio's Commentary on
Giovanni Pico's Kabbalistic Thesis." *JWCI,* 24 (1961):
145-56.

1902 ————. "Giovanni Pico's Book of Job." *JWCI,* 32
(1969): 172-99.

1903 Wohl, Hellmut. "Martin V and the Revival of the Arts
in Rome." *Rome in the Renaissance* (item 300),
pp.171-83.

1904 Woodhouse, J.R. "Some Humanist Techniques of Vincenzio
Borghini." *Italian Quarterly,* 15, nos.58-59 (1971):
59-80. On late Renaissance Florentine humanist.

1905 Yates, Frances A. *Giordano Bruno and the Hermetic
Tradition.* London: Routledge and Kegan Paul, 1964.

1906 ————. "Giovanni Pico della Mirandola and Magic."
*L'opera e il pensiero di Giovanni Pico della Miran-
dola.* Florence: Istituto Nazionale di Studi sul
Rinascimento, 1965, vol.1, pp.159-96.

1907 Zimmermann, T.C. Price. "Paolo Giovo and the Evolution of Renaissance Art Criticism." *Cultural Aspects
of the Italian Renaissance* (item 280), pp.406-24.

1908 ————. "Renaissance Symposia." *Essays Presented to
Myron P. Gilmore* (item 275), vol.1, pp.363-74.
Mainly on the works of Paolo Giovio.

1909   ————, and Saul Levin.   "Fabio Vigile's Poem of the
          Pheasant: Humanist Conviviality in Renaissance Rome."
          Rome in the Renaissance (item 300), pp.265-78.

See also items 387, 394, 409, 414, 420, 429, 430, 453, 466-67,
          488, 496, 538, 551, 574, 584, 620-21, 802-3, 816, 819,
          827, 831, 838, 2425, 2466, 2520-21, 2547, 2550, 2568,
          2629, 2925, 2961, 3040.

XV. THE AGE OF ERASMUS

Perhaps no figure has ever dominated an era of European letters as did Desiderius Erasmus (1469-1535) the literature and
thought of the first quarter of the sixteenth century. Born
in Holland the son of a priest, Erasmus was educated in the
devotio moderna at Deventer before he moved to Paris where he
discovered his life-long antipathy for medieval Latin schooling and scholastic philosophy. Travelling to England in 1499,
Erasmus soon became a friend of Thomas More, learned the rudi-
ments of Greek, and embarked upon his program of returning
Christianity to its apostolic principles and showing its con-
sistency with the teachings of the best of ancient philosophy
and ethics. Erasmus' *oeuvre* falls into several genres: works
on education and proverbial wisdom, such as the *Adages* and
Enchiridion, were balanced by his satires, including his famous
critique of the corruptions of church and society in *The
Praise of Folly*. His extensive correspondence provides a
tasteful and intimate mirror of his age, while the latter part
of his life was devoted to the editing and translating of the
Bible and the Greek and Latin Fathers.

Consonant with Erasmus' importance for European humanism,
the beginnings of the Protestant Reformation, and sixteenth-
century cultural history, the bibliography on the man and his
works is enormous, as are the English translations of his
writings from his own time onward. The massive project sponsored by the University of Toronto Press, *The Collected Works
of Erasmus*, will eventually issue all of Erasmus' works in
authoritative English versions, and his letters and treatises
already available in that series should be used in preference
to other translations. But since the Toronto Erasmus will be
some years in the making, I have listed all significant
English renderings of his works as well as important secondary
literature and recent bibliographies including the exhaustive
three-volume guide in French by Jean-Claude Margolin, which
covers in all languages the period from 1936 to 1970.

A. BIBLIOGRAPHY

1910   Baker-Smith, Dominic. "Erasmus Research in Great
        Britain." *Erasmus in English*, 7 (1975): 33-34.

1911   Bradshaw, Brendan. "Interpreting Erasmus." *Journal of
        Ecclesiastical History*, 33 (1982): 596-610.

1912   Coppens, Joseph. "Bibliographia Erasmia." *Scrinium
        Erasmianum*, ed. J. Coppens. Leiden: Brill, 1969,
        vol.2, pp.621-78.

1913   Devereux, E.J. *A Checklist of English Translations of
        Erasmus to 1700*. Oxford Bibliographical Society.
        Oxford: Bodleian Library, 1968. 2d ed. 1983.

1914   Jones, Rosemary Devonshire. *Erasmus and Luther*.
        Clarendon Bibliographies. Oxford: Clarendon Press,
        1968.

1915   Manschreck, Clyde L. "Erasmus: Recent Studies--A
        Review Article." *Church History*, 41 (1972): 524-27.

1916   Margolin, Jean-Claude. *Douze années de bibliographie
        erasmienne 1950-1961*. Paris: Vrin, 1963.

1917   ————. *Neuf années de bibliographie erasmienne 1962-
        1970*. Paris: Vrin; Toronto: University of Toronto
        Press, 1977.

1918   ————. *Quatorze années de bibliographie erasmienne
        1936-1949*. Paris: Vrin, 1969.

1919   Nelson, E.W. "Recent Literature Concerning Erasmus."
        Journal of Modern History, 1 (1929): 88-102.

1920   Reedijk, Cornelis. "Erasmus in 1970." *BHR*, 32 (1970):
        449-66.

1921   Schoek, R.J.   "The Place of Erasmus Today."   *Trans-
        actions of the Royal Society of Canada*, ser.4, 8
        (1970): 287-98.

1922   Stunt, Timothy F.   "Desiderius Erasmus: Some Recent
        Studies."   *Evangelical Quarterly*, 42 (1970): 230-35.

1923   Thompson, Craig R.   "Erasmus Research in the United
        States."   *Erasmus in English*, 5 (1972): 1-5.

1924   Thomson, D.F.S.   "The Quincentenary of Erasmus and
        Some Recent Books."   *University of Toronto Quarterly*,
        39 (1970): 181-85.

                    B.   *WORKS BY ERASMUS*

                    1.   SELECTED WORKS

1925   DeMolen, Richard L., ed.   *Erasmus*.   London: Edward
        Arnold, 1973.   A collection of documents and short
        selections in English translation.

1926   Dolan, John P., ed. & trans.   *The Essential Erasmus*.
        New York: New American Library, 1964.   Includes
        translations of the *Praise of Folly*, the *Complaint
        of Peace, Concerning the Immense Mercy of God, The
        Handbook of the Militant Christian*, and other works.

1927   Jackson, W.T.H., ed.   *Essential Works of Erasmus*.   New
        York: Bantam Books, 1965.   Includes the *Praise of
        Folly*, and selections from the letters and *Collo-
        quies*.

1928   Olin, John C., ed.   *Christian Humanism and the Refor-
        mation: Selected Writings of Erasmus with the Life
        of Erasmus by Beatus Rhenanus*.   New York: Harper and
        Row, 1965.   2nd rev. ed. New York: Fordham Univer-
        sity Press, 1975.   Mainly selections of Erasmus'
        letters and *The Paraclesis*.

2. *ADAGES*

1929   *Adages, Iil to Iv100,* trans. M.M. Phillips and annota-
        ted by R.A.B. Mynors. Collected Works of Erasmus
        31. Toronto: University of Toronto Press, 1982. The
        first volume of the definitive translation.

1930   Phillips, M.M. *The Adages of Erasmus: A Study with
        Translations.* Cambridge: Cambridge University Press,
        1964. An ample selection.

1931   ————. *Erasmus and His Times, A Shortened Version of
        the Adages of Erasmus.* Cambridge: Cambridge Univer-
        sity Press, 1967.

1932   *Proverbs or Adages,* trans. R. Taverner. London: R.
        Banks, 1539; repr. with introd. DeWitt T. Starnes.
        Gainesville, Fla.: Scholars' Facsimiles and Reprints,
        1956. A brief selection.

1933   *Proverbs or Adages,* trans. R. Taverner. London: R.
        Banks, 1539; repr. Amsterdam: Da Capo, 1969. The
        English Experience, 124.

3. *COLLOQUIES*

1934   Bailey, N., trans. *The Colloquies of Erasmus,* ed. E.
        Johnson. London: Reeves and Turner, 1878.
        A reissue of the 1725 complete translation.

1935   *The Colloquies of Erasmus,* trans. Craig R. Thompson.
        Chicago: University of Chicago Press, 1965. Contains
        the only complete modern translation.

1936   *Ten Colloquies,* trans. Craig R. Thompson. Indianapolis:
        Bobbs-Merrill, 1957.

1937   DeVocht, Henry, ed. *The Earliest English Translation
        of Erasmus' Colloquia, 1536-1566.* Louvain: Librarie
        Universitaire, Uystpruyst, 1928.

1938   Spurgeon, Dickie A., ed. *Tudor Translations of the
        Colloquies of Erasmus 1536-1582.* Delmar, N.Y.:
        Scholars' Facsimiles and Reprints, 1972.

1939   Thompson, Craig R. *Inquisitio de fide: A Colloquy,*
       1524. New Haven: Yale University Press, 1950. Latin
       text with revision of English translation by Nathan
       Bailey in 1725.

                         4.   LETTERS

1940   *The Correspondence of Erasmus,* trans. R.A.B. Mynors and
       D.F.S. Thomson. 6 vols. to date. Collected Works
       of Erasmus, Vols.1-6. Toronto: University of Toronto
       Press, 1974-1982. Published translations with
       annotations of letters 1-992 covering the years from
       1484 to 1519. .

1941   *The Epistles of Erasmus,* 3 vols., trans. Francis M.
       Nichols. London: Longmans, 1901-1918; repr. New
       York: Russell and Russell, 1962. Translations of the
       letters only to 1519.

1942   Hillerbrand, Hans J., ed. and trans. Marcus Haworth,
       S.J. *Erasmus and His Age. Selected Letters of*
       Desiderius Erasmus. New York: Harper and Row, 1970.
       Ample selection of Erasmus' correspondence.

1943   *A Selection from the Letters of Erasmus and His Circle,*
       ed. G.S. Facer. London: Bell, 1951.

1944   *Erasmus in Cambridge: The Cambridge Letters of Erasmus,*
       trans. D.F.S. Thomson with introd. and commentary
       H.C. Porter. Toronto: University of Toronto Press,
       1963.

1945   Rouschausse, Jean. *Erasmus and Fisher: Their Corres-*
       pondence, 1511-1524. Paris: Vrin, 1968. Includes
       English translation of thirteen letters from Erasmus
       to Fisher.

1946   Madigan, Laverne, trans. *A Letter about Sir Thomas*
       More from Erasmus of Rotterdam to Ulrich Hutten.
       Dated: 23 July, 1519. New York: Privately Printed,
       1935. Includes Latin text.

5. *PRAISE OF FOLLY*

1947   *The Praise of Folie,* trans. Sir Thomas Chaloner and
        ed. Clarence H. Miller. Early English Text Society,
        no.257. London: Oxford University Press, 1965.

1948   *The Praise of Folly,* trans. Hoyt Hopewell Hudson.
        Princeton: Princeton University Press, 1941; repr.
        Princeton: Princeton University Press, 1970.

1949   *Praise of Folly,* trans. Leonard F. Dean. Chicago:
        Packard and Co., 1946.

1950   *Praise of Folly and Letter to Martin Dorp 1515,*
        trans. Betty Radice and introd. and notes A.H.T.
        Levi. Baltimore: Penguin, 1971.

1951   *The Praise of Folly,* trans. with introd. and commen-
        tary by Clarence H. Miller. New Haven: Yale Uni-
        versity Press, 1979. The best translation with
        full notes and useful distinction between the text
        of 1511 and later editions.

6. *ENCHIRIDION*

1952   *A Book Called in Latyn Enchiridion militis christiani.*
        The English Experience, no.156. London: Wynkyn de
        Worde, 1533; repr. Amsterdam: Da Capo, 1969.

1953   *Handbook of the Militant Christian,* trans. John P.
        Dolan. Notre Dame, Ind.: Fides Publishers, 1962;
        repr. Dolan, *The Essential Works of Erasmus* (item
        1926).

1954   *Enchiridion Militis Christiani,* trans. Raymond
        Himelick. Bloomington, Ind.: Indiana University
        Press, 1963.

1955   *Enchiridion,* trans. M. Spinka. *Advocates of Reform*
        (item 332), pp.295-382.

7. EDUCATIONAL WORKS

1956   Woodward, William H. *Desiderius Erasmus Concerning*
        the Nature and Aims of Education. Cambridge: At the
        University Press, 1904; repr. with foreword by Craig
        R. Thompson. Classics in Education, 19. New York:
        Teachers College, Columbia University, 1964. Con-
        tains partial, free translation of *De ratione studii,*
        better used in Toronto translation (item 1958).

1957   *Antibarbari/Parabolae,* ed. C.R. Thompson, with trans.
        M.M. Phillips and R.A.B. Mynors. Collected Works of
        Erasmus, 23. Toronto: University of Toronto Press,
        1978.

1958   *De copia/De ratione studii,* ed. C.R. Thompson with
        trans. Betty I. Knott and Brian McGregor. The Col-
        lected Works of Erasmus, 24. Toronto: University of
        Toronto Press, 1978.

1959   King, Donald B., and H. David Rix, trans. *On Copia of*
        Words and Ideas (De utraque verborem, [sic] *ac rerum*
        copia). Milwaukee: Marquette University Press, 1963.

1960   "Ciceronianus," in I. Scott, *Controversies over the*
        Imitation of Cicero (item 436), part 2, pp.19-130.

1961   *The Education of Children (De pueris statim ac liber-*
        aliter instituendis), trans Richard Sherry. London:
        I. Day, 1550; repr. Gainesville, Fla.: Scholars'
        Facsimiles and Reprints, 1961.

1962   "Compendium Rhetorices, by Erasmus: A Translation, by
        H.H. Hudson," in *Studies in Speech and Drama in*
        Honor of Alexander M. Drummond. Ithaca: Cornell
        University Press, 1944, pp.326-40.

1963   Born, Lester K., trans. *The Education of a Christian*
        Prince. Records of Civilization, Sources and
        Studies, 27. New York: Columbia University Press,
        1936; repr. New York: Norton, 1965.

8. POLEMICAL WORKS

1964 "De libero arbitrio," in *Luther and Erasmus: Free Will and Salvation*, ed. and trans. E.G. Rupp with A.N. Marlow. The Library of Christian Classics, 17. London: SCM Press, 1969, pp.35-97.

1965 Winter, Ernst F., trans. *Discourse on Free Will [by] Erasmus and Luther*. New York: Ungar, 1961. Abridged translation.

1966 *The Polemics of Erasmus of Rotterdam and Ulrich von Hutten*, trans. R.J. Klawiter. Notre Dame, Ind.: University of Notre Dame Press, 1977.

1967 *The "Julius Exclusus" of Erasmus*, trans. P. Pascal with introd. J.K. Sowards. Bloomington, Ind.: Indiana University Press, 1968.

1968 *The Complaint of Peace, Translated from the Querela Pacis (A.D. 1521) of Erasmus*. Chicago: Open Court, 1917.

1969 MacKail, J.W. *Erasmus Against War (Querela Pacis)*. Boston: Merrymount Press, 1907.

1969 "Peace Protests (*Querela pacis*)," in J. Chapiro *Erasmus and Our Struggle for Peace*. Boston: Beacon Press, 1950.

9. OTHER WORKS

1970 "Laurentius Valla's Annotations to the New Testament," trans. P.L. Nyhus in *Forerunners of the Reformation* (item 327), pp.308-15.

1971 Udall, Nicholas, trans. *The First Tome or Volume of the Paraphrases of Erasmus upon the Newe Testament*. London: Edwarde Whitechurch, 1548.

1972 *Prefaces to the Fathers, the New Testament on Study*, ed. Robert Peters. Menston, Eng.: Scholar Press, 1970. Publishes only the Latin text, but contains

valuable commentary on Erasmus' editions of the
Bible and Church Fathers.

1973   "On the Philosophy of Christ," (*Paraclesis*) in *Renais-
        sance Philosophy, Vol.2, The Transalpine Thinkers,*
        trans. and ed. H. Shapiro and A.B. Fallico. New
        York: Random House, 1969, pp.149-62.

1974   "Erasmus' Letter to Carondelet, The Preface to His
        Edition of St. Hilary of Poitiers, 1523," trans.
        J.C. Olin in his *Six Essays on Erasmus.* New York:
        Fordham University Press, 1979, pp.93-120.

1975   *Apothegmes,* trans. Nicholas Udall. The English Exper-
        ience, 99. London: Richard Grafton, 1542; repr.
        Amsterdam: Da Capo, 1969.

1976   *The Comparation of a Vyrgin and a Martyr (1523),* trans.
        Thomas Paynell. London: Thomae Bertheleti, 1537;
        repr. with introd. by W.J. Hirten. Gainesville,
        Fla.: Scholars' Facsimiles and Reprints, 1970.

1977   *De Contemptu Mundi (1488?),* trans. Thomas Paynell.
        London: T. Bertheleti, 1533; repr. with introd. by
        W.J. Hirten. Gainesville, Fla.: Scholars' Facsimiles
        and Reprints, 1967.

1978   "A Devoute treatise upon the 'Pater Noster' ...".
        Moreana, 9 (Feb. 1966): 65-92; 10 (May 1966): 91-110;
        11 (Sept. 1966): 109-18. The modernized version of
        the English translation of 1524 by Margaret Roper
        with modern French version by Sister M.C. Robineau
        on facing pages.

1979   *The Immense Mercy of God (De immensa misericordia Dei,
        1524),* trans. E.H. Hulme. San Francisco: California
        State Library, 1940.

1980   *A Lytle Treatise of the Maner and Forme of Confession,
        made by the Most Excellent and Famous Clerk M. Eras.
        of Roterdame.* New York: Da Capo, 1975. Facsimile of
        1535 edition.

1981   *The Lives of Jehan Vitrier and John Colet by Desiderius
        Erasmus,* trans. J.H. Lupton. London: George Bell and
        Sons, 1883.

1982   *Pilgrimages to St. Mary of Walsingham and St. Thomas of
        Canterbury (Peregrinatio Religionis Erga)*, trans.
        John Gough Nichols. London: John Murray, 1875.

1983   *Preparation to Deathe*. London: Thomae Bertheleti,
        1538; repr. Amsterdam: Da Capo, 1975.

1984   "The 'Tyrannicida' of Erasmus, trans. C.S. Rayment."
        Speech Monographs, 26 (1959): 233-47.

1985   *Utile dolce; or Truethes Libertie*. London: N. Ling,
        1535; repr. Amsterdam: Da Capo, 1973.

                        C. STUDIES

1986   Adams, Robert P. "Erasmus' Ideas of His Role as a
        Social Critic ca.1480-1500." *Renaissance News,* 11
        (1958): 11-16.

1987   Aldridge, John W. *The Hermeneutic of Erasmus*. Rich-
        mond: John Knox, 1966.

1988   Allen, P.S. *The Age of Erasmus*. Oxford: Clarendon
        Press, 1914; repr. New York: Russell and Russell,
        1963.

1989   ———. *Erasmus: Lectures and Wayfaring Sketches*.
        Oxford: Clarendon Press, 1934.

1990   Allen, Mrs. P.S. "Erasmus on Peace." *Bijdraagen voor
        Vaderlandsche Geschiedenis en Oudheidkunde,* 7th ser.,
        7 (1936): 235-46.

1991   Anderson, Jaynie. "Erasmus and the Siren." *Erasmus
        in English,* 11 (1981-1982): 8-12.

1992   Anderson, Marvin. "Erasmus the Exegete." *Concordia
        Theological Monthly,* 40 (1969): 722-33.

1993   Appelt, Theodore C. *Studies in the Content and Sources
        of Erasmus' "Adagia."* Chicago: Privately Printed,
        1942.

1994   Bailey, J.W. "Erasmus and the Textus Receptus."
        Classical Quarterly, 17 (1940): 271-79. On
        Erasmus' edition of the New Testament.

1995   Bainton, Roland H. "Erasmus and Luther and the
        'Dialog Julius Exclusus.'" *Vierhundertfunzig Jahre
        Lutherische Reformation, Festschrift Franz Lau,* ed.
        H. Junghans, et al. Leipzig: Evangelische Verlag-
        anstalt, 1967, pp.17-26.

1996   ————. *Erasmus of Christendom.* New York: Scribner's,
        1969.

1997   ————. "The Paraphrases of Erasmus." *ARG,* 57
        (1966): 67-76.

1998   ————. "The *Querela Pacis* of Erasmus, Classical and
        Christian Sources." *ARG,* 42 (1951): 32-48.

1999   ————. "The Responsibilities of Power According to
        Erasmus of Rotterdam." *Essays in Honor of Hajo
        Holborn,* ed. L. Kreiger and F. Stern. Garden City,
        N.Y.: Doubleday, 1967, pp.54-63.

2000   Belladonna, Rita. "Bartolomeo Carli Piccolomini's
        Attitudes towards Religious Ceremonies Compared to
        That of Erasmus and That of Luther." *BHR,* 42 (1980):
        421-26.

2001   Bentley, Jerry H. "Erasmus, Jean Le Clerc, and the
        Principle of the Harder Reading." *RQ,* 31 (1978):
        309-21.

2002   ————. "Erasmus' *Annotationes in Novum Testamentum*
        and the Textual Criticism of the Gospel." *ARG,* 67
        (1976): 33-53.

2003   ————. "New Testament Scholarship at Louvain in the
        Early Sixteenth Century." *SMRS,* n.s. 2 (1979): 51-
        79.

2004   Berger, Harry J. "Utopian Folly: Erasmus and More on
        the Perils of Misanthropy." *English Literary Renais-
        sance,* 12 (1982): 271-90.

2005   Bietenholz, Peter G. *Basle and France in the Sixteenth
        Century: the Basle Humanists and Printers in Their
        Contacts with Francophone Culture.* Geneva: Droz,
        1971.

2006 ————. "The Biographical Register." *Erasmus in English,* 9 (1978): 24.

2007 ————. "Ethics and Early Printing: Erasmus' Rules for the Proper Conduct of Authors." *Humanities Association Review,* 26 (1975): 180-95.

2008 ————. "Erasmus and the Anabaptists." *Erasmus in English,* 2 (1971): 8.

2009 ————. "Erasmus' View of More." *Moreana,* 5 (1964): 5-16.

2010 ————. *History and Biography in the Work of Erasmus of Rotterdam.* Travaux d'Humanisme et Renaissance, 87. Geneva: Droz, 1966.

2011 ————. "Humanistic Ventures into Psychology: Etienne Dolet's Polemic against Erasmus." *Essays Presented to Myron P. Gilmore* (item 275), vol.1, pp.21-36.

2012 Bloch, Eileen. "Erasmus and the Froben Press: The Making of an Editor." *Library Quarterly,* 35 (1964): 109-20.

2013 Born, Lester K. "Some Notes on the Political Theories of Erasmus." *Journal of Modern History,* 2 (March 1930): 226-36.

2014 Bouyer, Louis. *Erasmus and the Humanist Experiment,* trans. Francis X. Murphy. London: Geoffrey Chapman, 1959.

2015 ————. "Erasmus in Relation to the Medieval Biblical Tradition." *The Cambridge History of the Bible,* ed. G.W.H. Lampe. Cambridge: Cambridge University Press, 1969, vol.2, pp.492-508.

2016 Boyle, Marjorie O'Rourke. *Christening Pagan Mysteries: Erasmus in Pursuit of Wisdom.* Toronto: University of Toronto Press, 1981.

2017 ————. "The Eponyms of 'Desiderius Erasmus.'" *RQ,* 30 (1977): 12-23.

2018 ————. *Erasmus on Language and Method in Theology.* Toronto and Buffalo: University of Toronto Press, 1977.

2019   ————. "Erasmus' Prescription for Henry VIII: Logo-
        therapy." *RQ*, 31 (1978): 161-72.

2020   ————. "Weavers, Farmers, Tailors, Travellers, Masons,
        Prostitutes, Pimps, and Other Theologians." *Erasmus
        in English*, 3 (1971): 1-7.

2021   Bradshaw, Brendan. "The Christian Humanism of Erasmus."
        Journal of Theological Studies, n.s. 33 (1982): 411-
        47.

2022   Bruce, A.K. *Erasmus and Holbein*. London: Muller, 1936.

2023   Bywater, Ingraham. *The Erasmian Pronunciation of Greek
        and Its Predecessors*. London: Fronde, 1908.

2024   Callahan, Virginia Woods. "The Erasmus-Alciati Friend-
        ship." *Acta Conventus Neo-latini Louvaniensis* (item
        288), pp.133-41.

2025   ————. "The Mirror of Princes. Erasmian Echoes in
        Alciati's Emblematum Liber." *Acta Conventus Neo-
        latini Amstelodamensis* (item 305), pp.183-96.

2026   Campbell, William E. "Erasmus in England." *Dublin
        Review*, 422 (July 1942): 36-49.

2027   ————. *Erasmus, Tyndale, and More*. London: Eyre
        and Spottiswoode, 1949.

2028   Carley, James. "Four Poems in Praise of Erasmus by
        John Leland." *Erasmus in English*, 11 (1981-1982):
        26-27.

2029   Caspari, F. "Erasmus on the Social Functions of Chris-
        tian Humanism." *JHI*, 8 (1947): 78-106.

2030   Chomarat, Jacques. "Grammar and Rhetoric in the Para-
        phrases of the Gospels by Erasmus." *Erasmus of
        Rotterdam Society Yearbook*, 1 (1981): 30-68.

2031   Christian, Lynda. "The Figure of Socrates in Erasmus'
        Works." *The Sixteenth-Century Journal*, 3 (1972):
        1-10.

2032   ————. "The Metamorphoses of Erasmus' 'Folly.'" *JHI*,
        32 (1971): 284-94.

2033   Clarke, M.L.   "The Educational Writings of Erasmus."
       Erasmus in English, 8 (1976): 23-31.

2034   Clough, Cecil H.   "Erasmus and the Pursuit of English
       Royal Patronage in 1517 and 1518." *Erasmus of
       Rotterdam Society Yearbook,* 1 (1981): 126-40.

2035   Clutton, George.   "An Emblem by Holbein for Erasmus
       and More." *JWI,* 1 (1937-1938): 63-66.

2036   Cole, H.N.   "Erasmus and His Diseases." *Journal of
       the American Medical Association,* 148 (1952): 529-31.

2037   Colie, Rosalie L.   "Some Notes on Burton's Erasmus."
       RQ, 20 (1967): 335-41.

2038   Colish, Marcia L.   "Seneca's *Apocolocyntosis* as a Pos-
       sible Source for Erasmus' *Julius Exclusus.*" *RQ,*
       29 (1976): 361-68.

2039   Colledge, Edmund, O.S.A.   "Erasmus, the Brethren of
       the Common Life, and the Devotio moderna." *Erasmus
       in English,* 7 (1975): 2-4.

2040   Coppens, J., ed.   *Scrinium Erasmianum,* 2 vols.   Leiden:
       Brill, 1969.

2041   Dallmann, William.   "Erasmus' Pictures of Church Con-
       ditions." *Concordia Theological Monthly,* 11 (1940):
       100-07, 179-88, 266-80.

2042   ————.   "Erasmus on Luther." *Concordia Theological
       Monthly,* 9 (1938): 660-74, 735-36.

2043   Dekker, A.M.M.   "Dedekind, Erasmus and Navagero: Three
       Emendations." *HL,* 28 (1979): 342-43.

2044   DeMolen, Richard L.   "Erasmus' Commitment to the Canons
       Regular of St. Augustine." *RQ,* 26 (1973): 437-43.

2045   ————.   "Erasmus on Childhood." *Erasmus of Rotterdam
       Society Yearbook,* 2 (1982): 25-46.

2046   ————, ed.   *Erasmus of Rotterdam. A Quincentennial
       Symposium.*   New York: Twayne, 1971.

2047   ————, ed.   *Essays on the Works of Erasmus.*   New Haven:
       Yale University Press, 1978.   Superb collection with

treatment of each of Erasmus' major works by well-
qualified scholars.

2048   Devereux, E.J. "The Publication of the English *Para-
       phrases* of Erasmus." *BJRL*, 51 (1968-1969): 348-67.

2049   ———. "English Translations of Erasmus, 1522-1557."
       Editing Sixteenth-Century Texts, ed. R.J. Schoeck.
       Toronto: University of Toronto Press, 1966, pp.43-58.

2050   ———. "Tudor Uses of Erasmus on the Eucharist."
       ARG, 62 (1971): 38-52.

2051   Di Cesare, Mario. "Erasmus' 'Pacificator' and Girolamo
       Vida." *Moreana*, 13 (1967): 25-44.

2052   Dolan, John P. *The Influence of Erasmus, Witzel and
       Cassander in the Church Ordinances and Reform Pro-
       posals of the United Duchies of Cleve during the
       Middle Decades of the 16th Century.* Reformations-
       geschichtliche Studien und Text, 83. Münster:
       Aschendorffsche, 1957.

2053   Dorey, T.A., ed. *Erasmus.* Studies in Latin Litera-
       ture and Its Influence. London: Routledge and Kegan
       Paul, 1970. Important studies on various works.

2054   Drummond, Robert B. *Erasmus. His Life and Character
       as Shown in His Correspondence and Works,* 2 vols.
       London: Smith, Elder, 1873.

2055   Elliot-Binns, Leonard. *Erasmus the Reformer.* 2nd ed.
       London: Methuen, 1923.

2056   Engelhardt, George John. "Medieval Vestiges in the
       Rhetoric of Erasmus." *PMLA*, 63 (1948): 739-44.

*   *Erasmus in English.* A Newsletter Published by Univer-
       sity of Toronto Press. Toronto, 1970-. Aims to
       serve as a clearing-house for information about
       Erasmus and report on the progress of the Collected
       Works of Erasmus, published by the University of
       Toronto Press. Cited above as item 11.

2057   Emerton, Ephraim. *Desiderius Erasmus of Rotterdam.*
       New York: Putnam's Sons, 1899.

2058   Faludy, George. *Erasmus.* New York: Stein and Day, 1970.

2059   Faulkner, J.A. *Erasmus: The Scholar.* Cincinnati:
        Jennings and Graham, 1907.

2060   Ferguson, Wallace K. *Erasmus and Christian Humanism,*
        B.K. Smith Lecture. Houston: University of Saint
        Thomas, 1963.

2061   ————. "Renaissance Tendencies in the Religious
        Thought of Erasmus." *JHI,* 15 (1954): 499-508.

2062   Fernandez, José A. "Erasmus on the Just War." *JHI,*
        34 (1973): 209-26.

2063   Friedman, Jerome. "Sixteenth-Century Christian-
        Hebraica: Scripture and the Renaissance Myth of the
        Past." *The Sixteenth-Century Journal,* 11 (1980):
        67-86.

2064   Froude, J.A. *Life and Letters of Erasmus, Lectures*
        Delivered at Oxford 1893-4. New York: Scribner's,
        1927; repr. New York: AMS Press, 1971. Includes
        copious translations from the letters.

2065   Garrod, H.W. "Erasmus and His English Patrons." *The*
        Library, ser.5, 4 (1949-1950): 1-13.

2066   Gavin, J.A., and Clarence H. Miller. "Erasmus: Addi-
        tions to Listrius; Commentary on 'The Praise of
        Folly.'" *Erasmus in English,* 11 (1981-1982): 19-26.

2067   ————, and Thomas M. Walsh. "The *Praise of Folly* in
        Context: The Commentary of Girardus Listrius." *RQ,*
        24 (1971): 193-210.

2068   Geanakoplos, Deno J. "Erasmus and the Aldine Academy
        of Venice, A Neglected Chapter in the Transmission
        of Graeco-Byzantine Learning to the West." *Greek,*
        Roman & Byzantine Studies, 3 (1960): 107-34.

2069   Gee, John Archer. "John Byddell and the First Publi-
        cation of Erasmus' *Enchiridion* in English." *Journal*
        of English Literary History, 4 (1937): 43-59.

2070   ————. "Margaret Roper's Version of Erasmus' 'Pre-
        catio Dominica' and the Apprenticeship behind Early
        Tudor Translation." *Review of English Studies,* 13
        (1937): 257-71.

2071   Gerlo, A.   "The *Opus de Conscribendis Epistolis* of
        Erasmus and the Tradition of the *Ars Epistolica*."
        *Classical Influences on European Culture A.D. 500-
        1500* (item 277), pp.103-14.

2072   Giese, Rachel.   "Erasmus and the Fine Arts."   *Journal
        of Modern History*, 7 (1935): 257-79.

2073   ————.   "Erasmus' Greek Studies."   *Classical Journal*,
        29 (1934): 517-26.

2074   ————.   "Erasmus in Effigy."   *South Atlantic Quarterly*,
        44 (1945): 195-201.

2075   ————.   "Erasmus' Knowledge and Estimate of the Ver-
        nacular Language."   *Romanic Review*, 18 (1937): 3-18.

2076   Gilmore, Myron P.   "Anti-Erasmian in Italy: The Dia-
        logue of Ortensio Lando on Erasmus' Funeral."   *JMRS*,
        4 (1974): 1-14.

2077   ————.   "*De modis disputandi*: The Apologetic Works of
        Erasmus."   *Florilegium Historiale* (item 302), pp.63-
        88.

2078   ————.   "Erasmus and Alberto Pio, Prince of Carpi."
        Action and Conviction in Early Modern Europe (item
        299), pp.299-318.

*   ————.   *Humanists and Jurists: Six Studies in the
        Renaissance*.   Cambridge, Mass.: Harvard University
        Press, 1963.   Cited above as item 227.

2079   ————.   "Italian Reactions to Erasmian Thought."
        Itinerarium Italicum (item 298), pp.61-115.

2080   Gilson, Etienne.   "Erasmus and the Continuity of Clas-
        sical Culture."   *Erasmus in English*, 1 (1970): 2-7.

2081   Gleason, John B.   "The Birth Dates of John Colet and
        Erasmus of Rotterdam: Fresh Documentary Evidence."
        RQ, 32 (1979): 73-76.

2082   Godin, André.   "The *Enchiridion Militis Christiani*:
        The Modes of an Origenian Appropriation."   *Erasmus
        of Rotterdam Society Yearbook*, 2 (1982): 47-79.

2083   Green, Lowell C. "The Bible in Sixteenth-Century
        Humanist Education." *Studies in the Renaissance,* 19
        (1972): 112-32.

2084   ————. "Erasmus, Luther, and Melanchthon on the
        magnus consensus: The Problem of the Old and New in
        the Reformation and Today." *Lutheran Quarterly,*
        27 (1975): 364-81.

2085   ————. "The Influence of Erasmus upon Melanchthon,
        Luther and the Formula of Concord in the Doctrine of
        Justification." *Church History,* 43 (1974): 183-200.

2086   Green, Otis H. "Additional Data on Erasmus in Spain."
        Modern Language Quarterly, 10 (1949): 47-48.

2087   Grendler, Marcella and Paul. "The Survival of Erasmus
        in Italy." *Erasmus in English,* 8 (1976): 2-22.

2088   Guggisberg, Hans R. "The Amerbach Correspondence."
        Erasmus in English, 3 (1971): 25-28.

2089   Gundersheimer, Werner L. "Erasmus, Humanism and the
        Christian Cabala." *JWCI,* 26 (1963): 38-52.

2090   Guppy, H. "Desiderius Erasmus." *BJRL,* 20 (1936):
        245-57.

2091   ————. "William Tyndale, Scholar and Martyr." *BJRL,*
        20 (1936): 258-67.

2092   Hardin, Richard F. "The Literary Conventions of
        Erasmus' 'Education of a Christian Prince': Advice
        and Aphorism." *RQ,* 35 (1982): 151-63.

2093   Harvey, E. Ruth. "A Preliminary List of Names for
        Erasmus' Correspondence." *Erasmus in English,* 4
        (1972): 3-25. See also Bietenholz (item 2006).

2094   Headley, John. "Gattinars, Erasmus, and the Imperial
        Configurations of Humanism." *ARG,* 71 (1980): 64-98.

2095   Henderson, Judith Rice. "Euphues and His Erasmus."
        English Literary Renaissance, 12 (1982): 135-61.

2096   Heninger, S.K., Jr. "Pythagorean Symbols in Erasmus'
        Adagia." *RQ,* 21 (1968): 162-65.

2097   Hirsch, Elizabeth F.   "Erasmus and Portugal."   *BHR*,
        32 (1970): 539-57.

2098   ————.   "The Friendship of Erasmus and Damião de Goes."
        Proceedings of the American Philosophical Society,
        95 (1951): 556-68.

2099   Hoffman, Manfred.   "Erasmus and Religious Toleration."
        Erasmus of Rotterdam Society Yearbook, 2 (1982): 80-
        106.

2100   Hollis, Christopher.   *Erasmus*.   Milwaukee: Bruce, 1933.

2101   Huizinga, Johan.   *Erasmus of Rotterdam*, trans. F. Hop-
        man, with a selection of *Letters of Erasmus*, trans.
        B. Flower.   New York: Scribner's, 1924; repr. London:
        Phaidon, 1952; repr. as *Erasmus and the Age of Refor-
        mation*. New York: Harper and Row, 1957.   The last
        edition omits the translation of the selection of
        Erasmus' letters.

2102   ————.   "In Commemoration of Erasmus."   *Men and
        Ideas*, trans. J.S. Holmes and H. van Marle.   New
        York: Meridian, 1959, pp.310-26.

2103   Hutton, James.   "Erasmus and France: The Propaganda
        for Peace."   *Studies in the Renaissance*, 6 (1961):
        103-27.

2104   Hyma, Albert.   *The Brethren of the Common Life*.   Grand
        Rapids: Eerdmans, 1950.

2105   ————.   *The Christian Renaissance: A History of the
        "Devotio moderna."*   New York: Century, 1925; repr.
        Hamden, Ct.: Archon, 1965.

2106   ————.   *Erasmus and the Humanists*.   New York: Crofts,
        1930.

2107   ————.   "Erasmus and the Oxford Reformers."   *Bij-
        draagen voor Vaderlandsche Geschiedenis en Oudheid-
        kunde*, 7th ser., 7 (1936): 132-54.

2108   ————.   "Erasmus and the Oxford Reformers (1493-
        1503)."   *Nederlands Archief voor Kerkgeschiedenis*,
        n.s. 25 (1932): 69-92.

2109   ———. "Erasmus and the Reformation in Germany."
        MH, 8 (1954): 99-104.

2110   ———. "Erasmus and the Sacrament of Matrimony."
        ARG, 48 (1957): 145-64.

2111   ———. *The Life of Desiderius Erasmus*. Assen: Van
        Gorcum, 1972.

2112   ———. *The Youth of Erasmus*. University of Michigan
        Publications. History and Political Science, Vol.10.
        Ann Arbor: University of Michigan Press, 1930; repr.
        New York: Russell and Russell, 1968.

2113   IJsewijn, J. "The Declamatio Lovaniensis de tutelae
        severitate. Students against Academic Authority at
        Louvain in 1481." *Lias*, 3 (1976): 5-31.

2114   ———. "The Coming of Humanism in the Low Countries."
        Itinerarium Italicum (item 298), pp.193-301.

2115   ———. "Humanism and Humanist Literature in the Low
        Countries before 1500." *Classical Influences on
        European Culture A.D. 500-1500* (item 277), pp.115-18.

2116   ———. "A Passage of Erasmus, *De pueris instituendis*,
        Explained." *HL*, 23 (1974): 384-85.

2117   ———, W. Lourdaux, and E. Persons. "Adam Jordaens
        (1449-1494), an Early Humanist at Louvain." *HL*, 22
        (1973): 83-99.

2118   Jacob, E.F. "Christian Humanism in the Late Middle
        Ages." *Europe in the Later Middle Ages* (item 285),
        pp.437-65.

2119   Jarrott, C.A.L. "Erasmus' Biblical Humanism." *Stud-
        ies in the Renaissance*, 17 (1970): 119-52.

2120   Kaiser, Walter Jacob. *Praisers of Folly: Erasmus,
        Shakespeare, Rabelais*. Harvard Studies in Compara-
        tive Literature, 25. Cambridge, Mass.: Harvard
        University Press, 1963.

2121   Kaufman, Peter Iver. "The Disputed Date of Erasmus'
        Liber Apologeticus." *MH*, n.s. 10 (1981): 141-57.

2122   ————. "John Colet and Erasmus' *Enchiridion*." *Church History*, 46 (1977): 296-312.

2123   Kay, W. David. "Bartholomew Fair: Ben Jonson in Praise of Folly." *English Literary Renaissance*, 6 (1976): 299-316.

2124   ————. "Erasmus' Learned Joking: the Ironic Use of Classical Wisdom in *The Praise of Folly*." *Texas Studies in Literature and Language*, 19 (1977): 247-67.

2125   Kinney, D. "Erasmus' *Adagia*: Midwife to the Rebirth of Learning." *JMRS*, 11 (1981): 169-92.

2126   Kittelson, James M. "Capito and Erasmus." *Erasmus in English*, 11 (1981-1982): 12-19.

2127   Kleinhaus, R.G. "Luther and Erasmus: Another Perspective." *Church History*, 39 (1970): 459-69.

2128   Klucas, Joseph A. "Erasmus and Erasmians on Education in Sixteenth-Century Portugal." *Erasmus of Rotterdam Society Yearbook*, 1 (1981): 69-88.

2129   Knott, Betty I. "Erasmus' Use of Sources in *De copia*." *Erasmus in English*, 11 (1981-1982): 2-7.

2130   Koch, A.F.C. *The Year of Erasmus' Birth*. Utrecht: Haentjens, Dekker and Gumbert, 1969.

2131   Kristeller, Paul Oskar. "Erasmus from an Italian Perspective." *RQ*, 23 (1970): 1-14.

2132   ————. "A Little-Known Letter of Erasmus and the Date of His Encounter with Reuchlin." *Florilegium Historiale* (item 302), pp.53-61.

2133   ————. "Two Unpublished Letters to Erasmus." *Renaissance News*, 14 (Spring 1961): 6-14.

2134   Krivatsky, Peter. "Erasmus' Medical Milieu." *Bulletin of the History of Medicine*, 47 (1975): 113-54.

2135   Krodel, Gottfried G. "Erasmus-Luther: On Theology, On Method, Two Results." *Concordia Theological Monthly*, 41 (1970): 648-67.

2136   ————. "Luther, Erasmus and Henry VIII." *ARG*, 53
          (1962): 60-78.

2137   Levi, A.H.T. "Erasmus, the Early Jesuits and the
          Classics." *Classical Influences on European Culture
          A.D. 1500-1700* (item 278), pp.223-38.

2138   Locher, Gottfried. "Zwingli and Erasmus." *Erasmus in
          English,* 10 (1979-1980): 2-11.

2139   Longhurst, John E. *Erasmus and the Spanish Inquisi-
          tion: The Case of Juan de Valdes.* Albuquerque: Uni-
          versity of New Mexico Press, 1950.

2140   McConica, James K. "Erasmus and the *Julius*: A Humanist
          Reflects on the Church." *The Pursuit of Holiness*
          (item 304), pp.444-77.

2141   ————. "The Riddle of 'Terminus.'" *Erasmus in
          English,* 2 (1971): 2-7.

2142   McCullough, C. Douglas. "The Concept of Law in the
          Thought of Erasmus." *Erasmus of Rotterdam Society
          Yearbook,* 1 (1981): 89-112.

2143   McLuhan, Marshall. "Erasmus: The Man and the Masks."
          Erasmus in English, 3 (1971): 7-10.

2144   McSorely, Harry S. "Erasmus and the Primacy of the
          Roman Pontiff: Between Conciliarism and Papalism."
          ARG, 65 (1974): 37-54.

2145   Maguire, John B. "Erasmus' Biographical Masterpiece:
          Hieronymi Stridonensis Vita." *RQ,* 26 (1973): 265-73.

2146   Major, J. Russell. "The Renaissance Monarchy as Seen
          by Erasmus, More, Seyssel, and Machiavelli." *Action
          and Conviction in Early Modern Europe* (item 299),
          pp.17-31.

2147   Mangan, John Joseph. *The Life, Character and Influ-
          ence of Desiderius Erasmus of Rotterdam,* 2 vols.
          New York: Macmillan, 1927.

2148   Mansfield, Bruce. "Erasmus in the Nineteenth Century.
          The Liberal Tradition." *Studies in the Renaissance,*
          15 (1968): 193-219.

2149   ———. "Erasmus and the Mediating School." *Journal of Religious History*, 4.4 (1967): 302-16.

2150   ———. *Phoenix of His Age: Interpretations of Erasmus c.1550-1750*. Toronto: University of Toronto Press, 1979.

2151   ———. "The Three Circles of Erasmus of Rotterdam." *Colloquium: The Australian and New Zealand Theological Review*, 4 (1972): 4-11.

2152   ———. "Erasmus of Rotterdam: Evangelical." *Erasmus in English*, 6 (1973): 1-5.

2153   Marc'hadour, G. "Erasmus' Paraphrase of the 'Pater Noster' (1523) with Its English Translation by Margaret Roper (1524)." *Moreana*, 7 (1964): 9-64.

2154   Marsh, David. "Erasmus on the Antithesis of Body and Soul." *JHI*, 37 (1976): 673-88.

2155   Meagher, John C., and Richard Schoeck. "On Erasmus' *The Godly Feast*." *Erasmus in English*, 3 (1971): 10-12.

2156   Metzger, Bruce M. "Erasmus; Edition of the New Testament." *The Text of the New Testament*. Oxford: Clarendon Press, 1968, pp.98-103.

2157   Meyer, Carl S. "Erasmus and Reuchlin." *Moreana*, 24 (1969): 65-80.

2158   ———. "Erasmus on the Study of Scriptures." *Concordia Theological Monthly*, 40 (1969): 734-46.

2159   ———. "Christian Humanism and the Reformation: Erasmus and Melanchthon." *Concordia Theological Monthly*, 41 (1970): 637-47.

2160   Miller, Clarence H. "Current English Translations of *The Praise of Folly*: Some Corrections." *Philological Quarterly*, 45 (1966): 718-33.

2161   ———. "The Epigrams of Erasmus and More: A Literary Diptych." *Erasmus of Rotterdam Society Yearbook*, 1 (1981): 8-29.

2162   ————. "Some Medieval Elements and Structural Unity
        in Erasmus' *The Praise of Folly.*" *RQ*, 27 (1974):
        499-512.

2163   ————. "Three Sixteenth-Century Manuscripts of
        Erasmus' *Moriae Encomium.*" *Manuscripta*, 22 (1978):
        173-76.

2164   Miller, Clement A. "Erasmus on Music." *Musical
        Quarterly*, 52 (1966): 332-49.

2165   Minnich, Nelson H., and W.W. Meissner. "The Character
        of Erasmus." *American Historical Review*, 83 (1978):
        577-624.

2166   Moholi, Joan. "English-Hungarian Connections in the
        Humanist Circle of Erasmus of Rotterdam." *History*,
        32 (1947): 60-62.

2167   Moore, John A. "A Note on Erasmus and Fray Luis de
        Granada." *Romance Notes*, 9 (1968): 314-19.

2168   Mozley, J.F. "The English 'Enchiridion' of Erasmus,
        1533." *Review of English Studies*, 20 (1944): 97-
        107.

2169   Murray, Robert H. *Erasmus and Luther. Their Atti-
        tude to Toleration*. London: Society for Promoting
        Christian Knowledge, 1920.

2170   Murray, W.A. "Erasmus and Paracelsus." *BHR*, 20
        (1958): 560-64.

2171   Nash, Charles A. "The Relation of Erasmus to the
        Reformation." *Bibliotheca Sacra*, 95 (1938): 309-28,
        445-60; 96 (1939): 51-56.

2172   Nurse, Peter H. "Erasmus and Bonaventure Des Périers."
        BHR, 30 (1968): 53-64.

2173   Nuttall, Geoffrey F. "Cross-reference Table between
        LB and Opus Epistolarum." *Erasmus in English*, 3
        (1971): 18-23.

2174   O'Donnell, Sister Anne M. "Rhetoric and Style in
        Erasmus' *Enchiridion militis Christiani.*" *Studies in
        Philology*, 77 (1980): 26-49.

2175   Olin, John C. "Erasmus and His Edition of St. Hilary."
        Erasmus in English, 9 (1978): 8-13.

2176   ———. "Erasmus and St. Jerome." *Thought,* 54 (1979):
        313-21.

2177   ———. *Six Essays on Erasmus, and a Translation of
        Erasmus' Letter to Carondelet, 1523.* New York:
        Fordham University Press, 1979.

2178   ———, James D. Smart and Robert E. McNally, eds.
        *Luther, Erasmus and the Reformation: A Catholic-
        Protestant Reappraisal.* New York: Fordham Univer-
        sity Press, 1969.

2179   O'Malley, John W. "Erasmus and Luther, Continuity and
        Discontinuity as a Key to Their Conflict." *The Six-
        teenth-Century Journal,* 5 (1974): 47-65.

2180   Packer, James I. "Luther against Erasmus." *Concordia
        Theological Monthly,* 37 (1966): 207-21.

2181   Panofsky, Erwin. "Erasmus and the Visual Arts." *JWCI,*
        32 (1969): 200-27.

2182   Parker, Douglas H. "The English 'Enchiridion militis
        Christiani' and Reformation Politics." *Erasmus in
        English,* 5 (1972): 16-21.

2183   ———. "Religious Polemics and Two Sixteenth-Century
        English Editions of Erasmus' *Enchiridion Militis
        Christiani, 1545-1561.*" *Renaissance and Reformation,*
        9 (1973): 94-107.

2184   Payne, John B. "Erasmus and Lefèvre d'Etaples as
        Interpreters of Paul." *ARG,* 65 (1974): 54-83.

2185   ———. *Erasmus: His Theology of the Sacraments.*
        Richmond: John Knox, 1970.

2186   ———. "Erasmus: Interpreter of Romans." *Sixteenth-
        Century Essays and Studies,* ed. Carl S. Meyer. St.
        Louis: Foundation for Reformation Research, 1971,
        vol.2, pp.1-35.

2187   Pease, Arthur S. "Things without Honor." *Classical
        Philology,* 21 (1936): 27-42. Discusses Classical and
        Renaissance mock encomia such as *Praise of Folly.*

2188   Perreiah, Alan. "Humanistic Critiques of Scholastic
        Dialectic." *The Sixteenth-Century Journal*, 13
        (1982): 3-22.

2189   Peters, Robert. "Erasmus and the Fathers: Their Prac-
        tical Value." *Church History*, 36 (1967): 354-61.

2190   Phelps, Wayne H. "Philip Gerrard, Translator of
        Erasmus." *Erasmus in English*, 9 (1978): 14-15.

2191   Phillips, Margaret Mann. "Erasmus and Biography."
        University of Toronto Quarterly, 42 (1973): 185-201.

2192   ────. "Erasmus and Propaganda." *Modern Language
        Review*, 37 (1942): 1-17.

2193   ────. *Erasmus and the Northern Renaissance*.
        London: Macmillan, 1949; repr. New York: Collier,
        1965. Perhaps still the best introduction to
        Erasmus and his works.

2194   ────. "Erasmus in France in the Later Sixteenth
        Century." *JWCI*, 34 (1971): 246-61.

2195   ────. "Erasmus on the Tongue." *Erasmus of Rotter-
        dam Society Yearbook*, 1 (1981): 113-25.

2196   ────. "The Mystery of the Metsys Portrait."
        Erasmus in English, 7 (1975): 18-21.

2197   ────. "Nicolas Bourbon and Erasmus." *Acta Conventus
        Neo-latini Amstelodamensis* (item 305), pp.859-66.

2198   Pigman, G.W., III. "Imitation and the Renaissance
        Sense of the Past: The Reception of Erasmus' *Cicero-
        nianus*." *JMRS*, 9 (1979): 155-77.

2199   Pineas, Rainer. "Erasmus and More: Some Contrasting
        Theological Opinions." *Renaissance News*, 13 (1960):
        298-300.

2200   Popkin, Richard H. *The History of Scepticism from
        Erasmus to Spinoza*, new ed. Berkeley and Los Angeles:
        University of California Press, 1979.

2201   Post, R.R. *The Modern Devotion*. Leiden: Brill, 1968.

2202   Rabil, Albert, Jr. *Erasmus and the New Testament: The Mind of a Christian Humanist.* San Antonio, Tex.: Trinity University Press, 1972.

2203   ———. "Erasmus' Paraphrases of the Gospel of John." *Church History,* 48 (1979): 142-55.

2204   Radice, Betty. "Holbein's Marginal Illustrations to the *Praise of Folly.*" *Erasmus in English,* 7 (1975): 9-17.

2205   Rea, John D. "Jaques in Praise of Folly." *Modern Philology,* 17 (1919-1920): 465-69.

2206   Reardon, Bernard M.G. "Erasmus and the Reformation." *Downside Review,* 92 (1974): 221-32.

2207   Rebhorn, Wayne A. "Erasmian Education and the *Convivium Religiosum.*" *Studies in Philology,* 69 (1972): 131-49.

2208   ———. "The Metamorphoses of Moria: Structure and Meaning in *The Praise of Folly.*" *PMLA,* 89 (1974): 463-76.

2209   ———. "Thomas More's Enclosed Garden: Utopia and Renaissance Humanism." *English Literary Renaissance,* 6 (1976): 140-55.

2210   Rechtien, John G. "A 1520 French Translation of the *Moriae Encomium.*" *RQ,* 27 (1974): 23-35.

2211   Redeker, Hans. *Man Not Citizen: Erasmus in Our Time.* Amsterdam: P.N. van Kampen, 1969.

2212   Reedijk, Cornelis. "What Is Typically Dutch in Erasmus." *Delta,* 2, 4 (1959-1960): 35-44.

2213   Reynolds, E.E. *Thomas More and Erasmus.* London: Burns & Oates, 1965.

2214   Rice, Eugene F., Jr. "Erasmus and the Religious Tradition." *JHI,* 11 (1950): 177-206; repr. *Renaissance Essays* (item 290), pp.162-86.

2215   Rieger, James Henry. "Erasmus, Colet, and the Schoolboy Jesus." *Studies in the Renaissance,* 9 (1962): 187-94.

2216   Rix, Herbert David. "The Editions of Erasmus' *De
        copia.*" *Studies in Philology*, 43 (1946): 595-618.

2217   Rothschild, Herbert B. "Blind and Purblind: A Reading
        of *The Praise of Folly.*" *Neophilologus*, 54 (1970):
        223-34.

2218   Rummel, Erika. "The Use of Greek in Erasmus' Letters."
        HL, 30 (1981): 55-92.

2219   Ryan, Lawrence V. "Art and Artifice in Erasmus' *Con-
        vivium Profanum.*" *RQ*, 31 (1978): 1-16.

2220   ————. "*Erasmi Convivia*: The Banquet Colloquies of
        Erasmus." *MH,* n.s. 8 (1977): 201-15.

2221   Salmon, Albert. "Democracy and Religion in the World
        of Erasmus." *Review of Religion*, 14 (1950): 227-49.

2222   Salmon, Vivien. "A Pioneer of the 'Direct Method' in
        the Erasmus Circle." *Latomus*, 19 (1960): 567-77.

2223   Scheible, Heinz. "Melanchthon's Correspondence."
        Erasmus in English, 6 (1973): 11-13.

2224   Schenk, W. "That Erasmian Idea." *The Hibbert Journal*,
        48 (1950): 257-65.

2225   ————. "Erasmus and Melanchthon." *Heythrop Journal*,
        8 (1967): 249-59.

2226   ————. "Three Circles: Erasmus on the Clergy, Rulers
        and Education of the Laity." *The Dublin Review*, 224
        (1950): 66-81.

2227   Schevill, Rudolph. "Erasmus and Spain." *Hispanic
        Review*, 7 (1939): 93-116.

2228   ————. "Erasmus and the Fate of a Liberalistic Move-
        ment Prior to the Counter Reformation." *Hispanic
        Review,* 5 (1937): 103-23.

2229   Schram, Hugh R. "John of Garland and Erasmus on the
        Principle of Synonomy." *University of Texas Studies
        in English*, 30 (1951): 24-39.

2230   Screech, M.A. *Ecstasy and the Praise of Folly.* London:
        Duckworth, 1980.

2231   Scribner, R.W. "The Erasmians and the Beginning of
       the Reformation in Erfurt." *Journal of Religious
       History,* 9 (1976): 3-31.

2232   ————. "The Social Thought of Erasmus." *Journal of
       Religious History,* 6.1 (1970): 3-26.

2233   Item deleted.

2234   Siirala, Aarne. *Divine Humanness,* trans. T.A.
       Kantonen. Philadelphia: Fortress Press, 1970.
       Includes a discussion of Erasmus on free will.

2235   Silver, Larry. "Prayer and Laughter: Erasmian Elements
       in Two Late Metsys Panels." *Erasmus in English,* 9
       (1978): 17-23.

2236   Smith, Preserved. *Erasmus.* New York: Harper and
       Brothers, 1923; repr. New York: Ungar, 1962. A study
       of his life, ideals and place in history.

2237   ————. *A Key to the Colloquies of Erasmus.* Harvard
       Theological Studies, 12. Cambridge, Mass.: Harvard
       University Press, 1927; repr. New York: Kraus, 1969.

2238   Southgate, W.M. "Erasmus: Christian Humanism and Poli-
       tical Theory." *History,* 40 (1955): 240-54.

2239   Sowards, Jesse K. "Erasmus and the Apologetic Text-
       book: A Study of *De Duplici Copia Rerum ac Verborum.*"
       Studies in Philology, 55 (1958): 122-35.

2240   ————. *Desiderius Erasmus.* Boston: Twayne, 1975.

2241   ————. "Erasmus and the Education of Women." *The
       Sixteenth-Century Journal,* 13 (1982): 77-89.

2242   ————. "Erasmus and the Making of Julius Exclusus."
       Wichita State University Studies, 40.3 (1964): 3-16.

2243   ————. "Erasmus in England, 1509-1514." *Wichita
       State University Studies,* 37.2 (1962): 3-70.

2244   ————. "Thomas More, Erasmus and Julius II: A Case
       of Advocacy." *Moreana,* 24 (1969): 81-99.

2245   ————. "The Two Lost Years of Erasmus." *Studies in
       the Renaissance,* 9 (1962): 161-86.

2246 Spinka, Matthew. "Two Early Representatives of Human-
ism: Erasmus and Montaigne." *Christian Thought from
Erasmus to Berdyaev*, ed. M. Spinka. Englewood Cliffs,
N.J.: Prentice-Hall, 1962, pp.14-22.

2247 Spitz, Lewis G. "Erasmus." *Reformers in Profile, Advocates of Reform 1300-1600,"* ed. B.A. Gerrish. Philadelphia: Fortress Press, 1967, pp.60-83.

2248 Stenger, Genevieve. "*The Praise of Folly* and its *Par-
erga*." *MH*, n.s. 2 (1971): 97-117.

2249 Swain, Barbara. *Fools and Folly during the Middle Ages
and the Renaissance*. New York: Columbia University
Press, 1932.

2250 Sylvester, Richard S. "The Problem of Unity in *The
Praise of Folly*." *English Literary Renaissance*, 6
(1976): 125-39.

2251 Telle, Emile V. "'To everything there is a season....':
Ways and Fashions in the Art of Preaching on the Eve
of the Religious Upheaval in the Sixteenth Century."
Erasmus of Rotterdam Yearbook, 2 (1982): 13-24.

2252 Tentler, Thomas N. "Forgiveness and Consolation in the
Religious Thought of Erasmus." *Studies in the
Renaissance*, 12 (1965): 110-33.

2253 Thompson, Craig R. "Better Teachers than Scotus or
Aquinas." *Medieval and Renaissance Studies*, 2 (1966):
114-45.

2254 ————. "Erasmus as Internationalist and Cosmopolitan."
ARG, 46 (1955): 167-95.

2255 ————. "Erasmus, More and the Conjuration of Spirits:
The Possible Source of a Practical Joke." *Moreana*,
24 (1969): 45-50.

2256 ————. "Erasmus' Translation of Lucian's *Longaevi*."
Classical Philology, 35 (1940): 397-415.

2257 ————. "Scripture for the Ploughboy and Some Others."
*Studies in the Continental Background of Renaissance
Literature: Essays Presented to John L. Lievsay*, ed.
D.B. Randall and G.W. Williams. Durham, N.C.: Duke
University Press, 1977, pp.3-28. On Tyndale and
Erasmus' *Paraclesis*.

2258   ————. "Some Greek and Grecized Words in Renaissance
          Latin." *American Journal of Philology*, 64 (1943):
          333-35. By More and Erasmus.

2259   ————. "The Translations of Lucian by Erasmus and
          St. Thomas More." *Revue belge de philologie et
          d'histoire,* 18 (1939): 855-81; 19 (1940): 5-35.
          Also issued in book form, Ithaca: Cornell Univer-
          sity Press, 1940.

2260   Thompson, Geraldine. *Under Pretext of Praise: Satiric
          Mode in Erasmus' Fiction.* Toronto: University of
          Toronto Press, 1974.

2261   ————. "'Water wonderfully clear': Erasmus and Figur-
          ative Writing." *Erasmus in English,* 5 (1972): 5-10.

2262   ————. "Erasmus and the Tradition of Paradox."
          Studies in Philology, 61 (1964): 41-63.

2263   Tobriner, Marian Leona. "Juan Luis Vives and
          Erasmus." *Moreana,* 24 (1969): 35-44.

2264   Tournoy, G. "Franciscus Cremensis and Antonius Gratia
          Dei. Two Italian Humanists, Professors at Louvain
          in the Fifteenth Century." *Lias,* 3 (1976): 32-73.

2265   Tracy, James D. *"Against the 'Barbarians'*: The Young
          Erasmus and His Humanist Contemporaries." *The Six-
          teenth-Century Journal,* 11 (1980): 3-23.

2266   ————. "Erasmus and the Arians: Remarks on the *Con-
          sensus Ecclesiae." Catholic Historical Review,* 67
          (1981): 1-10.

2267   ————. "Erasmus Becomes a German." *RQ,* 21 (1968):
          281-88.

2268   ————. *Erasmus: The Growth of a Mind.* Travaux
          d'humanisme et Renaissance, 125. Geneva: Droz, 1972.

2269   ————. "The 1489 and 1494 Versions of Erasmus' *Anti-
          barbarorum Liber." HL,* 20 (1971): 81-120.

2270   ————. *The Politics of Erasmus: A Pacifist Intellec-
          tual and His Political Milieu.* Toronto: University
          of Toronto Press, 1978.

2271   Trapp, J.B. "Peter Meghen 1466/7-1540, Scribe and Courier." *Erasmus in English*, 11 (1981-1982): 28-35.

2272   Trinkhaus, Charles. "Erasmus, Augustine, and the Nominalists." *ARG*, 67 (1976): 5-32.

2273   Van der Laan, N. "Erasmus' Satire: Julius exclusus e coelis." *Stemmen des Tijds*, 25 (1936): 529-72.

2274   Verbeke, G., and J. IJsewijn, eds. *The Late Middle Ages and the Dawn of Humanism Outside Italy, Proceedings of the International Conference Louvain May 11-13, 1970.* Hague: Martinus Nijhoff and Leuven: University Press, 1972. Fifteen essays mainly on the spread of humanism to France and the Low Countries.

2275   Von Richthofen, Erich. "A Spanish Inquisitor's Objections to Erasmus." *Erasmus in English*, 7 (1975): 4-6.

2276   Walsh, James E. "The 'Querela Pacis' of Erasmus: The 'Lost' French Translation." *Harvard Library Bulletin*, 17 (1969): 374-84.

2277   Walsh, R. "The Coming of Humanism to the Low Countries: Some Italian Influences at the Court of Charles the Bold." *HL*, 25 (1976): 146-97.

2278   Watson, Donald Gwynn. "Erasmus' *Praise of Folly* and the Spirit of Carnival." *RQ*, 32 (1979): 333-54.

2279   Item deleted.

2280   Watson, Philip. "Erasmus, Luther, and Aquinas." *Concordia Theological Monthly*, 40 (1969): 747-58.

2281   Weiss, James Michael. "Ecclesiastes and Erasmus. The Mirror and the Image." *ARG*, 65 (1974): 83-108.

2282   Wells, William. "Erasmus and the Praise of Wisdom." *University of North Carolina Extension Bulletin*, 35 (1956): 5-17.

2283   Welsford, Enid. *The Fool.* London: Faber & Faber, 1935; repr. New York: Anchor Books, 1961. Contains extensive discussion of *The Praise of Folly*.

2284   White, Olive B.   "Richard Taverner's Interpretation of
        Erasmus in *Proverbs or Adagies.*" *PMLA*, 592 (1944):
        928-43.

2285   Whitney, J.P.   "Erasmus."   *EHR*, 35 (1920): 1-25.

2286   Williams, G.H.   "Erasmus and the Reformers on Non-
        Christian Religions and *Salus Extra Ecclesiam.*"
        Action and Conviction in Early Modern Europe (item
        299), pp.319-70.

2287   Williams, Kathleen, ed.   *Twentieth-Century Interpreta-
        tions of "The Praise of Folly."*   Englewood Cliffs,
        N.J.: Prentice-Hall, 1969.

2288   Yost, John K.   "German Protestant Humanism and the
        Early English Reformation: Richard Taverner and
        Official Translation."   *BHR*, 32 (1970): 613-25.

2289   ————.   "Taverner's Use of Erasmus and the Protest-
        antization of English Humanism."   *RQ,* 23 (1970):
        266-76.

2290   Zantuan, Konstanty.   "Erasmus and the Cracow Human-
        ists: The Purchase of His Liberty by Laski."   *Polish
        Review,* 10 (1965): 3-36.

2291   Zweig, Stefan.   *Erasmus of Rotterdam*, trans. E. and C.
        Paul.   New York: Viking, 1934.   A misleading popular-
        ization.

See also items 346, 455, 474, 2345, 2347, 2381, 2420, 2527,
      2538, 2697, 2723, 2733, 2871, 2918, 2959, 2992.

XVI. HUMANISM IN GREAT BRITAIN

More than any other northern country, England was influenced
by the thought, interests and style of Italian culture in the
fifteenth century. For an account of this transmission of
culture, turn to the works of G.B. Parks, R.J. Mitchell, and,
most of all, Roberto Weiss. By the end of the fifteenth century, Greek studies were well established in England and the
Oxford Reformers, headed by the Dean of St. Paul's, John
Colet, began to use the critical philological methods of Valla,
Poliziano and others, to understand biblical texts as well as
the classical heritage. In the next generation, Sir Thomas
More came to dominate English humanism, and with his classic
work *Utopia*, even created a new and enduring literary genre.
More has received the lion's share of scholarship devoted to
English humanism, and his complete works will soon be available in a critical edition with facing English translation
published by Yale University Press. More, too, has generated
very different critical approaches, including those of R.W.
Chambers, J.H. Hexter, G. Marc'hadour, and E. Surtz, as well
as recent monographs of A. Fox, B. Gogan, J.A. Guy, and G.M.
Logan. For bibliographical guides to More and the period, see
the essays of J.P. Jones and R.J. Schoeck, and for background,
the works of A.G. Dickens, G.R. Elton, and Denys Hay.

A. BIBLIOGRAPHY

2292   Baumann, Frederick L. "Review Article: Sir Thomas
        More." *Journal of Modern History,* 4 (1932): 604-15.

2293   Dees, Jerome S. *Sir Thomas Elyot and Roger Ascham, A
        Reference Guide.* Boston: G.K. Hall, 1980.

2294   Gibson, Reginald Walter, and J. Max Patrick. *St.
        Thomas More: A Preliminary Bibliography of His Works
        and of Moreana to the Year 1750. With a Bibliography
        of Utopia.* New Haven and London: Yale University
        Press, 1961.

2295   Jones, Judith P. "Recent Studies in More." *English
        Literary Renaissance,* 9 (1979): 442-58. Full critical
        bibliography from 1945 to 1976.

2296   Levine, Mortimer. *Tudor England, 1485-1603.* Cambridge:
        Cambridge University Press, 1968. A fine bibliog-
        raphy valuable for Chap.14 on intellectual history.

2297   Read, Conyers. *Bibliography of British History, Tudor
        Period, 1485-1603,* 2nd ed. Oxford: Clarendon Press,
        1959. The standard bibliography on Tudor England
        with much on humanism in Chap.10, on cultural and
        social history.

2298   Reynolds, Ernest Edwin. *Sir Thomas More, Bibliographi-
        cal Series.* London: Longmans, Green, 1965.

2299   Schoeck, R.J. "Recent Studies in the English Renais-
        sance." *Studies in English Literature,* 10 (1970):
        215-50.

2300   Sullivan, Frank, and Majie Padberg Sullivan. *Moreana--
        Materials for the Study of St. Thomas More.* Los
        Angeles: Loyola University of Los Angeles, 1964-1971.
        Fully annotated list of secondary works by author to
        late sixties.

B. *WORKS BY BRITISH HUMANISTS*

1. THE YALE EDITION OF THE WORKS OF ST. THOMAS MORE

2301   *The History of King Richard III*, ed. R.S. Sylvester.
        The Yale Edition of the Complete Works of St. Thomas
        More, Vol.2. New Haven: Yale University Press, 1963.

2302   *Translations of Lucian*, ed. Craig R. Thompson. The
        Yale Edition of the Complete Works of St. Thomas More,
        Vol.3 (part 1). New Haven: Yale University Press,
        1974.

2303   *Utopia*, ed. Edward Surtz, S.J., and J.H. Hexter. The
        Yale Edition of the Complete Works of St. Thomas More,
        Vol.4. New Haven: Yale University Press, 1965.

2304   *Responsio ad Lutherum*, ed. John M. Headley, and trans.
        Sister Scholastica Mandeville. The Yale Edition of
        the Complete Works of St. Thomas More, Vol.5. New
        Haven: Yale University Press, 1969.

2305   *A Dialogue Concerning Heresies*, ed. T. Lawlor and G.
        Marc'hadour. The Yale Edition of the Complete Works
        of St. Thomas More, Vol.6 (parts 1 and 2). New
        Haven: Yale University Press, 1982.

2306   *The Confutation of Tyndale's Answer*, ed. Louis A.
        Schuster, R.C. Marius, J.P. Lusardi, and R.J. Schoeck.
        The Yale Edition of the Complete Works of St. Thomas
        More, Vol.8. New Haven: Yale University Press, 1973.

2307   *The Apology*, ed. J.B. Trapp. The Complete Works of
        St. Thomas More, Vol.9. New Haven: Yale University
        Press, 1979.

2308   *Treatise on the Passions; Treatise on the Blessed Body,
        Instructions and Prayers*, ed. Garry E. Haupt. The
        Complete Works of St. Thomas More, Vol.13. New
        Haven: Yale University Press, 1976.

2309   *De Tristitia Christi*, ed. Clarence H. Miller. The Yale
        Edition of the Complete Works of St. Thomas More,
        Vol.14 (parts 1 and 2). New Haven: Yale University
        Press, 1976.

2. TRANSLATIONS OF MORE'S *UTOPIA*

2310   Adams, Robert M., ed. and trans. *Utopia, by Sir Thomas
        More*. New York: W.W. Norton and Co., 1975.

2311   Campbell, Mildred, ed. *"The Utopia" of Sir Thomas More
        Including Roper's Life of More and Letters of More
        and His Daughter Margaret*. New York: W.J. Black,
        1947.

2312   Gallagher, Ligeia, ed. *More's Utopia and Its Critics*.
        Chicago: Scott, Foresman, 1964. Includes the *Utopia*
        in Robinson's translation of 1551 and some modern
        criticism.

2313   Lupton, J.H., ed. *Utopia, in Latin and English*.
        Oxford: Oxford University Press, 1895.

2314   Robinson, Ralph, trans. *Utopia*. London: 1556; repr.
        London: A. Murry, 1869.

2315   Surtz, E., ed. *Utopia, Selected Works of St. Thomas
        More*. New Haven: Yale University Press, 1961. The
        best translation and edition.

2316   Turner, Paul, trans. *Utopia*. Baltimore: Penguin,
        1965.

3. WORKS OF MORE IN OTHER EDITIONS

2317   *The English Works*, 2 vols. London: 1557; repr. London:
        Scolar Press, 1978. Facsimile reprint of William
        Rastell's famous black-letter edition; the most com-
        plete edition of More's works in print.

2318   *The English Works*, ed. W.E. Campbell, with introd. and
        notes by A.W. Reed. 2 vols. London: Eyre and
        Spottiswoode, 1931. Facsimile of part of the black-
        letter text of William Rastell's edition of 1557 with
        modern English versions of the following works:
        *Early Poems, Life of Pico della Mirandola, Richard
        III, The Four Last Things* in Vol.1, and *Dialogue
        concerning Tyndale* in Vol.2. The edition projected
        in seven volumes was never completed.

2319   *The Apologye of Syr Thomas More*, ed. A.I. Taft. Early
        English Text Society, original series, 180. London:
        Oxford University Press, 1930.

2320   *A Dialogue of Comfort against Tribulation*, ed. with
        introd. Frank Manley. The Yale Edition of the Com-
        plete works of St. Thomas More; Selected Works. New
        Haven: Yale University Press, 1977.

2321   *Saint Thomas More. A Dialogue of Comfort against Tribu-
        lation*, ed. Leland Miles. Bloomington and London:
        Indiana University Press, 1965.

2322   *The Essential Thomas More*, ed. James J. Green and John
        P. Dolan. New York: The New American Library, 1967.

2323   *The Latin Epigrams of Thomas More*, ed. and trans.
        Leicester Bradner and Charles A. Lynch. Chicago:
        University of Chicago Press, 1953.

2324   *The History of King Richard III and Selections from the
        English and Latin Poems*, ed. R.S. Sylvester. The
        Yale Edition of the Works of St. Thomas More, Selec-
        ted Works. New Haven: Yale University Press, 1976.

2325   *Selected Letters*, trans. Elizabeth F. Rogers. The Yale
        Edition of the Works of St. Thomas More, Modernized
        Series. New Haven: Yale University Press, 1961.

2326   *Thomas More's Prayer Book, A Facsimile Reproduction of
        the Annotated Pages*, transcribed and trans. with
        introd. L.L. Martz and R.S. Sylvester. New Haven:
        Yale University Press, 1969.

2327   *A Translation of St. Thomas More's 'Responsio ad
        Lutherum,'* trans. Gertrude J. Donnelly. Washington,
        D.C.: Catholic University of America Press, 1962.

2328   *The Tower Works: Devotional Writings*, ed. Garry E.
        Haupt. The Yale Edition of the Complete Works of
        St. Thomas More, Selected Works. New Haven: Yale
        University Press, 1979.

4. WORKS BY OTHER BRITISH HUMANISTS

2329   Boece, Hector. *The Chronicles of Scotland*, trans.
        John Bellenden. Edinburgh: Thomas Davidson, 1536;
        repr. Bannatyne Club, 1821, 2 vols.; re-ed. from MS
        by R.W. Chambers and Edith C. Batho, *Scottish Text
        Society*, ser.3,10, 15 (1936-1941).

2330   Colet, John. *An Exposition of St. Paul's Epistle to
        the Romans*, ed. and trans. J.H. Lupton. London:
        Bell and Daldy, 1873.

2331   ————. *An Exposition of St. Paul's Epistle to the
        Corinthians*, ed. and trans. J.H. Lupton. London:
        Bell and Daldy, 1876.

2332   ————. *A Treatise on the Sacraments of the Church*,
        ed. and trans. J.H. Lupton. London: Bell and Daldy,
        1867.

2333   ————. *Opuscula quaedam theologica* (Commentary on
        I Peter [unfinished]; On the Composition of Christ's
        Mystical Body the Church; Exposition of St. Paul's
        Epistle to the Romans; Letters to Radulphus on the
        Mosaic Account of the Creation), ed. and trans. J.H.
        Lupton. London: Bell, 1876.

2334   ————. *The Sermon Made to the Convocation at Paulis*,
        trans. Thomas Lupset. London: Thomae Bertheleti
        [1530?]; repr. J.H. Lupton, *The Life of Colet*, 2nd
        ed. Hamden, Ct.: Shoe String Press, 1961.

2335   ————. *Two Treatises on the Hierarchies of Dionysius
        (Super opera Dionysii)*, ed. and trans. J.H. Lupton.
        London: Bell and Daldy, 1869.

2336   Fisher, John Cardinal, St. *The Defence of the Priest-
        hood against Luther*, trans. P.E. Hallett. London:
        Burns & Oates, 1935.

2337   Foxe, John. *Two Latin Comedies by John Foxe the Mar-
        tyrologist: Titus et Gesippus, Christus Triumphans*,
        ed. and trans. J.H. Smith. Ithaca: Cornell Univer-
        sity Press, 1973.

2338   Pace, Richard. *The Benefit of a Liberal Education (De
        fructu qui ex doctrina percipitur)*, ed. and trans.
        Frank Manley and Richard S. Sylvester. New York:
        Ungar, 1967.

2339   Pole, Reginald Cardinal. *The Defense of the Unity of
        the Church*, trans. Joseph G. Dwyer. Westminster,
        Md.: Newman Press, 1965.

2340   Roper, William. *The Life of Sir Thomas More, in Two
        Early Tudor Lives*, ed. R.S. Sylvester and D.P.
        Harding. New Haven: Yale University Press, 1962.

2341   Stapleton, Thomas. *The Life and Illustrious Martyrdom
        of Sir Thomas More*, trans. Philip E. Hallett, ed.
        E.E. Reynolds. London: Burns & Oates, 1966.

2342   Vergil, Polydore. *The Anglica Historia*, in part, ed.
        and trans. Denys Hay. Camden Society, ser.3, 74
        (1950).

2343   ————. *The English History (Anglica Historia)*, part
        trans. anon. (16th c), ed. Sir Henry Ellis as *Three
        Books of English History*. Camden Society, 29 (1844).

                            C. STUDIES

2344   Adams, J.W.L. "Scottish Neo-Latin Poetry." *Acta Con-
        ventus Neo-latini Amstelodamensis* (item 305), pp.1-9.

2345   Adams, Robert P. *The Better Part of Valor: More,
        Erasmus, Colet, and Vives, on Humanism, War, and
        Peace, 1496-1535*. Seattle: University of Washington
        Press, 1962.

2346   ————. "Bold, Bawdry and Open Manslaughter. The
        English New Humanist Attack on Medieval Romance."
        The Huntington Library Quarterly, 23 (1959/60): 33-48.

2347   ————. "Designs by More and Erasmus for a New Social
        Order." *Studies in Philology*, 42 (1945): 131-45.

2348   ————. "The Social Responsibilities of Science in
        Utopia, New Atlantis and After." *JHI*, 10 (1949):
        374-98; repr. *Renaissance Essays* (item 290), pp.137-
        61.

2349   Ady, C.M.   "Italian Influences on English History dur-
       ing the Period of the Renaissance." *History,* 9
       (1924-25): 288-301.   On acceptance of Italian ideas
       in sixteenth-century England.

2350   Africa, Thomas W.   "Thomas More and the Spartan Mirage."
       Historical Reflections, 6 (1979): 343-52.

2351   Allen, C.G.   "The Sources of 'Lily's Latin Grammar': A
       Review of the Facts and Some Further Suggestions."
       The Library, ser.5, 9 (1954): 85-100.   Fundamental on
       this important sixteenth-century grammar.

2352   Allen, Judson B.   "Commentary as Criticism: The Text,
       Influence, and Literary Theory of the 'Fulgentius
       Metaphored' of John Ridewall." *Acta Conventus Neo-
       latini Amstelodamensis* (item 305), pp.25-47.

2353   Allen, Peter R.   "*Utopia* and European Humanism: The
       Function of the Prefatory Letters and Verses."
       Studies in the Renaissance, 10 (1963): 91-107.

2354   Allen, P.S.   "Linacre and Latimer in Italy." *EHR,* 18
       (1903): 514-17.

2355   ————.   "A Sixteenth-Century School." *EHR,* 10 (1895):
       738-42.

2356   Allen, Ward.   "Hythloday and the Root of All Evil."
       Moreana, 29-32 (1971): 51-59.

2357   ————.   "Speculation on St. Thomas More's Use of
       Hesychius." *Philological Quarterly,* 40 (1967): 156-
       66.

2358   ————.   "The Tone of More's Farewell to *Utopia*: A
       Reply to J.H. Hexter." *Moreana,* 51 (1976): 108-18.
       A reply to Hexter's essay, "Intention, Words, and
       Meaning: The Case of More's *Utopia*," (item 2504).

2359   Ames, Russell.   *Citizen Thomas More and His Utopia.*
       Princeton: Princeton University Press, 1948.

2360   Armstrong, Elizabeth.   "English Purchases of Printed
       Books from the Continent 1465-1526." *EHR,* 94 (1979):
       268-90.

2361   Armstrong, John. "An Italian Astrologer at the Court
        of Henry VII." *Italian Renaissance Studies* (item
        289), pp.433-54.

2362   Aston, Margaret. "Lollardy and the Reformation: Sur-
        vival or Revival." *History,* 49 (1964): 149-70.

2363   Atkins, J.W.H. *English Literary Criticism: The Renais-
        sance.* London: Methuen, 1947.

2364   Atkins, Sidney H. "Certain of Sir Thomas More's Epi-
        grams Translated by Stanihurst." *Modern Language
        Review,* 26 (1931): 338-40.

2365   Avineri, Schlomo. "War and Slavery in More's *Utopia.*"
        International Review of Social History, 7 (1962):
        260-90.

2366   Baerwald, Friedrich. "Humanism and Social Ambivalence."
        Thought, 42 (1967): 543-60.

2367   Baker, Howard H. "Thomas More as a Student at Oxford."
        Moreana, 43-44 (1974): 5-11.

2368   Baker-Smith, D. *Thomas More and Plato's Voyage.* An
        Inaugural Lecture Given on 1st June 1978 at Univer-
        sity College, Cardiff. Cardiff: University College
        Cardiff Press, 1978.

2369   Baldwin, T.W. *William Shakespear's 'Small latine and
        lesse Greeke,'* 2 vols. Urbana: University of Illi-
        nois Press, 1944. The great study of the place of
        the classics in Renaissance curriculum.

2370   Barber, M.J. "The Englishman Abroad in the Fifteenth
        Century." *MH,* 11 (1957): 69-77.

2371   Barker, Arthur E. "*Clavis Moreana:* The Yale Edition of
        Thomas More." *The Journal of English and Germanic
        Philology,* 65 (1966): 318-30; repr. *Essential Articles*
        (item 2719), pp.215-28.

2372   Barnes, J.W. "Irony and the English Apprehension of
        Renewal." *Queen's Quarterly,* 73 (1966): 357-76.

2373   Bassett, Bernard. *Born for Friendship: The Spirit of
        Sir Thomas More.* London: Burns & Oates, 1965.

2374   Bennett, H.S. *English Books and Readers, 1475 to 1557.*
        Cambridge: At the University Press, 1952.

2375   ————. "Science and Information in English Writings
        of the Fifteenth Century." *Modern Language Review,*
        39 (1944): 1-8.

2376   Bennett, Josephine Waters. "Andrew Holes: A Neglected
        Harbinger of the English Renaissance." *Speculum,* 19
        (1944): 314-35.

2377   Berger, Harry, Jr. "The Renaissance Imagination:
        Second World and Green World." *The Centennial
        Review,* 9 (1965): 36-77.

2378   Berneri, Marie Louise. *Journey Through Utopia.*
        London: Routledge and Kegan Paul, 1950.

2379   Bevington, David M. "The Dialogue in *Utopia*: Two
        Sides to the Question." *Studies in Philology,* 58
        (1961): 496-509.

2380   Bierman, Judah. "Science and Society in the *New Atlan-
        tis* and Other Renaissance Utopias." *PMLA,* 78 (1963):
        492-500.

2381   Bietenholz, Peter G. "Erasmus' View of More."
        Moreana, 5 (1965): 5-16.

2382   Binder, James. "More's *Utopia* in English: A Note on
        Translation." *Modern Language Notes,* 62 (1947):
        370-76; repr. *Essential Articles* (item 2719), pp.
        229-33.

2383   Binns, J.W., ed. *The Latin Poetry of English Poets.*
        London: Routledge and Kegan Paul, 1974. Treats
        mainly those of the seventeenth century.

2384   ————. "William Gager's *Meleager* and *Ulysses Redux.*"
        *The Drama of the Renaissance: Essays for Leicester
        Bradner,* ed. Elmer M. Blistein. Providence, R.I.:
        Brown University Press, 1970, pp.27-41.

2385   Birchenough, E. and J., and G. Marc'hadour. "More's
        Appointment as Chancellor and His Resignation."
        Moreana, 12 (1966): 71-80.

2386   Bleich, David. "More's *Utopia*: Confessional Modes."
        American Imago, 28 (1971): 24-52. A psychological
        interpretation of More.

2387   Boewe, Charles. "Human Nature in More's *Utopia*." *The
        Personalist,* 41 (1960): 303-09.

2388   Bolchazy, L.J., ed. *A Concordance of St. Thomas More,
        and a Frequency Word List.* Hildesheim and New York:
        Olms, 1978.

2389   Borsa, M. "Correspondence of Humphrey, Duke of Glou-
        cester, and Pier Candido Decembrio." *EHR,* 19 (1904):
        509-26.

2390   Bradner, Leicester. *Musae Anglicanae: A History of
        Anglo-Latin Poetry, 1500-1925.* New York: Modern
        Language Association of America; and London: Oxford
        University Press, 1940.

2391   Bradshaw, Brendan. "More on Utopia." *Historical
        Journal,* 24 (1981): 1-24. Important study of Utopia
        as a critique of humanist ideals of reform as well
        as of contemporary sixteenth-century corruption.

2392   Bridgett, Thomas Edward. *The Life and Writings of Sir
        Thomas More.* London: Burns and Oates, 1891.

2393   Bush, Douglas. *Classical Influences in Renaissance
        Literature.* Cambridge, Mass.: Harvard University
        Press, 1952.

2394   ————. *The Renaissance and English Humanism.*
        Toronto: University of Toronto Press, 1939.

2395   Byron, Brian. *Loyalty in the Spirituality of St.
        Thomas More.* Bibliotheca Humanistica et Reforma-
        torica, Vol.4. Nieuwkeep: De Graaf, 1972.

2396   ————. "The Fourth Count of More's Indictment."
        Moreana, 10 (1966): 33-46.

2397   Campbell, W.E. *More's Utopia and His Social Teaching.*
        London: Eyre & Spottiswoode, 1930.

2398   Carpenter, Nan C. "St. Thomas More and Music: The
        Epigrams." *RQ,* 30 (1977): 24-28.

2399   Caspari, F. *Humanism and the Social Order in Tudor England.* New York: Teachers' College Press, 1954.

*   Cassirer, Ernst. *The Platonic Renaissance in England,* trans. James P. Pettegrove. London: Nelson, 1953. See item 501.

2400   Cespedes, Frank V. "The Final Book of Polydore Vergil's *Anglica historia*: Persecution and the Art of Writing." *Viator,* 10 (1979): 397-432.

2401   Chambers, R.W. "More's 'History of Richard III.'" *Modern Language Review,* 23 (1928): 405-23.

2402   ————. *The Place of Thomas More in English Literature and History.* London: Longmans, Green, 1937.

2403   ————. "The Saga and Myth of Sir Thomas More." *Proceedings of the British Academy,* 12 (1926): 179-225.

2404   ————. "Some Sequences of Thought in Shakespeare in the 147 lines of 'Sir Thomas More.'" *Modern Language Review,* 26 (1931): 251-80.

2405   ————. *Thomas More.* New York: Harcourt Brace, 1935.

2406   Charlton, Kenneth. *Education in Renaissance England.* London: Routledge and Kegan Paul, 1965.

2407   Chillington, Carol A. "Playwrights at Work: Henslowe's, Not Shakespeare's, Book of Sir Thomas More." *English Literary Renaissance,* 10 (1980): 439-79.

2408   Ciorgnescu, Alexandre. "Utopia: Land of Cocaigne and the Golden Age." *Diogenes,* 75 (Fall 1971): 85-121.

2409   Clebsch, William. *England's Earliest Protestants.* New Haven: Yale University Press, 1964.

2410   ————. "John Colet and the Reformation." *Anglican Theological Review,* 38 (1955): 167-77.

2411   Clough, Cecil H. "Federigo Veterani Polydore Vergilis 'Anglica Historia' and Baldassare Castiglione's 'Epistola'.... " *EHR,* 82 (1967): 772-83.

2412   ————. "Thomas Linacre, Cornelio Vitelli, and Humanistic Studies at Oxford." *Linacre Studies: Essays*

on the *Life and Work of Thomas Linacre, c.1460-1524,*
ed. F. Maddison, M. Pelling, and C. Webster. Oxford:
Clarendon Press, 1977, pp.1-23.

2413   ———. "The Relations between the English and Urbino
        Courts, 1474-1508." *Studies in the Renaissance,* 14
        (1967): 202-18.

2414   Coles, Paul. "The Interpretation of More's *Utopia.*"
        Hibbert Journal, 56 (1958): 365-70.

2415   Coogen, Robert. Petrarch and More's Concept of For-
        tune." *Italica,* 46 (1969): 167-75.

2416   ———. "Petrarch and Thomas More." *Moreana,* 21
        (1969): 19-30.

2417   ———. "Petrarch's Latin Prose and the English
        Renaissance." *Studies in Philology,* 68 (1971):
        270-91.

2418   Cooper, Sister M. Scholastica, O.S.B. "More and the
        Letter to Martin Dorp." *Moreana,* 6 (1965): 37-44.

2419   Copenhaven, Brian P. "The Historiography of Dis-
        covery in the Renaissance: The Sources and Composi-
        tion of Polydore Vergil's *De Inventoribus Rerum,* I-
        III." *JWCI,* 41 (1978): 192-214.

2420   Crofts, Richard A. "Renaissance Expressions of Socie-
        tal Responsibility: Thomas More, Desiderius Erasmus,
        and Thomas Muntzer." *The Sixteenth-Century Journal,*
        3 (1972): 11-24.

2421   Crosset, John. "More and Seneca." *Philological
        Quarterly,* 40 (1961): 577-80.

2422   Davis, J.C. "More, Morton, and the Politics of Accom-
        modation." *Journal of British Studies,* 9.2 (1970):
        27-49.

2423   ———. *Utopia and the Ideal Society: A Study of
        English Utopian Writings, 1516-1700.* New York:
        Cambridge University Press, 1980.

2424   Dean, Leonard F. "Literary Problems in More's *Richard
        III.*" *PMLA,* 58 (1943): 22-41; repr. in *Essential
        Articles* (item 2719), pp.315-25.

2425   De la Mare, A.C.   "Vespasiano da Bisticci and Gray."
       JWCI, 20 (1957): 174-76.   Includes letters of 1448.

2426   Delcourt, Joseph.   "Saint Thomas More and France."
       Traditio, 5 (1947): 285-310.

2427   Denholm-Young, N.   "Richard of Bury."   *TRHS*, 4th ser.,
       20 (1937): 135-68.

2428   Derrett, J. Duncan M.   "Gemistus Plethon, The Essences,
       and More's *Utopia*."   *BHR*, 27 (1965): 579-606.

2429   ————.   "Sir Thomas More and the Nun of Kent."
       Moreana, 15-16 (1967): 267-84.

2430   ————.   "The 'New' Document on Thomas More's Trial."
       Moreana, 3 (1964): 5-19.

2431   Dickens, Arthur Geoffrey.   *The English Reformation*.
       London: B.T. Batsford, 1964.

2432   Donner, H.W.   *Introduction to Utopia*.   London: Sedgwick
       and Jackson, 1945.

2433   Donno, E.S.   "Thomas More and *Richard III*."   *RQ*, 35
       (1982): 401-47.

2434   Dorsch, T.S.   "Sir Thomas More and Lucian: An Inter-
       pretation of *Utopia*."   *Archiv für das Studium der
       Neueren Sprachen und Literaturen*, 203 (1966-67):
       345-63.

2435   Doyle, Charles C.   "The Popular Aspects of Sir Thomas
       More's Latin Epigrams."   *Southern Folklore Quarterly*,
       37 (1973): 87-89.

2436   ————.   "*Utopia* and the Proper Place of Gold: Classi-
       cal Sources and Renaissance Analogues."   *Moreana*,
       31-32 (1971): 47-49.

2437   Duhamel, P. Albert.   "The Oxford Lectures of John Colet:
       An Essay Defining the English Renaissance."   *JHI*, 14
       (1953): 493-510.

2438   ————.   "Medievalism of More's *Utopia*."   *Studies in
       Philology*, 52 (1955): 99-126; repr. in *Essential
       Articles* (item 2719), pp.234-50.

2439   Durkan, John. "Giovanni Ferrerio and Religious Human-
        ism in Sixteenth-Century Scotland." *Religion and
        Humanism* (item 301), pp.181-94.

2440   Eden, P.T. "William Gray, Bishop of Ely, and Three
        Oxford Manuscripts of Seneca." *Classica et Mediae-
        valia,* 21 (1960): 29-42.

2441   Eilson, K.J. "Ascham's *Toxophilus* and the Rules of
        Art." *RQ,* 29 (1976): 30-51.

2442   Einstein, Lewis. *The Italian Renaissance in England.*
        New York: Columbia University Press, 1902.

2443   Elliot, Robert C. "The Shape of Utopia." *ELH,* 30
        (1963): 317-34.

2444   Elton, G.R. "The Real Thomas More." *Reforming Prin-
        ciple and Practice: Essays in Honour of Arthur Geof-
        frey Dickens,* ed. P.N. Brooks. London: Scolar
        Press, 1980, pp.21-31.

2445   ————. *Reform and Reformation: England, 1509-1558.*
        Cambridge, Mass.: Harvard University Press, 1977.

2446   ————. "Thomas More, Councillor (1517-1529)." *St.
        Thomas More: Action and Contemplation,* ed. Richard S.
        Sylvester. New Haven: Yale University Press, 1972.

2447   Emden, A.B. *A Biographical Register to the University
        of Oxford to A.D. 1500,* 3 vols. Oxford: Oxford Uni-
        versity Press, 1957-1959. Invaluable for careers of
        early English humanists.

2448   Evans, John X. "The Kingdom within More's *Utopia.*"
        Moreana, 55-56 (1977): 5-21.

2449   Fenlon, Dermot. "England and Europe: Utopia and Its
        Aftermath." *TRHS,* ser.5, 25 (1975): 115-36.

2450   ————. "The New Learning, the New Religion and the
        Law." *Historical Journal,* 17 (1974): 185-95.
        A review essay on works on French and English human-
        ism.

2451   ————. "Thomas More and Tyranny." *Journal of Eccles-
        iastical History,* 32 (1981): 453-76.

2452   Ferguson, Arthur B. *Articulate Citizen and the English Renaissance.* Durham, N.C.: Duke University Press, 1965.

2453   ————. "'By Little and Littel': The Early Tudor Humanists on the Development of Man." *Florilegium Historiale* (item 302), pp.126-50.

2454   ————. *Clio Unbound. Perception of the Social and Cultural Past in Renaissance England.* Duke Monographs in Medieval and Renaissance Studies, 2. Durham, N.C.: Duke University Press, 1979.

2455   ————. "John Twyne: A Tudor Humanist and the Problem of Legend." *Journal of British Studies,* 9.1 (1969): 24-44.

2456   ————. "Reginald Pecock and the Renaissance Sense of History." *Studies in the Renaissance,* 13 (1966): 147-65.

2457   Fideler, Paul A. "Christian Humanism and Poor Law Reform in Early Tudor England." *Societas,* 4 (1974): 269-85.

2458   Fisher, R.M. "Thomas Cromwell, Humanism and Educational Reform, 1530-40." *BIHR,* 50 (1977): 151-63.

2459   Fleisher, Martin. *Radical Reform and Political Persuasion in the Life and Writings of Thomas More.* Travaux d'humanisme et Renaissance, 132. Geneva: Droz, 1973.

2460   Flesseman-Van Leer, E. "The Controversy about Ecclesiology between Thomas More and William Tyndale." *Nederlands Archief voor Kerkgeschiedenis,* 44 (1960): 65-86.

2461   ————. "The Controversy about Scripture and Tradition between Thomas More and William Tyndale." *Nederlands Archief voor Kerkgeschiedenis,* 43 (1959): 143-64.

2462   Flynn, Vincent Joseph. "Englishmen in Rome during the Renaissance." *Modern Philology,* 36 (1938-39): 121-38.

2463   Fox, Alistair. *Thomas More, History and Providence*.
        New Haven: Yale University Press, 1982.

2464   Franciscius, Andreas. *Two Italian Accounts of Tudor
        England, a Journey to London in 1497, a Picture of
        English Life under Queen Mary*, trans. Cesare V.
        Malfatti. Barcelona: Sociedad Alcanaza de Artes,
        1953.

2465   Fyfe, W.H. "Tacitus' *Germania* and More's *Utopia*."
        *Proceedings and Transactions of the Royal Society of
        Canada*, 3rd ser., 30 (1936): sec.II, 57-59.

2466   Gabrieli, Vittorio. "Giovanni Pico and Thomas More."
        Moreana, 15-16 (1967): 43-57.

2467   Gaertner, Johannes. "Latin Verse Translations of the
        Psalms, 1500-1620." *Harvard Theological Review*, 49
        (1956): 271-305. A basic bibliography.

2468   Gee, J.A. *Thomas Lupset*. New Haven: Yale University
        Press, 1928.

2469   Gogan, Brian. *The Common Corps of Christendom: Eccles-
        iological Themes in the Writings of Sir Thomas More*.
        Leiden: Brill, 1982.

2470   Gordon, Walter M. "The Argument of Comedy in Thomas
        More's Dialogue Concerning Heresies." *Renaissance
        and Reformation*, 16 (1980): 13-22.

2471   ———. "The Monastic Achievement and More's Utopian
        Dream." *MH*, n.s. 9 (1979): 199-214.

2472   ———. "A Scholastic Problem in Thomas More's Contro-
        versy with John Frith." *Harvard Theological Review*,
        69 (1976): 131-49.

2473   Green, Lawrence D. "Modes of Perception in the *Mir-
        ror for Magistrates*." *The Huntington Library
        Quarterly*, 44 (1980/81): 117-33.

2474   Greenslade, S.L. "The Morean Renaissance." *Journal of
        Ecclesiastical History*, 24 (1974): 395-403.

2475   Greg, Walter W. *Pastoral Poetry and Pastoral Drama: A
        Literary Inquiry with Special Reference to the Pre-
        Restoration Stage in England*. London: Bullen, 1907;
        repr. New York: Russell and Russell, 1959.

2476   Guss, Donald L. "Wyatt's Petrarchism: An Instance of
        Creative Imitation in the Renaissance." *The Hunting-*
        ton Library Quarterly, 29 (1965/66): 1-15.

2477   Guy, John A. *The Public Career of Sir Thomas More.*
        New Haven: Yale University Press, 1980.

2478   ————. "Thomas More as a Successor to Wolsey."
        Thought, 52 (1977): 275-92.

2479   Haas, Steven W. "Simon Fish, William Tyndale, and Sir
        Thomas More's 'Lutheran Conspiracy.'" *Journal of*
        Ecclesiastical History, 23 (1972): 125-36.

2480   Haines, Roy M. "The Practice and Problems of a Fif-
        teenth-Century Bishop: The Episcopate of William
        Gray." *Mediaeval Studies,* 34 (1972): 435-61.

2481   Hale, J.R. *England and the Italian Renaissance.*
        London: Faber and Faber, 1954.

2482   Hall, Anne Drury. "Tudor Prose Style: English Human-
        ists and the Problem of a Standard." *English Lite-*
        rary Renaissance, 7 (1977): 267-96.

2483   Hampsher-Monk, Iain. "Civic Humanism and Parliamentary
        Reform: The Case of the Society of the Friends of the
        People." *Journal of British Studies,* 18.2 (1979):
        70-89.

2484   Hanham, Alison. *Richard III and His Early Historians,*
        1483-1535. Oxford: Clarendon Press, 1975.

2485   Hansot, Elisabeth. *Perfection and Progress: Two Modes*
        of Utopian Thought. Cambridge, Mass.: MIT Press,
        1924.

2486   Harbison, E. Harris. "The Intellectual as Social
        Reformer: Machiavelli and Thomas More." *Rice*
        Institute Pamphlets, 44 (1957): 1-46.

2487   Hardin, Richard F. "Humanism and History at the Inns
        of Court: John Ross of the Inner Temple." *Res Pub-*
        lica Litterarum, 1 (1978): 101-12.

2488   Harrier, Richard. "Invention in Tudor Literature: His-
        torical Perspectives." *Philosophy and Humanism*
        (item 293), pp.370-86.

2489   Haselden, R.B.   "A Scribe and Printer in the Fifteenth
        Century." *The Huntington Library Quarterly,* 2
        (1938-39): 205-11.

2490   Haugaard, William P.   "Renaissance Patristic Scholar-
        ship and Theology in Sixteenth-Century England."
        The Sixteenth Century Journal, 10 (1979): 37-60.

2491   Haupt, Garry E.   "The Personal and Impersonal in the
        Late Works of Sir Thomas More." *Interpretations:
        Studies in Language and Literature,* 6 (1974): 14-23.

2492   Hay, Denys.   "The Early Renaissance in England." *From
        Renaissance to Counter Reformation* (item 279), pp.95-
        112.

2493   ———.   "England and the Humanities in the Fifteenth
        Century." *Itinerarium Italicum* (item 298), pp.305-
        67.

2494   ———.   "The Life of Polydore Vergil of Urbino."
        JWCI, 12 (1949): 131-51.

2495   ———.   "A Note on More and the General Council."
        Moreana, 15-16 (1967): 249-52.

2496   ———.   *Polydore Vergil: Renaissance Historian and
        Man of Letters.* Oxford: Clarendon Press, 1952.

2497   Headley, John M.   "More Against Luther: On Laws and
        the Magistrate." *Moreana,* 15-16 (1967): 211-24.

2498   ———.   "The New Debate on More's Political Career."
        Thought, 52 (1977): 269-74.

2499   ———.   "Thomas More and Luther's Revolt." *ARG,* 60
        (1969): 145-60.

2500   ———.   "Thomas More and the Papacy." *Moreana,* 41
        (1974): 5-10.

2501   Heath, T.G.   "Another Look at Thomas More's *Richard.*"
        Moreana, 19-20 (1968): 11-19.

2502   Heiserman, A.R.   "Satire in the *Utopia.*" *PMLA,* 78
        (1963): 163-74.

2503   Herbrüggen, H. Schulte. "More's *Utopia* as Paradigm."
        Utopie und Anti-Utopie. Bochum-Langendreer, 1960,
        pp.16-37; repr. *Essential Articles* (item 2719), pp.
        251-62.

2504   Hexter, J.H. "Intention, Words, and Meaning: The Case
        of More's *Utopia*." *New Literary History*, 6 (1975):
        529-41.

2505   ————. *More's Utopia. The Biography of an Idea*.
        Princeton: Princeton University Press, 1952; repr.
        with epilogue, New York: Harper and Row, 1965.

2506   ————. "Thomas More: On the Margins of Modernity."
        Journal of British Studies, 1.1 (1961): 20-37.

2507   ————. "Utopia and Geneva." *Action and Conviction
        in Early Modern Europe* (item 299), pp.77-89.

2508   ————. *The Vision of Politics on the Eve of the
        Reformation: More, Machiavelli, and Seyssel*. New
        York: Basic Books, 1973.

2509   Hinton, R.W.K. "English Constitutional Theories from
        Sir John Fortescue to Sir John Eliot." *EHR*, 75
        (1960): 410-25.

2510   Hitchcock, James. "Thomas More and the *Sensus Fidel-
        ium*." *Theological Studies*, 36 (1975): 145-54.

2511   Hogrefe, Pearl. *The Sir Thomas More Circle: A Program
        of Ideas and Their Impact on Secular Drama*. Urbana:
        University of Illinois Press, 1959.

2512   Hollis, Christopher. *Thomas More*. Milwaukee: Bruce,
        1934.

2513   Holmes, George. "Cardinal Beaufort and the Crusade
        against the Hussites." *EHR*, 88 (1973): 721-50.

2514   Hoopes, Robert. *Right Reason in the English Renais-
        sance*. Cambridge, Mass.: Harvard University Press,
        1962.

2515   Hudson, Hoyt H. "John Leyland's List of Early English
        Humanists." *The Huntington Library Quarterly*, 2
        (1938/39): 301-04.

2516   ———. *The Epigram in the English Renaissance.*
        Princeton: Princeton University Press, 1947.

2517   Hyma, Albert. "The Continental Origins of English
        Humanism." *The Huntington Library Quarterly,* 4
        (1940/41): 1-25.

2518   Jardine, Lisa. "Humanism and the Sixteenth-Century
        Cambridge Arts Course." *History of Education,* 4
        (1975): 16-31.

2519   ———. "The Place of Dialectic in Sixteenth-Century
        Cambridge." *Studies in the Renaissance,* 21 (1974):
        31-62.

2520   Jayne, Sears. "Ficino and the Platonism of the
        English Renaissance." *Comparative Literature,* 4
        (1952): 214-38.

2521   ———. *John Colet and Marsilio Ficino.* London:
        Oxford University Press, 1963.

2522   Jenkins, Claude. *Sir Thomas More.* Canterbury:
        Friends of Canterbury Cathedral, 1935.

2523   Johnson, Robbin S. *More's 'Utopia': Ideal and Illu-
        sion.* New Haven: Yale University Press, 1969.

2524   Jones, Judith P. "The *Philebus* and the Philosophy of
        Pleasure in Thomas More's *Utopia.*" *Moreana,* 31-32
        (1971): 61-69.

2525   ———. "The Structure of Thomas More's *A Dialogue of
        Comfort.*" *Selected Papers: Shakespeare and Renais-
        sance Association of West Virginia,* 2 (1978): 20-29.

2526   ———. *Thomas More.* Twayne's English Authors Series,
        247. Boston: Twayne, 1979.

2527   Kaufman, Peter I. "John Colet and Erasmus' *Enchiri-
        dion.*" *Church History,* 46 (1977): 296-312.

2528   ———. "John Colet's *Opus de sacramentis* and Clerical
        Anticlericalism: The Limitations of 'Ordinary
        Wayes.'" *Journal of British Studies,* 22 (1982):
        1-22.

2529   Kautsky, Karl. *Thomas More and His Utopia,* trans. H.J.
       Stenning. London: A. & C. Black, 1927. (First German
       ed. 1888); repr. New York: Russell and Russell, 1959.

2530   Kay, W. David. "Jonson's *Urbane Gallants*: Humanistic
       Contexts for *Epicoene.*" *The Huntington Library
       Quarterly,* 34 (1975/76): 251-66.

2531   Kelley, Donald R. "The Conscience of the King's 'Good
       Servant.'" *Thought,* 52 (1977): 293-99.

2532   Kendall, Paul Murray, ed. *Richard III: The Great
       Debate, Including Sir Thomas More's History of King
       Richard III and Horace Walpole's Historic Doubts on
       the Life and Reign of Richard III.* London: The
       Folio Society, 1955.

2533   Khanna, Lee Cullen. "No Less Real Than Ideal: Images
       of Women in More's Work." *Moreana,* 55-56 (1977):
       35-51.

2534   ————. "Utopia: The Case for Open-Mindedness in the
       Commonwealth." *Moreana,* 31-32 (1971): 91-105.

2535   Kinney, Arthur F. "Rhetoric and Poetic: Humanist Fic-
       tion in the Renaissance." *ELH,* 43 (1976): 413-43.

2536   ————. *Rhetoric and Poetic in Thomas More's 'Utopia.'*
       Humana Civilitas, Vol.5. Malibu: Undena Publica-
       tions, 1979.

2537   Kinney, Daniel. "More's *Letter to Dorp*: Remapping the
       Trivium." *RQ,* 34 (1981): 179-211.

2538   Klawiter, R. "Thomas More, Erasmus and Ulrich von
       Hutten." *Moreana,* 67-68 (1980): 17-30.

2539   Knox, R., et al. *The Fame of Blessed Thomas More.*
       London: Sheed and Ward, 1929.

2540   Koebner, Richard. "The Imperial Crown of This Realm."
       BIHR, 26 (1953): 29-52.

2541   Koehl, Richard. "Pineas' *Thomas More and Tudor Polem-
       ics.*" *Philosophy and Rhetoric,* 4 (1971): 181-82.

2542   Krey, A.C. "Padua in the English Renaissance." *The
        Huntington Library Quarterly,* 10 (1946/47): 129-34.

2543   Kristeller, Paul Oskar. "Thomas More as a Renaissance
        Humanist." *Moreana,* 65-66 (1980): 5-22.

2544   Kuhn, Joaquin. "The Function of Psalm 90 in Thomas
        More's *Dialogue of Comfort.*" *Moreana,* 22 (1969):
        61-67.

2545   Law, Robert Adger. "The Text of 'Shakespeare's Plu-
        tarch.'" *The Huntington Library Quarterly,* 6
        (1942/43): 197-203.

2546   Lehmberg, Stanford E. *Sir Thomas Elyot, Tudor Human-
        ist.* Austin: University of Texas Press, 1960.

2547   ————. "Sir Thomas More's Life of Pico della Miran-
        dola." *Studies in the Renaissance,* 3 (1956): 61-74.

2548   ————. "English Humanists, the Reformation, and the
        Problem of Counsel." *ARG,* 52 (1961): 74-91.

2549   Levin, Carole. "A Good Prince: King John and Early
        Tudor Propaganda." *The Sixteenth-Century Journal,*
        11 (1980): 23-32.

2550   Levine, Joseph M. "Reginald Pecock and Lorenzo Valla
        on the 'Donation of Constantine.'" *Studies in the
        Renaissance,* 20 (1973): 118-43.

2551   Levy, F.J. *Tudor Historical Thought.* San Marino,
        Ca.: The Huntington Library, 1967.

2552   Lewis, C.S. *English Literature in the Sixteenth Cen-
        tury Excluding Drama.* The Oxford History of English
        Literature, III. Oxford: Clarendon Press, 1954.

2553   Liljegren, S.B. *Studies on the Origin and Early Tra-
        dition of English Utopian Fiction.* Uppsala: Lunde-
        quistska Bokhandeln, 1961.

2554   Lind, L.R. "'Citizen Thomas More': A Review." *Renais-
        sance News,* 2 (1949): 69-70.

2555   Logan, George M. *The Meaning of More's 'Utopia.'*
        Princeton: Princeton University Press, 1982.

2556 Lucas, Peter G. "The Growth and Development of English Literary Patronage in the Later Middle Ages and Early Renaissance." *The Library,* ser.6, 4 (1982): 209-48. With full bibliography.

2557 Luttrell, Anthony. "Giovanni Contarini, A Venetian at Oxford: 1392-1399." *JWCI,* 29 (1966): 424-32.

2558 Lynch, C.A. "On St. Thomas More, an Epitaph of Uncertain Origin." *Renaissance News,* 15 (Spring 1962): 1-2.

2559 MacDonald, William W. "Saint Thomas More and the Historian." *American Benedictine Review,* 21 (1970): 428-38.

2560 McConica, James K. *English Humanists and Reformation Politics under Henry VIII and Edward VI.* Oxford: Clarendon Press, 1965.

2561 ————. "Humanism and Aristotle in Tudor Oxford." *EHR,* 94 (1979): 291-317.

2562 McCutcheon, Elizabeth. "Denying the Contrary: More's Use of Litotes in the *Utopia.*" *Moreana,* 31-32 (1971): 107-21; repr. *Essential Articles* (item 2719), pp. 263-74.

2563 ————. "Thomas More, Raphael Hythlodaeus, and the Angel Raphael." *Studies in English Literature,* 9 (1969): 21-38.

2564 McIntosh, Marjorie K. "Sir Anthony Cooke: Tudor Humanist, Educator, and Religious Reformer." *Proceedings of the American Philosophical Society,* 119 (1975): 233-50.

2565 McKinnon, Dana G. "The Marginal Glosses in More's *Utopia*: The Character of the Commentator." *Renaissance Papers* (1970): 11-19.

2566 McLean, Antonia. *Humanism and the Rise of Science in Tudor England.* New York: Neale Watson Academic Publications, Inc., 1972.

2567 McMillin, Scott. "*The Book of Sir Thomas More*: A Theatrical View." *Modern Philology,* 68 (1970): 10-24.

2568   McNulty, Robert. "Bruno at Oxford." *Renaissance News,*
        13 (Winter 1960): 300-06.

2569   Major, John M. *Sir Thomas Elyot and Renaissance Human-*
        ism. Lincoln: University of Nebraska Press, 1964.

2570   Manuel, Frank E., and Fritzie P. Manuel. *Utopian*
        Thought in the Western World. Cambridge, Mass.:
        Harvard University Press, 1979.

2571   Marc'hadour, Germain. *The Bible in the Works of St.*
        Thomas More, 5 vols. Nieuwkoop: De Graaf, 1969-1971.

2572   ————. "Erasmus Englished by Margaret More." *The*
        Clergy Review, 43 (1958): 78-91.

2573   ————. "Hugh Latimer and Thomas More." *Moreana,* 18
        (1968): 29-48.

2574   ————. "The Latin Vulgate in the Prose of Sixteenth-
        Century Humanists." *Acta Conventus Neo-latini*
        Amstelodamensis (item 305), pp.682-89.

2575   Marius, Richard C. "The Pseudonymous Patristic Text in
        Thomas More's Confutation." *Moreana,* 15-16 (1967):
        253-66.

2576   ————. "Thomas More and the Early Church Fathers."
        Traditio, 24 (1968): 379-407; repr. *Essential*
        Articles (item 2719), pp.402-20.

2577   Marriot, J.A.R. *The Life of John Colet.* London:
        Methuen, 1933.

2578   Martin, J.W. "The Marian Regime's Failure to Under-
        stand the Importance of Printing." *The Huntington*
        Library Quarterly, 44 (1980/81): 231-47.

2579   Martz, L.L. "The Design of More's *Dialogue of Com-*
        fort." *Moreana,* 15-16 (1967): 331-46.

2580   ————. "More as Author: The Virtue of Digression."
        Moreana, 62 (1979): 105-19.

2581   ————. "Thomas More: The Sacramental Life." *Thought,*
        52 (1977): 300-18.

2582   ————, and Richard Sylvester. "Thomas More's Prayer
        Book." *Yale University Library Gazette*, 43 (1968):
        53-80.

2583   Masek, Rosemary. "The Humanistic Interests of the
        Early Tudor Episcopate." *Church History*, 39 (1970):
        5-17.

2584   Mason, Harold Andrew. *Humanism and Poetry in the Early
        Tudor Period: An Essay*. London: Routledge and Kegan
        Paul, 1959.

2585   Mattingly, Garrett. "A Humanist Ambassador." *Journal
        of Modern History*, 4 (1932): 175-85.

2586   Maynard, Theodore. *Humanist as Hero: The Life of Sir
        Thomas More*. New York: Hafner Publishing Co., 1971.

2587   Mermel, Jerry. "Preparations for a Politic Life: Sir
        Thomas More's Entry into the King's Service." *JMRS*,
        7 (1977): 53-66.

2588   Miles, Leland. "Boethius and Thomas More's *Dialogue
        of Comfort*." *English Language Notes*, 3 (1965): 97-
        101.

2589   ————. *John Colet and the Platonic Tradition*.
        La Salle, Ind.: Open Court, 1961.

2590   ————. "More's *Dialogue of Comfort* as a First
        Draft." *Studies in Philology*, 63 (1966): 126-34.

2591   ————. "Patristic Comforters in More's *Dialogue of
        Comfort*." *Moreana*, 8 (1965): 9-20.

2592   ————. "Persecution and the *Dialogue of Comfort*:
        A Fresh Look at the Charges against Thomas More."
        Journal of British Studies, 5.1 (1965): 19-30.

2593   ————. "The Platonic Source of *Utopia's* 'Minimum
        Religion.'" *Renaissance News*, 9 (Summer 1956): 83-
        90.

2594   ————. "Platonism and Christian Doctrine: The Re-
        vival of Interest in John Colet." *Philosophical
        Forum*, 21 (1963-64): 87-103.

2595   ———. "Thomas More: Disenchanted Saint." *Litera-*
        ture and Society, ed. Bernice Slote. Lincoln: Uni-
        versity of Nebraska Press, 1964, pp.65-84.

2596   ———. "With a Coal? The Composition of Thomas More's
        Dialogue of Comfort." *Philological Quarterly*, 45
        (1966): 437-42.

2597   Miller, Clarence H. "The English Translation in the
        Yale *Utopia*: Some Corrections." *Moreana*, 9 (1966):
        57-64.

2598   Mitchell, Rosamond J. "A Renaissance Library: The Col-
        lection of John Tiptoft, Earl of Worcester." *The*
        Library, ser.4, 18 (1937-1938): 67-83.

2599   ———. "English Law Students at Bologna in the Fif-
        teenth Century." *EHR*, 51 (1936): 270-87.

2600   ———. "English Students at Padua, 1460-1475."
        TRHS, ser.4, 19 (1936): 101-18.

2601   ———. "English Students in Early Renaissance Italy."
        Italian Studies, 7 (1952): 62-81.

2602   ———. *John Free, From Bristol to Rome in the Fif-*
        teenth Century. London: Longmans, Green, 1955.

2603   ———. *John Tiptoft*. London: Longmans, Green, 1938.

2604   ———. "Thomas Linacre in Italy." *EHR*, 50 (1933):
        696-98.

2605   Moore, Michael J., ed. *Quincentennial Essays on St.*
        Thomas More. Boone, N.C.: 1978. Albion 10, Sup-
        plement, 1978.

2606   Morgan, Alice B. "Philosophic Reality and Human Con-
        struction in the *Utopia*." *Moreana*, 39 (1973): 15-
        24.

2607   Morgan, Arthur E. *Nowhere Was Somewhere: How History*
        Makes Utopias and How Utopias Make History. Chapel
        Hill: University of North Carolina Press, 1946.

2608   Morison, Stanley, and Nicholas Baker. *The Likeness of*
        Thomas More. London: Burns and Oates, 1963.

2609 Morton, A.L. *The English Utopia.* London: Lawrence
      and Wishart, 1952.

2610 Mozley, J.F. *William Tyndale.* London: S.P.C.K.,
      1937.

2611 Murray, Francis A. "Feminine Spirituality in the More
      Household." *Moreana,* 27/28 (1970): 92-102.

2612 Nadeau, Ray. "Thomas Farnaby: Schoolmaster and
      Rhetorician of the English Renaissance." *Quarterly
      Journal of Speech,* 36 (1950): 340-44.

2613 Nagel, Alan F. "Lies and the Limitable Inane: Contra-
      diction in More's *Utopia.*" *RQ,* 26 (1973): 173-80.

2614 Nelson, William. "The Friendship of Thomas More and
      John Colet: An Early Document." *Modern Language
      Quarterly,* 1 (1940): 459-60.

2615 ————. "Thomas More, Grammarian and Orator." *PMLA,*
      58[1] (1943): 337-52; repr. *Essential Articles* (item
      2719), pp.150-60.

2616 ————, ed. *Twentieth-Century Interpretations of
      Utopia.* Englewood Cliffs, N.J.: Prentice-Hall, 1968.

2617 Neuman, Harry. "On the Platonism of More's *Utopia.*"
      Social Research, 33 (1966): 495-512.

2618 Newman, W.L. "The Correspondence of Humphrey, Duke of
      Gloucester, and Pier Candido Decembrio." *EHR,* 20
      (1905): 484-93.

2619 Noreña, Carlos G. "Juan Luis Vives and Henry VIII."
      Renaissance and Reformation, 12 (1976): 85-88.

2620 Norland, Howard B. "The Role of Drama in More's Lite-
      rary Career." *The Sixteenth-Century Journal,* 13
      (Winter 1982): 59-75.

2621 O'Malley, Charles D. *English Medical Humanism: Thomas
      Linacre and John Caius.* Lawrence: University of
      Kansas Press, 1964.

2622 O'Malley, John W. "Thomas More's Spirituality Com-
      pared." *Thought,* 52 (1977): 319-23.

2623   Orme, Nicholas. *English Schools in the Middle Ages*.
         London: Methuen, 1973.

2624   O'Sullivan, Richard. "John Manyngham: An Early Tudor
         Humanist." *Bodleian Library Record*, 7 (1962): 28-39.

2625   ————. "St. Thomas More and Lincoln's Inn." *The
         Catholic Lawyer*, 3 (1957): 71-80; repr. *Essential
         Articles* (item 2719), pp.161-68.

2626   Parker, T.M. "Sir Thomas More's Utopia." *Essays in
         Modern English Church History*, ed. G.V. Bennett and
         J.D. Walsh. New York: Oxford University Press, 1966,
         pp.1-17.

2627   Parks, George B. "The Decline and Fall of the English
         Renaissance Admiration of Italy." *The Huntington
         Library Quarterly*, 31 (1967/68): 341-57.

2628   ————. *The English Traveler to Italy: The Middle
         Ages (to 1527)*. Stanford: Stanford University
         Press, 1954.

2629   ————. "Pico della Mirandola in Tudor Translation."
         Philosophy and Humanism (item 293), pp.352-69.

2630   Parmiter, Geoffrey de C. "St. Thomas More and the
         Oath." *Downside Review*, 78 (1965): 1-13.

2631   Partee, Morriss Henry. "Sir Thomas Elyot on Plato's
         Aesthetics." *Viator*, 1 (1970): 327-35.

2632   Paul, Leslie. *Sir Thomas More*. London: Faber and
         Faber, 1954.

2633   Peggram, Reed Edwin. "The First French and English
         Translations of Sir Thomas More's 'Utopia.'"
         Modern Language Review, 35 (1940): 330-40.

2634   Peters, Robert. "John Colet's Knowledge and Use of
         Patristics." *Moreana*, 22 (1969): 45-59.

2635   ————. "Utopia and More's Orthodoxy." *Moreana*, 31-
         32 (1971): 147-55.

2636   Pineas, Rainer. "George Joye's Controversy with
         Thomas More." *Moreana*, 38 (1973): 27-36.

2637   ————. "More versus Tyndale: A Study of Controversial
        Technique." *Modern Language Quarterly,* 24 (1963):
        144-50.

2638   ————. "Polemical *Exemplum* in Sixteenth-Century Reli-
        gious Controversy." *BHR,* 28 (1966): 393-96.

2639   ————. "Sir Thomas More's Controversy with Christopher
        Saint-German." *Studies in English Literature,* 1
        (1961): 49-62.

2640   ————. *Thomas More and Tudor Polemics.* Bloomington:
        Indiana University Press, 1968.

2641   ————. "Thomas More's Controversy with Simon Fish."
        Studies in English Literature, 7 (1967): 15-28.

2642   ————. "Thomas More's Use of Humor as a Weapon of
        Religious Controversy." *Studies in Philology,* 58
        (1961): 97-114.

2643   ————. "Thomas More's *Utopia* and Protestant Polemics."
        Renaissance News, 17 (1964): 197-201.

2644   Pollard, A.F. "The Making of Sir Thomas More's *Richard
        III.*" *Historical Essays in Honour of James Tait,* ed.
        J.G. Edwards, V.H. Galbraith, and E.F. Jacob. Man-
        chester: Printed for the Subscribers, 1933, pp.223-38.

2645   Porter, H.C. "The Gloomy Dean and the Law: John
        Colet, 1466-1519." *Essays in Modern English Church
        History,* ed. G.V. Bennett and J.B. Walsh. New York:
        Oxford University Press, 1966, pp.18-43.

2646   ————. *Reformation and Reaction in Tudor Cambridge.*
        Cambridge: Cambridge University Press, 1958.

2647   Potter, G.R. *Sir Thomas More (1478-1535).* London:
        L. Parsons, 1925.

2648   Prescott, Anne Lake. "English Writers and Beza's Latin
        Epigrams: The Uses and Abuses of Poetry." *Studies
        in the Renaissance,* 21 (1974): 83-117.

2649   ————. "Renaissance References to Thomas More."
        Moreana, 70 (1981): 5-24.

2650   Quattrocki, E. "Injustice, Not Conciliarship: The
        Theme of Book One of *Utopia*." *Moreana*, 31-32
        (1971): 19-28.

2651   Radford, Lewis Bostock. *Henry Beaufort, Bishop, Chan-
        cellor, Cardinal*. London: Sir Isaac Pitman and
        Sons, Ltd., 1908.

2652   Raitiere, Martin N. "More's *Utopia* and *The City of
        God*." *Studies in the Renaissance*, 20 (1973): 144-
        68.

2653   Ramsay, G.D. "A Saint in the City: Thomas More at
        Mercers' Hall, London." *EHR*, 97 (1982): 269-88.

2654   Reiss, Timothy. "*Utopia* and Process: Text and Anti-
        Text." *Substance*, 8 (1974): 101-25.

2655   Reiter, Robert E. "On the Genre of Thomas More's
        Richard III." *Moreana*, 25 (1970): 5-16.

2656   Reynolds, E.E. *The Field Is Won: The Life and Death
        of St. Thomas More*. London: Burns and Oates, 1968.

2657   ————. *Margaret Roper*. New York: P.J. Kenedy, 1960.

2658   ————. *Saint Thomas More*. London: Burns and Oates,
        1953.

2659   ————. *The Trial of St. Thomas More*. New York: P.J.
        Kenedy, 1964.

2660   ————. "An Unnoticed Document." *Moreana*, 1 (1963):
        12-17. On More's trial.

2661   Rhodes, Dennis E. "Battista Guarini and a Book at
        Oxford." *JWCI*, 37 (1974): 349-53.

2662   Rice, Eugene F., Jr. "John Colet and the Annihilation
        of the Natural." *Harvard Theological Review*, 45
        (1952): 141-62.

2663   Richardson, David. "Humanistic Intent in Surrey's
        Aeneid." *English Literary Renaissance*, 6 (1976):
        204-19.

2664   Richardson, H.G. "An Oxford Teacher of the Fifteenth
        Century." *BJRL*, 23 (1939): 436-57.

2665   Ridley, Jasper. *Statesman and Saint, Cardinal Wolsey, Sir Thomas More and the Politics of Henry VIII*. New York: Viking, 1982.

2666   Routh, Enid M. *Sir Thomas More and His Friends, 1477-1535*. London: Oxford University Press, 1934.

2667   Rudat, Wolfgang E.H. "More's Raphael Hythloday: Missing the Point in *Utopia* Once More?" *Moreana*, 69 (1981): 41-64.

2668   ————. "Thomas More and Hythloday: Some Speculations on *Utopia*." *BHR*, 43 (1981): 123-27.

2669   Ryan, Lawrence. "Walter Haddon: Elizabethan Latinist." *The Huntington Library Quarterly*, 17 (1953/54): 99-124.

2670   Scarisbrick, John J. "Thomas More: The King's Good Servant." *Thought*, 52 (1977): 249-68.

2671   Schaeffer, John D. "Socratic Method in More's *Utopia*." *Moreana*, 69 (1981): 5-20.

2672   Schenck, Wilhelm. *Reginald Pole: Cardinal of England*. London: Longmans, Green, 1950.

2673   Schmidt, Albert J. "Thomas Wilson and the Tudor Commonweal: An Essay in Civic Humanism. *The Huntington Library Quarterly*, 23 (1959/60): 49-60.

2674   ————. "Thomas Wilson, Tudor Scholar-Statesman." *The Huntington Library Quarterly*, 20 (1956/57): 205-18.

2675   Schmitt, Charles B. "John Case and Machiavelli." *Essays Presented to Myron P. Gilmore* (item 275), pp.231-40.

2676   Schoeck, Richard J. *The Achievement of Thomas More: Aspects of His Life and Works*. Victoria, B.C.: English Literary Studies, University of Victoria, 1976.

2677   ————. "More, Plutarch, and King Agis: Spartan History and the Meaning of *Utopia*." *Philological Quarterly*, 35 (1956): 366-75; repr. *Essential Articles* (item 2719), pp.275-80.

2678   ———. "Neo-latin Legal Literature." *Acta Conventus
        Neo-latini Lovaniensis* (item 288), pp.577-88.

2679   ———. "A Nursery of Correct and Useful Institutions:
        On Reading More's *Utopia* as a Dialogue." *Moreana,*
        22 (1969): 19-32; repr. *Essential Articles* (item
        2719), pp.281-89.

2680   ———. "On the Spiritual Life of St. Thomas More."
        Thought, 52 (1977): 324-27.

2681   ———. "Sir Thomas More and Lincoln's Inn Revels."
        Philological Quarterly, 29 (1950): 426-30.

2682   ———. "Sir Thomas More, Humanist and Lawyer." *Uni-
        versity of Toronto Quarterly,* 34 (1964): 1-14; repr.
        Essential Articles (item 2719), pp.569-79.

2683   ———. "Thomas More's 'Dialogue of Comfort' and the
        Problem of the Real Grand Turk." *English Miscellany,*
        20 (1969): 23-37.

2684   Schuster, Sister Mary Faith, O.S.B. "Philosophy of Life
        and Prose Style in Thomas More's *Richard III* and
        Francis Bacon's *Henry VIII*." *PMLA,* 70 (1955): 474-87.

2685   Scott-Craig, T.S.K. "Thomas More's 1518 Letter to the
        University of Oxford." *Renaissance News,* 1 (1948):
        17-24.

2686   Seeber, Hans Ulrich. "Hythloday as Preacher and a Pos-
        sible Debt to Macrobius." *Moreana,* 31-32 (1971):
        71-86.

2687   Seebohm, Frederick. *The Oxford Reformers: Colet, Eras-
        mus, and More,* ed. Hugh E. Seebohm. London: 1867;
        repr. New York: Dutton, 1914.

2688   Sheldrake, Philip. "Authority and Consensus in Thomas
        More's Doctrine of the Church." *The Heythrop Journal,*
        20 (1979): 146-72.

2689   Simon, Elliot P. "Thomas More's *Utopia*: Creating an
        Image of the Soul." *Moreana,* 69 (1981): 21-40.

2690   Simon, Joan. "The Reformation and English Education."
        Past and Present, 11 (April 1957): 48-65.

2691   Skinner, Q. "History and Ideology in the English Ref-
        ormation." *The Historical Journal,* 8 (1965): 151-78.

2692   ————. "More's *Utopia.*" *Past and Present,* 38 (Dec.
        1967): 153-68.

2693   Slavin, Arthur J. "Profitable Studies: Humanists and
        Government in Early Tudor England." *Viator,* 1 (1970):
        307-25.

2694   Smith, John Hazel. "John Foxe on Astrology." *English
        Literary Renaissance,* 1 (1971): 210-25.

2695   Smith, Margery H. "Some Humanist Libraries in Early
        Tudor Cambridge." *The Sixteenth-Century Journal,* 5
        (1974): 15-34.

2696   Sowards, J.K. "Some Factors in the Re-Evaluation of
        Thomas More's *Utopia.*" *Northwest Missouri State
        College Studies,* 16 (1952): 31-58.

2697   ————. "Thomas More, Erasmus, and Julius II: A Case
        of Advocacy." *Moreana,* 21-24 (1969): 81-99.

2698   Stevens, Irma Ned. "Aesthetic Distance in the *Utopia.*"
        Moreana, 43-44 (1974): 13-24.

2699   Stout, Harry S. "Marsilius of Padua and the Henrician
        Reformation." *Church History,* 43 (1974): 308-18.

2700   Surtz, Edward L., S.J. "Interpretations of Utopia."
        Catholic Historical Review, 38 (1952): 156-74.

2701   ————. "John Fisher and the Scholastics." *Studies in
        Philology,* 55 (1958): 136-53.

2702   ————. "Logic in Utopia." *Philological Quarterly,*
        29 (1950): 389-401.

2703   ————. "More's *Apologia Pro Utopia Sua.*" *Modern
        Language Quarterly,* 19 (1958): 319-24.

2704   ————. "More's Friendship with Fisher." *Moreana,*
        15-16 (1967): 115-33; repr. *Essential Articles* (item
        2719), pp.169-79.

2705   ————. "Oxford Reformers and Scholasticism."
        Studies in Philology, 47 (1950): 547-56.

2706   ———. *The Praise of Pleasure: Philosophy, Education,*
        and Communism in More's Utopia. Cambridge, Mass.:
        Harvard University Press, 1957.

2707   ———. *The Praise of Wisdom: A Commentary on the Re-*
        ligious and Moral Problems and Backgrounds of St.
        Thomas More's "Utopia." Chicago: Loyola University
        Press, 1957.

2708   ———. "Richard Pace's Sketch of Thomas More."
        Journal of English and Germanic Philology, 57 (1958):
        36-50; repr. *Essential Articles* (item 2719), pp.180-88.

2709   ———. "St. Thomas More and His Utopian Embassy of
        1515." *Catholic Historical Review,* 39 (1953): 272-97.

2710   ———. "The Setting for More's Plea for Greek in the
        Utopia." Philological Quarterly, 35 (1956): 353-65.

2711   ———. "Sources, Parallels and Influences: Supplemen-
        tary to the Yale *Utopia." Moreana,* 9 (1966): 5-12.

2712   ———. "Thomas More and Great Books." *Philological*
        Quarterly, 32 (1953): 43-57.

2713   Sylvester, Richard S. "The 'Man for all Seasons' Again:
        Robert Whittington's Verses to Sir Thomas More." *The*
        Huntington Library Quarterly, 26 (1962/63): 147-54.

2714   ———. "A Part of His Own: Thomas More's Literary
        Personality in His Early Works." *Moreana,* 15-16
        (1967): 29-42.

2715   ———. "Si Hythlodaeo Credimus: Vision and Revision in
        Thomas More's *Utopia." Soundings,* 51 (1968): 271-89;
        repr. *Essential Articles* (item 2719), pp.290-301.

2716   ———. "Thomas More: Humanist in Action." *Medieval*
        and Renaissance Studies, 1 (1966): 125-37; repr.
        Essential Articles (item 2719), pp.462-69.

2717   ———. "Three Dialogues." *Moreana,* 64 (1980): 65-78.
        On More's *Utopia, Dialogue Concerning Heresies,* and
        Dialogue of Comfort.

2718   ———, ed. *St. Thomas More: Action and Contemplation.*
        Proceedings of the Symposium Held at St. John's Uni-
        versity, October 9-10, 1970. New Haven and London:
        Yale University Press, 1972.

2719   ———, and G.P. Marc'hadour, eds. *Essential Articles for the Study of Sir Thomas More*. Hamden, Ct.: Archon Books, 1977. Contains items 2382, 2424, 2438, 2503, 2562, 2576, 2615, 2625, 2677, 2679, 2682, 2704, 2708, 2715, 2716, 2761, 2762.

2720   Thomas, Patricia. "The First English Petrarchans." *The Huntington Library Quarterly*, 22 (1958/59): 85-105.

2721   ———. "Sir Thomas Wyatt: Classical Philosophy and English Humanism." *The Huntington Library Quarterly*, 25 (1961-62): 79-96.

2722   Thompson, Craig R. "The Humanism of More Reappraised." *Thought*, 52 (1977): 229-48.

2723   Thompson, J.A.K. "Erasmus in England." *Vorträge der Bibliothek Warburg*, 9 (1930-31): 64-82.

2724   Thomson, D.F.S. "The Latin Epigram in Scotland: The Sixteenth Century." *Phoenix*, 11 (1957): 63-78.

2725   Thomson, S. Harrison. *Latin Handbooks of the Later Middle Ages, 1100-1500*. New York: Cambridge University Press, 1969.

2726   Tilley, Arthur. "Greek Studies in England in the Early Sixteenth Century." *EHR*, 53 (1938): 221-39, 438-56.

2727   Todd, Margo. "Humanists, Puritans and the Spiritualized Household." *Church History*, 49 (1980): 18-34.

2728   Trapp, J.B. "Dame Christian Colet and Thomas More." *Moreana*, 15-16 (1967): 103-13.

2729   ———. "John Colet and the *Hierarchies* of the Pseudo-Dionysus." *Religion and Humanism* (item 293), pp. 127-48.

2730   Traugott, John. "A Voyage to Nowhere with Thomas More and Jonathan Swift: *Utopia* and *The Voyage of the Houyhnhnms*. *Sewanee Review*, 69 (1961): 534-65.

2731   Tromly, Frederic B. "'A Rueful Lamentation' of Elizabeth: Thomas More's Transformation of Didactic Lament." *Moreana*, 53 (1977): 45-56.

2732   Tucker, E.F.J.   "Ruggle's *Ignoramus* and Humanistic
        Criticism of the Language of the Common Law."   *RQ,*
        30 (1977): 341-50.

2733   Ulback, Edward.   "Erasmus and His Writings."   *Biblio-
        theca Sacra,* 94 (1937): 175-96.

2734   Ullman, B.L.   "Manuscripts of Duke Humphrey of Glou-
        cester."   *EHR,* 52 (1937): 670-72.

2735   Valeri Bayne, Diane.   "Richard Hyrde and the More
        Circle."   *Moreana,* 45 (1975): 5-16.

2736   Vickers, K.H.   *Humphrey, Duke of Gloucester.*   London:
        Constable, 1907.

2737   Vocht, Henry de.   *Acta Thomae Mori: History of the
        Reports of His Trial and Death with an Unedited Con-
        temporary Narrative.*   Louvain: Louvain University
        Press, 1947.

2738   Vos, Alvin.   "The Humanism of Toxophilus: A New Source."
        English Literary Renaissance, 6 (1976): 187-203.

2739   Wallace, Karl R.   "Rhetorical Exercises in Tudor Edu-
        cation."   *Quarterly Journal of Speech,* 22 (1936):
        28-51.

2740   Weinberg, Carole.   "Thomas More and the Use of English
        in Early Tudor Education."   *Moreana,* 59-60 (1978):
        21-30.

2741   Weiner, Andrew D.   "Raphael's Eutopia and More's
        Utopia: Christian Humanism and the Limits of Reason."
        The Huntington Library Quarterly, 34 (1975/76): 1-27.

2742   Weiss, Roberto.   *Humanism in England during the Fif-
        teenth Century.*   3rd ed.   Oxford: Blackwell, 1967.

2743   ————.   "Humphrey Duke of Gloucester and Tito Livio
        Frulovisi."   *Fritz Saxl, 1890-1948* (item 283), pp.
        218-27.

2744   ————.   "John Tiptoft, Earl of Worcester, and Ludovico
        Carbone."   *Rinascimento,* 8.2 (1957): 209-12.

2745   ————.   "Leonardo Bruni Aretino and Early English Hu-
        manism."   *Modern Language Review,* 36 (1941): 443-48.

2746   ————. "New Light on Humanism in England during the
        Fifteenth Century." *JWCI*, 14 (1951): 21-33.

2747   ————. "Notes on Thomas Linacre." *Miscellanea
        Giovanni Mercati* (item 295), pp.373-80.

2748   ————. "The Earliest Catalogues of the Library of
        Lincoln College." *Bodleian Quarterly Record*, 8
        (1935-38): 343-59. On William Gray.

2749   ————. "The Study of Greek in England during the
        Fourteenth Century." *Rinascimento*, 2.3-4 (1950-
        1951): 209-40.

2750.   White, Thomas. "Aristotle and *Utopia*." *RQ*,
        (1976): 635-76.

2751   ————. "*Festivitas, Utilitas, et Opes*: The Conclud-
        ing Irony and Philosophical Purpose of Thomas More's
        Utopia." *Albion*, 10 (Supplement, 1978): 135-50.

2752   Whitney, Edward Allen. "Erasmianism and Divine Right."
        The Huntington Library Quarterly, 2 (1938-39): 373-
        98.

2753   ————, and P.P. Cram. "Polydore Vergil's Will."
        TRHS, ser.4, 11 (1928): 117-36.

2754   Wilson, Dere K. *England in the Age of Thomas More*.
        Atlantic Highlands, N.J.: Humanities Press, 1980.

2755   Wilson, K.J. "More and Holbein: The Imagination of
        Death." *The Sixteenth-Century Journal*, 7 (1976):
        51-58.

2756   Wooden, Warren W. "Anti-Scholastic Satire in Sir
        Thomas More's *Utopia*." *The Sixteenth-Century
        Journal*, 8 (1977): 29-46.

2757   ————. "Satiric Strategy in More's *Utopia*: The Case
        of Raphael Hythloday." *Renaissance Papers*,
        (1977): 1-9.

2758   ————. "Thomas More and Lucian: A Study of Satiric
        Influence and Technique." *University of Mississippi
        Studies in English*, 13 (1972): 43-57.

2759   ————. "Utopia and Arcadia: An Approach to More's
        Utopia." *College Literature*, 6 (1979-1980): 30-40.

2760   Wortham, James. "Sir Thomas Elyot and the Translation
        of Prose." *The Huntington Library Quarterly*, 11
        (1947/48): 219-40.

2761   Zavala, Silvio. "Sir Thomas More in New Spain." *The
        Huntington Library Quarterly*, 10 (1947): 337-47;
        repr. *Essential Articles* (item 2719), pp.302-11.

2762   Zeeveld, William Gordon. "Apology for an Execution."
        Moreana, 15-16 (1967): 353-71; repr. *Essential
        Articles* (item 2719), pp.198-211.

2763   ————. *Foundations of Tudor Policy*. Cambridge, Mass.:
        Harvard University Press, 1948.

See also items 380, 417, 471, 501, 540-42, 545, 571, 587, 624,
        657, 674, 762, 1190, 1286, 2019, 2026-28, 2034, 2037,
        2049-50, 2065, 2069-70, 2081, 2091, 2107-8, 2161, 2179,
        2209, 2213, 2243-44, 2288-89, 2847, 2912.

XVII. HUMANISM IN FRANCE AND IBERIA

Works available in English by French and Iberian humanists
and studies on humanism in the two areas are, of course, far
less plentiful than those for England or the age of Erasmus.
In fact the works of only two figures, the French philosopher
and statesman, Jean Bodin (1530-1596) and the Spanish Erasmian Juan Luis Vives (1492-1540), have been much translated
into English. For French humanism in general see the surveys
of I.D. McFarlane and Franco Simone and the collection of
essays edited by W.L. Gundersheimer. For Spain see the studies of O.H. Green and E.F. Hirsch. Individual thinkers are
rather better served: consult the works of M.A. Screech and
L. Febvre on Rabelais, D.M. Frame on Montaigne, E.F. Rice on
Lefèvre d'Etaple, A.T. Grafton on Joseph Scaliger, and D.R.
Kelley on legal humanism.

A. WORKS BY FRENCH AND IBERIAN HUMANISTS

2764   Bodin, Jean. *Colloquium of the Seven about Secrets of the Sublime*, trans. with introd. by Marion Leathers Daniels Kuntz. Princeton: Princeton University Press, 1975.

2765   ———. *Method for the Easy Comprehension of History*, trans. Beatrice Reynolds. New York: Columbia University Press, 1945.

2766   ———. *Six Books of a Commonweal*, trans. Richard Knolles. London: Bishop, 1606; repr. ed. Kenneth Douglas McRae. Cambridge, Mass.: Harvard University Press; London: Oxford University Press, 1962.

2767   ———. *Six Books of a Commonweal*, trans. (abridged) M.J. Tooley. Oxford: Blackwell; New York: Macmillan, 1955.

2768   Calvin, Jean. *Calvin's Commentary on Seneca's "De Clementia,"* ed. and trans. Ford Lewis Battles and A.M. Hugo. Leiden: Brill, 1964.

2769   Goes, Damianus. *The Faith, Religion, and Manners of the Aethiopians*, trans. Edward Aston, in Jeannes Boemus, *The Manners, Lawes, and Customs of All Nations*. London: G. Eld, 1611.

2770   ———. *The Legacye or Embassate of Prester John vnto Emanuell, Kynge of Portyngale*, trans. John More. London: W. Rastell, 1533.

2771   Guevara, Antonio de. *The Dial of Princes*, trans. Thomas North. London: J. Waylande, 1557; repr. Amsterdam: Da Capo, 1968.

2772   Osorio, Hieronymus. *A Discourse of Civil and Christian Nobility*, trans. William Blandie. London: T. Marsh, 1576.

2773   ———. *The History of the Portuguese during the Reign
        of Emmanuel*, trans. James Gibbs. 2 vols. London:
        A. Millar, 1752.

2774   Scaliger, Joseph. *Autobiography*, ed. and trans. G.W.
        Henderson. Cambridge, Mass.: Harvard University
        Press, 1927.

2775   Secundus, Johannes. *Basia .... or the Kisses*, trans.
        Thomas Stanley. London: 1647; repr. London: Nonesuch
        Press, 1923.

2776   ———. *The Love Poems (Basia, Amores, Odae)*, trans.
        and ed. F.A. Wright. London: Routledge; New York:
        Dutton, 1930.

2777   Vives, Juan Luis. *Commentary on St. Augustine, The
        City of God*, trans. John Healey, *The Citie of God,
        with the Learned Commentary of Ioannis Lodovici
        Vives. London: G. Eld, 1610; repr. London: G. Eld,
        1620.*

2778   ———. *"A Fable about Man,"* trans. Nancy Lenkeith,
        The Renaissance Philosophy of Man (item 311), pp.387-
        93.

2779   ———. *The Instruction of a Christian Woman*, trans.
        Richard Hyrde. London: T. Berthelet, 1540. Extracts
        repr. in Foster Watson, *Vives and the Renascence Edu-
        cation of Women*. London: Arnold, 1912.

2780   ———. *Juan Luis Vives against the Pseudodialecti-
        cians: A Humanist Attack on Medieval Logic*, trans.
        and introd. by Rita Guerlac. Boston: D. Reidel,
        1979.

2781   ———. *Juan Luis Vives. In Pseudodialecticos. A
        Critical Edition*, trans. and introd. by Charles
        Fantazzi. Leiden: Brill, 1979.

2782   ———. *The Office and Duetie of an Husband*, trans.
        Thomas Paynell. London: J. Cawood, 1555.

2783   ———. *Tudor Schoolboy Life: The Dialogues (Linguae
        latinae exercitatio)*, trans. Foster Watson. London:
        Dent, 1908.

2784   ————. *Vives on Education (De tradendis disciplinis)*,
          trans. Foster Watson. Cambridge: Cambridge Univer-
          sity Press, 1913.

2785   ————. *Vives' Introduction to Wisdom: A Renaissance
          Textbook*, ed. Marian Leona Tobriner. New York:
          Teachers' College Press, 1968.

                          B. FRENCH HUMANISM

2786   Bakhtim, Mikhail. *Rabelais and His World*, trans.
          Helene Iswolsky. Cambridge, Mass.: M.I.T. Press,
          1968.

2787   Battenhouse, Roy W. "The Doctrine of Man in Calvin
          and in Renaissance Platonism." *JHI*, 10 (1949):
          447-71.

2788   Baxandall, Michael, and E.H. Gombrich. "Beroaldus on
          Francia." *JWCI*, 25 (1962): 113-15.

2789   Bouwsma, William J. *Concordia Mundi: The Career and
          Thought of Guillaume Postel (1510-1581)*. Cambridge,
          Mass.: Harvard University Press, 1957.

2790   ————. "Postel and the Significance of Renaissance
          Cabalism." *JHI*, 15 (1954): 218-32; repr. *Renais-
          sance Essays* (item 290), pp.252-66.

2791   Bowen, Barbara C. *The Age of Bluff, Paradox and Am-
          biguity in Rabelais and Montaigne*. Urbana: Univer-
          sity of Illinois Press, 1972.

2792   Brault, Gerard J. "Exploration and Discovery in
          French Literature from the Middle Ages to Rabelais."
          French Review, 53 (1979-80): 550-56.

2793   Breen, Quirinus. *John Calvin, A Study in French Human-
          ism*. Chicago: University of Chicago Press, 1931.

2794   Clements, Robert J. *Critical Theory and Practice of
          the Pleiade*. Cambridge, Mass.: Harvard University
          Press, 1942; repr. New York: Octagon, 1970.

2795   ————. "Ronsard and Ficino on the Four Furies." *The Romanic Review*, 45 (1954): 161-69.

2796   Connolly, James L. *Jean Gerson: Reformer and Mystic*. Louvain: Librarie Universitaire Uystpruyst, 1928.

2797   Cooper, Richard. "Rabelais and the *Topographia Antiquae Romae* of Marliani." *Etudes rabelaisiennes*, 14 (1978): 71-88.

2798   Copenhaver, Brian P. "Lefèvre d'Etaples, Symphorien Champier and the Secret Names of God." *JWCI*, 40 (1977): 189-211.

2799   ————. *Symphorien Champier and the Reception of the Occultist Tradition in Renaissance France*. The Hague and New York: Mouton, 1979.

2800   Denieul-Cormier, Anne. *A Time of Glory, The Renaissance in France, 1488-1559*, trans. Anne and Christopher Fremantle. Garden City, N.Y.: Doubleday, 1968.

2801   Davis, Natalie Zeman. "Poor Relief, Humanism, and Heresy: The Case of Lyon." *SMRH*, 5 (1968): 175-215.

2802   Derret, J.D.M. "Rabelaisian Kyrielles and Their Source." *Etudes rabelaisiennes*, 7 (1967): 83-89.

2803   Dickinson, Gladys. *Du Bellay in Rome*. Leiden: Brill, 1960.

2804   Dresden, Sem. "The Profile of the Reception of the Italian Renaissance in France." *Itinerarium Italicum* (item 298), pp.119-89.

2805   Febvre, Lucien P.V. *The Problem of Unbelief in the Sixteenth Century: The Religion of Rabelais*, trans. B. Gottlieb. Cambridge, Mass.: Harvard University Press, 1982.

2806   Frame, Donald M. *François Rabelais: A Study*. New York: Harcourt Brace Jovanovich, 1977.

2807   ————. *Montaigne's Discovery of Man: The Humanization of a Humanist*. New York: Columbia University Press, 1955.

2808   ———. "What Next in Montaigne Studies?" *French Review*, 36 (1962-63): 577-87.

2809   Franklin, Julian H. *Jean Bodin and the Sixteenth-Century Revolution in the Methodology of Law and History*. New York: Columbia University Press, 1963.

2810   Grafton, A. *Joseph Scaliger: A Study in the History of Classical Scholarship, Vol.1, Textual Criticism and Exegesis*. Oxford: Clarendon Press, 1983.

2811   Guerlac, Rita. "Vives and the Education of Gargantua." *Etudes rabelaisiennes*, 11 (1974): 63-72.

2812   Gundersheimer, W.L. "The Crisis of the Late French Renaissance." *Renaissance Studies in Honor of Hans Baron* (item 296), pp.791-808.

2813   ———, ed. *French Humanism, 1470-1600*. New York: Harper and Row, 1969.

2814   Hall, Basil. "From Biblical Humanism to Calvinist Orthodoxy." *Journal of Ecclesiastical History*, 31 (1980): 331-43.

2815   Harrie, Jeanne. "Duplessis-Mornay, Foix-Candale, and the Hermetic Religion of the World." *RQ*, 31 (1978): 499-514.

2816   Hartely, D.J. "A Little-known Latin Poem by Joachim Du Bellay." *BHR*, 41 (1979): 341-48.

2817   Hatzfeld, Helmut. "Christian, Pagan, and Devout Humanism in Sixteenth-Century France." *Modern Language Quarterly*, 12 (1951): 337-52.

2818   Hilgarth, J.N. *Ramon Lull and Lullism in Fourteenth-Century France*. Oxford: Clarendon Press, 1971.

2819   Hine, W.L. "Mersenne and Vanini." *RQ*, 29 (1976): 52-65.

2820   Hornik, Henry. "Three Interpretations of the French Renaissance." *Studies in the Renaissance*, 7 (1960): 43-66.

2821   Hufstader, Anselm. "Lefèvre d'Etaples and the Magdalen." *Studies in the Renaissance*, 16 (1969): 31-60.

2822   Huppert, George. "The Idea of Civilization in the
        Sixteenth Century." *Renaissance Studies in Honor of
        Hans Baron* (item 296), pp.757-70.

2823   ————. *The Idea of Perfect History: Historical Eru-
        dition and Historical Philosophy in Renaissance
        France.* Urbana: University of Illinois Press, 1970.

2824   Kalwies, H.H. "The First Verse Translation of *The
        Iliad* in Renaissance France." *BHR*, 40 (1978): 597-
        607.

2825   Keller, Abraham C. "Rabelais and the Renaissance Idea
        of Progress." *Renaissance News*, 2 (1949): 21-23.

2826   Kelley, Donald R. *The Beginning of Ideology, Conscious-
        ness and Society in the French Reformation.* New
        York: Cambridge University Press, 1981.

2827   ————. *Foundations of Modern Historical Scholarship.
        Language, Law and History in the French Renaissance.*
        New York: Columbia University Press, 1970.

2828   ————. "History as a Calling: The Case of La Popel-
        inière." *Renaissance Studies in Honor of Hans Baron*
        (item 296), pp.771-90.

2829   ————. "Louis Le Caron Philosophe." *Philosophy and
        Humanism* (item 293), pp.30-49.

2830   Kinser, Samuel. "Ideas of Temporal Change and Cul-
        tural Process in France, 1470-1535." *Renaissance
        Studies in Honor of Hans Baron* (item 296), pp.703-56.

2831   Kline, Michael B. *Rabelais and the Age of Printing.*
        Etudes rabelaisiennes, 4. Geneva: Droz, 1963.

2832   Krailsheimer, A.J. *Rabelais and the Franciscans.*
        Oxford: Clarendon Press, 1963.

2833   Kristeller, Paul Oskar. "Between the Italian Renais-
        sance and the French Enlightenment: Gabriel Naude
        as an Editor." *RQ*, 32 (1979): 41-72.

2834   ————. "The Myth of Renaissance Atheism and the
        French Tradition of Free Thought." *Journal of the
        History of Philosophy*, 6 (1968): 233-44.

2835 ————. "An Unknown Humanist Sermon on St. Stephen by
G. Fichet." *Mélanges E. Tisserant*. Vatican City:
Vol.6, pp.459-97.

2836 Kuntz, Marion Daniels. "Harmony and the *Heptaplomeres*
of Jean Bodin." *Journal of the History of Philosophy*, 12 (1974): 31-42.

2837 ————. "A New Link in the Correspondence of Guillaume
Postel." *BHR*, 41 (1979): 575-81.

2838 ————. "Paradoxes of the Colloquium Heptaplomeres
and Jean Bodin." *Acta Conventus Neo-latini Amstelodamensis* (item 305), pp.277-84.

2839 Lebeque, Raymond. "Rabelais, the Last of the Erasmians."
JWCI, 12 (1949): 91-100.

2840 Levi, A.H.T., ed. *Humanism in France at the End of the
Middle Ages and in the Early Renaissance*. Manchester:
Manchester University Press, 1970.

2841 Limbrick, Elaine. "Montaigne and Socrates." *Renaissance and Reformation*, 9 (1973): 46-57.

2842 Lindbreck, George. "Nominalism and the Problem of
Meaning as Illustrated by Pierre D'Ailly on Pre-
destination and Justification." *Harvard Theological
Review*, 52 (1959): 43-60.

2843 Linder, Robert D. "Calvinism and Humanism: The First
Generation." *Church History*, 44 (1975): 167-81.

2844 ————. "Pierre Viret's Ideas and Attitudes Concerning Humanism and Education." *Church History*, 34
(1965): 25-35.

2845 Logan, Marie-Rose. "Bovillus on Language." *Acta Conventus Neo-latini Amstelodamensis* (item 305), pp.
657-66.

2846 McFarlane, Ian D. "Jean Salmon Macrin (1490-1557)."
BHR, 21 (1959): 55-84, 311-49; 22 (1960): 73-89.

2847 ————. "George Buchanan in France." *Studies in
French Literature Presented to H.W. Lawton*, ed. J.C.
Ireson, I.D. McFarlane, and Garnett Rees. Manchester:

Manchester University Press; New York: Barnes and
Noble, 1968, pp.223-45.

2848   ————. *A Literary History of France, Renaissance
France 1470-1589.* London: Ernest Benn, 1974.

2849   ————. "Pierre de Ronsard and the Neo-Latin Poetry
of His Time." *Res Publica Litterarum*, 1 (1978):
117-205.

2850   McNeil, David O. *Guillaume Budé and Humanism in the
Reign of Francis I.* Geneva: Droz, 1975.

2851   Mandrou, Robert. *Introduction to Modern France 1500-
1640. An Essay in Historical Psychology*, trans.
R.E. Hallmark. New York: Holmes & Meier, 1976.

2852   Mann, Nicholas. "Petrarch's Role as a Moralist in
Fifteenth-Century France." *Humanism in France at
the End of the Middle Ages and in the Early Renaissance*, ed. A.T. Levi. Manchester: Manchester University Press, 1970, pp.26-29.

2853   Masters, G. Mallary. "Rabelais and Renaissance Figure
Poems." *Etudes rabelaisiennes*, 8 (1969): 51-68.

2854   Norton, Glyn P. *Montaigne and the Introspective Mind.*
The Hague and Paris: Mouton, 1975.

2855   Nugent, Donald. *Ecumenism in the Age of Reformation:
The Colloquy of Poissy.* Cambridge, Mass.: Harvard
University Press, 1974.

2856   Pegues, Frank. "Aubert de Guignicourt--Fourteenth-
Century Patron of Learning." *MH*, 9 (1955): 71-75.

2857   ————. "The Fourteenth-Century College of Aubert de
Guignicourt at Soissons." *Traditio*, 15 (1959): 428-
43.

2858   Phillips, Margaret Mann. "From the *Ciceronianus* to
Montaigne." *Classical Influences on European Culture
A.D. 1500-1700* (item 278), pp.191-97.

2859   Rebhorn, Wayne. "The Burdens and Joys of Freedom: An
Interpretation of the Five Books of Rabelais."
Etudes rabelaisiennes, 9 (1971): 71-90.

2860   Rice, Eugene F., Jr. "The 'De magia naturali' of
        Jacques Lefèvre d'Etaples." *Philosophy and Human-
        ism* (item 293), pp.19-29.

2861   ———. "The Humanist Idea of Christian Antiquity:
        Lefèvre d'Etaples and His Circle." *Studies in the
        Renaissance*, 9 (1962): 126-60.

2862   ———. "Jacques Lefèvre d'Etaples and the Medieval
        Christian Mystics." *Florilegium Historiale* (item
        302), pp.90-124.

2863   ———. "The Patrons of French Humanism, 1490-1520."
        Renaissance Studies in Honor of Hans Baron (item 296)
        pp.687-702.

2864   ———. *The Prefatory Epistles of Jacques Lefèvre
        d'Etaples and Related Texts*. New York: Columbia
        University Press, 1972.

2865   Roberts, A.E. "Pierre D'Ailly and the Council of
        Constance." *TRHS*, ser.4, 18 (1935): 123-42.

2866   Rose, Paul Lawrence. *Bodin and the Great God of
        Nature: The Moral and Religious Universe of a
        Judaiser*. Geneva: Droz, 1980.

2867   Rosen, K. "On the Publication of the *Rudimenta Gram-
        matices* in France." *Res Publica Litterarum*, 4
        (1981): 265-71.

2868   Screech, M.A. "Commonplaces of Law, Proverbial Wis-
        dom and Philosophy: Their Importance in Renaissance
        Scholarship (Rabelais, Joachim du Bellay, Montaigne)."
        *Classical Influences on European Culture A.D. 1500-
        1700* (item 278), pp.127-34.

2869   ———. "Eleven-Month Pregnancies: A Legal and Medi-
        cal Quarrel a propos of Gargantua, Chapter Three,
        Rabelais, Alciati and Tiraqueau." *Etudes rabelais-
        iennes*, 8 (1969): 91-106.

2870   ———. *Rabelais*. Ithaca: Cornell University Press,
        1979.

2871   ———. "Rabelais, Erasmus, Gilbertus Cognatus and
        Boniface Amerbach: A Link through the *Lucii Cuspidii
        Testamentum*." *Etudes rabelaisiennes*, 14 (1978): 43-
        46.

2872   ————. *The Rabelaisian Marriage. Aspects of
          Rabelais's Religion, Ethics and Comic Philosophy.*
          London: Edward Arnold, 1958.

2873   ————. "Some Aspects of Rabelais' *Almanachs* and on
          the *Pantagrueline Prognostication* (Astrology and
          Politics)." *Etudes rabelaisiennes*, 11 (1974): 1-8.

2874   ————. "Some Stoic Elements in Rabelais' Religious
          Thought (the Will--Destiny--Active Virtue)." *Etudes
          rabelaisiennes*, 1 (1956): 73-97.

2875   Sherman, M.A. "Political Propaganda and Renaissance
          Culture: French Reaction to the League of Cambrai,
          1509-1510." *The Sixteenth-Century Journal*, 8 (1977):
          97-128.

2876   Silver, Isidore. *Ronsard and the Hellenic Renaissance
          in France, Vol.1. Ronsard and the Greek Epic.* St.
          Louis: Washington University, 1961.

2877   ————. *Ronsard and the Hellenic Renaissance in
          France, Vol.2. Ronsard and the Grecian Lyre.*
          Geneva: Droz, 1981.

2878   Simone, Franco. *The French Renaissance, Medieval Tra-
          dition and Italian Influence in Shaping the Renais-
          sance in France,* trans. H. Gaston Hall. London:
          Macmillan, 1969.

2879   Smith, Malcom C. "The First Edition of Ronsard's
          'Recueil des nouvelles poesies.'" *BHR*, 36 (1974):
          613-20.

2880   ————. *Joachim Du Bellay's Veiled Victim. With an
          Edition of the Xenia.* Geneva: Droz, 1974.

2881   ————. "Joachim du Bellay's Renown as a Latin Poet."
          Acta Conventus Neo-latini Amstelodamensis (item 305),
          pp.928-42.

2882   Stevens, Linton C. "The Contribution of French Jurists
          to the Humanism of the Renaissance." *Studies in the
          Renaissance*, 1 (1954): 92-105.

2883   ————. "How the French Humanists of the Renaissance
          Learned Greek." *PMLA*, 651 (1950): 240-48.

2884   Stone, Donald, Jr. *France in the Sixteenth Century. A
        Medieval Society Transformed*. Westport, Ct.:
        Greenwood Press, 1969.

2885   Tate, Robert B. "Italian Humanism and Spanish Histor-
        iography of the Fifteenth Century." *BJRL*, 34
        (1951): 137-65.

2886   Tetel, Marcel. "The Humanistic Situation: Montaigne
        and Castiglione." *The Sixteenth-Century Journal*, 10
        (1979): 69-84.

2887   Thompson, Craig R. "Rabelais and 'Julius exclusus.'"
        Philological Quarterly, 22 (1943): 80-82.

2888   Tilley, Arthur. *The Dawn of the French Renaissance*.
        Cambridge: Cambridge University Press, 1918.

2889   ————. "Humanism under Francis I." *EHR*, 15 (1900):
        456-78.

2890   Trinkaus, Charles. "Renaissance Problems in Calvin's
        Theology." *Studies in the Renaissance*, 1 (1954):
        59-80.

2891   Victor, Joseph M. "Charles de Bovelles and Nicholas de
        Pax: Two Sixteenth-Century Biographies of Ramon Lull."
        Traditio, 32 (1976): 313-45.

2892   ————. *Charles de Bovelles, 1479-1553, An Intellec-
        tual Biography*. Geneva: Droz, 1978.

2893   ————. "The Revival of Lullism at Paris, 1499-1516."
        RQ, 28 (1975): 504-34.

2894   Wadsworth, James B. *Lyons 1473-1503, The Beginnings of
        Cosmopolitanism*. Cambridge, Mass.: Mediaeval Academy
        of America, 1962.

2895   Walker, D.P. "The 'Prisca Theologia' in France."
        JWCI, 17 (1954): 204-59.

See also items 422-24, 445, 454, 473, 500, 537, 589, 634, 658,
        669, 695, 2005, 2103, 2194, 2246, 2426.

C. *IBERIAN HUMANISM*

2896   Baker-Smith, Dominic. "Juan Vives and the *Somnium*
       Scipionis." *Classical Influences on European Cul-
       ture A.D. 1500-1700* (item 278), pp.239-44.

2897   Bell, Aubrey F.G. "Damião de Góes, a Portuguese
       Humanist." *Hispanic Review*, 9 (1941): 243-51.

2898   ————. "The Humanist Jerónymo Osório." *Revue hispan-
       ique*, 73 (1928): 525-56.

2899   Fucilla, Joseph G. "Angeriano and Antonio Ferreira."
       Philological Quarterly, 25 (1946): 89-92.

2900   ————. "A Peruvian Petrarchist: Diego D'Avalos y
       Figueroa." *Philological Quarterly*, 8 (1929): 355-68.

2901   ————. "Two Generations of Petrarchism and Petrarch-
       ists in Spain." *Modern Philology*, 27 (1929-30):
       277-95.

2902   Green, Otis H. *Spain and the Western Tradition: The
       Castilian Mind in Literature from 'El Cid' to
       Calderon*, 4 vols. Madison: University of Wisconsin
       Press, 1963-66.

2903   ————. *The Literary Mind of Medieval and Renaissance
       Spain*, introd. J.E. Keller. Lexington: University
       Press of Kentucky, 1970.

2904   Grey, Ernest. *Guevara, A Forgotten Renaissance Author*.
       The Hague: M. Nijhoff, 1973.

2905   Hamilton, Alastair. "A Flemish 'Erasmian' in the Spain
       of Charles V: The Case of Ana Del Valle." *BHR*, 41
       (1979): 567-73.

2906   Hamilton, Bernice. *Political Thought in Sixteenth-
       Century Spain: A Study of the Political Ideas of
       Vitoria, De Soto, Suarez, and Molina*. New York:
       Oxford University Press, 1963.

2907   Hirsch, Elisabeth F. *Damião de Goes. The Life and
       Thought of a Portuguese Humanist, 1502-1574*. The
       Hague: M. Nijhoff, 1967.

2908 ———. "Damiao de Góes' Contacts among the Diplo-
      mats." *BHR*, 23 (1961): 233-51.

2909 ———. "Michael Servetus and the Neoplatonic Tradi-
      tion." *BHR*, 42 (1980): 561-75.

2910 ———. "Portuguese Humanists and the Inquisition in
      the Sixteenth Century." *ARG*, 66 (1955): 47-67.

2911 IJsewijn, J. "J.L. Vives 1515-1517. A Reconsidera-
      tion of Evidence." *HL*, 26 (1977): 82-100.

2912 Lawrence, J.N.H. "Nuño de Guzmán and Early Spanish
      Humanism: Some Reconsiderations." *Medium Aevum*, 51
      (1982): 55-85.

2913 Longhurst, J.E. *Alfonso de Valdés and the Sack of
      Rome, Dialogue of Lactance and an Archdeacon.*
      Albuquerque: University of New Mexico Press, 1952.

2914 Lynn, Caro. *A College Professor of the Renaissance.
      Lucio Marineo among the Spanish Humanists.* Chicago:
      The University of Chicago Press, 1937.

2915 Nader, Helen. "'The Greek Commander' Hernán Núñez de
      Toledo, Spanish Humanist and Civic Leader." *RQ*,
      31 (1978): 463-85.

2916 Nieto, José C. *Juan de Valdés and the Origins of the
      Spanish and Italian Reformation.* Geneva: Droz, 1970.

2917 Noreña, Carlos G. *Juan Luis Vives.* The Hague: M.
      Nijhoff, 1970.

2918 ———. "Was Juan Luis Vives a Disciple of Erasmus?"
      Journal of the History of Philosophy, 7 (1969):
      263-72.

2919 Round, N.G. "Renaissance Culture and Its Opponents in
      Fifteenth-Century Castile." *Modern Language Review*,
      57 (1962): 204-15.

2920 Russell, Peter. "Arms versus Letters: Towards a Defi-
      nition of Spanish Fifteenth-Century Humanism."
      Aspects of the Renaissance (item 292), pp.47-58.

2921 Sinz, William. "The Elaboration of Vives' Treatises on
      the Arts." *Studies in the Renaissance*, 10 (1963):
      68-90.

2922   Spratlin, V.B. *Juan Latino, Slave and Humanist*. New
        York: Spinner Press, 1938.

2923   Tate, Robert B. "Lopez de Ayalo, Humanist Historian?"
        Hispanic Review, 25 (1957): 157-74.

2924   ————, and Ascori M. Mundó. "The Compendium of
        Alfonso de Palencia: A Humanist Treatise on the
        Geography of the Iberian Peninsula." *JMRS*, 5
        (1975): 253-78.

2925   Waswo, Richard. "The Reaction of Juan Luis Vives to
        Valla's Philosophy of Language." *BHR*, 42 (1980):
        595-609.

See also items 618, 890-91, 2086, 2097-98, 2128, 2139, 2167,
    2227, 2263, 2275, 2619, 2811, 2818, 2893.

XVIII. HUMANISM IN GERMANY AND THE LOWLANDS

The first great figure of German humanism is Nicholas
Cusanus, trained in Italy and imbued with the ideas of fifteenth-century Italian thought, best studied in the recent
monograph of P.M. Watts (item 3042). German humanism of the
late fifteenth century has often been viewed as aiding or
anticipating the outbreak of Luther's reformation. As yet
there is no synthesis of German humanism, but L. Spitz's
essay, "The Course of German Humanism" (item 3017), is a good
starting point; see also the studies of H.A. Oberman, Gerlad
Strauss, and Spitz himself. Major thinkers have been well
served, as in Hajo Holborn on Ulrich von Hutten, Charles
Nauert on Agrippa, Noel Brann on Trithemius, and Spitz and
L. Forster on Conrad Celtis.

A. SOURCES

2926 Agricola, Georgius. *De re metallica*, trans. H.C. and
L.H. Hoover. London: Mining Magazine, 1912; repr.
New York: Dover, 1960.

2927 Agrippa, Henricus Cornelius von Nettesheim. *The Fourth
Book of Occult Philosophy*, trans. Robert Turner.
London: Harrison, 1655.

2928 ————. *Of the Vainitie and Uncertaintie of Artes and
Sciences by Henry Cornelius Agrippa*, ed. Catherine M.
Dunn. Northridge: California State University, 1974.

2929 ————. *Three Books of Occult Philosophy*, trans. J.F.
London: Moule, 1651; repr. (Book I only) Chicago:
Hahn and Whitehead, 1898.

2930 ————. *A Treatise of the Nobilitie and Excellencie of
Womankynde*, trans. David Clapam. London: Berthelet,
1542.

2931 ————. *A Treatise of the Nobilitie and Excellencie of
Womankynde*, trans. Henry Care as *Female Preeminence*.
London: T.R., 1670.

2932 ————. *A Treatise of the Nobilitie and Excellencie
of Womankynde*, trans. Edward Fleetwood. London:
Ibbitson, 1652.

2933 Celtis, Conrad. *Selections from Conrad Celtis, 1459-
1508*, trans. Leonard Forster. Cambridge: Cambridge
University Press, 1948.

2934 Gnaphaeus, Gulielmus/William de Volder. *Acolastus, A
Latin Play of the Sixteenth Century*, ed. and trans.
W.E.D. Atkinson. London, Ont.: Humanities Depart-
ments of the University of Western Ontario, 1964.

299

2935   Hutten, Ulrich von. *De Morbo Gallico*, trans. Thomas
       Paynell. London: 1533; repr. as *Of the Wood Called
       Guaiacum*. London, 1540.

2936   ————. *Epistolae Obscurorum*. Latin text and trans.
       F.G. Stokes. London: Chatto & Windus, 1925; repr. of
       English only as *On the Eve of the Reformation*. New
       York: Harper and Row, 1964.

2937   Meinhardi, Andreas. *The Dialogus of Andreas Meinhardi:
       A Utopian Description of Wittenberg and Its Univer-
       sity, 1508*, ed. and trans. E.C. Reinke. Ann Arbor:
       Valparaiso University, 1976.

2938   Melanchthon, Philip. *The Loci Communes*, trans. Charles
       Leander Hill. Boston: Meador, 1944.

2939   ————. *On Christian Doctrine: Loci Communes, 1555*,
       trans. Clyde L. Manschreck. London & New York:
       Oxford University Press, 1965.

2940   ————. *Selected Writings*, trans. Charles Leander Hill,
       ed. E.E. Flack and L.J. Satre. Minneapolis, Minn.:
       Augsburg Publishing House, 1962.

2941   Nicholas of Cusa. *Nicholas of Cusa's Debate with John
       Wenck, A Translation and an Appraisal of De Ignota
       Litteratura and Apologia Doctae Ignorantiae*, ed. and
       trans. J. Hopkins. Minneapolis: Arthur J. Banning
       Press, 1981.

2942   ————. *Nicholas of Cusa on Learned Ignorance. A
       Translation and an Appraisal of De Docta Ignorantia*,
       ed. J. Hopkins. Minneapolis: Arthur J. Banning
       Press, 1981.

2943   ————. *Unity and Reform: Selected Writings of Nicolas
       de Cusa*, ed. John Patrick Dolan. South Bend, Ind.:
       University of Notre Dame Press, 1962.

2944   Spitz, Lewis W., Jr., ed. *The Northern Renaissance*.
       Englewood Cliffs, N.J.: Prentice-Hall, 1972.

2945   Trithemius, Johannes. *In Praise of Scribes (De laude
       scriptorum)*, ed. Klaus Arnold and trans. Roland
       Behrendt, O.S.B. Lawrence, Kan.: Coronado Press,
       1974.

B. *STUDIES*

2946   Bainton, Roland H. "Learned Women in the Europe of
        the Sixteenth Century." *Beyond Their Sex* (item 291),
        pp.117-28.

2947   Baumann, Fred E. "Mutianus Rufus and National Reli-
        gion: A Text Case." *RQ*, 29 (1976): 567-98.

2948   Behrendt, Roland, O.S.B. "Abbot John Trithemius."
        Revue Benedictine, 84 (1974): 212-29.

2949   Bernstein, E. *German Humanism*. Boston: Twayne, 1983.

2950   Best, Thomas W. *The Humanist Ulrich von Hutten*.
        Chapel Hill: University of North Carolina Press,
        1969.

2951   Bett, Henry. *Nicholas of Cusa*. London: Methuen,
        1932.

2952   Biechler, James E. "Nicholas of Cusa and the End of
        the Conciliar Movement: A Humanist Crisis of Identi-
        ty." *Church History*, 44 (1975): 5-21.

2953   ————. *The Religious Language of Nicholas of Cusa*.
        The American Academy of Religion Dissertation Series,
        no.8. Missoula, Mont.: Scholar's Press, 1972.

2954   Borchardt, Frank L. "Etymology in Tradition and in
        the Northern Renaissance." *JHI*, 29 (1968): 415-29.

2955   ————. *German Antiquity in Renaissance Myth*. Balti-
        more: Johns Hopkins Press, 1971.

2956   Bowen, Barbara C. "Cornelius Agrippa's *De Vanitate*:
        Polemic or Paradox." *BHR*, 34 (1972): 249-56.

2957   Brann, Noel L. *The Abbot Trithemius (1462-1516)*. *The
        Renaissance of Monastic Humanism*. Leiden: Brill,
        1981.

2958   ————. "Conrad Celtis and the 'Druid' Abbot Trithemius:
        An Inquiry into Patriotic Humanism. *Renaissance and
        Reformation*, n.s. 3 (1979): 16-28.

2959   ————. "The Shift from Mystical to Magical Theology
        in the Abbot Trithemius (1462-1516)." *Studies in
        Medieval Culture*, 11 (1977): 147-59.

2960   ————. "Was Paracelsus a Disciple of Trithemius?"
        The Sixteenth-Century Journal, 10 (1979): 71-82.

2961   Breen, Quirinus. "The Subordination of Philosophy to
        Rhetoric in Melanchthon: A Study of His Reply to G.
        Pico della Mirandola." *ARG*, 43 (1952): 13-28.

2962   Brennan, J.X. "Johannes Sesnbrutus: A Forgotten Hu-
        manist." *PMLA*, 75[2] (1960): 485-96.

2963   Cranz, F. Edward. "Cusanus, Luther and the Mystical
        Tradition." *Pursuit of Holiness* (item 304), pp.
        93-102.

2964   ————. "Saint Augustine and Nicholas of Cusa in the
        Traditions of Western Christian Thought." *Speculum*,
        28 (1953): 297-316.

2965   ————. "Transmutations of Platonism in the Develop-
        ment of Nicholas of Cusa and of Martin Luther."
        *Niccolò Cusano agli Inizi del Mondo Moderno. Atti
        del Congresso internazionale in occasione del V cen-
        tenario della morte di Niccolò Cusano, Bressanone,
        6-10 settembre 1964*. Florence: Sansoni, 1970, pp.73-
        103.

2966   Daniels, G.H., Jr. "Knowledge and Faith in the Thought
        of Cornelius Agrippa." *BHR*, 26 (1964): 326-40.

2967   Douglas, Richard M. "Talent and Vocation in Humanist
        and Protestant Thought." *Action and Conviction in
        Early Modern Europe* (item 299), pp.261-98.

2968   Dunn, E. Catherine. "Lipsius and the Art of Letter-
        Writing." *Studies in the Renaissance*, 3 (1956): 145-
        56.

2969   Fleischer, Manfred. "The Institutionalization of Hu-
        manism in Protestant Silesia." *ARG*, 66 (1975): 256-
        74.

2970   Gaier, Ulrich. "Sebastian Brant's 'Narrenschiff' and
        the Humanists." *PMLA*, 83 (1968): 266-70.

2971 Gilbert, William. "Sebastian Brant: Conservative Humanist." *ARG*, 46 (1955): 145-67.

2972 Gottschalk, H.B. "The Conclusion of Brant's 'De corrupto ordine vivendi pereuntibus.'" *Modern Language Review*, 77 (1982): 348-50.

2973 Grilli, Alberto. "Asterius to Rhenatus." *Res Publica Litterarum*, 1 (1978): 95-99.

2974 Grossman, M. *Humanism in Wittenberg, 1485-1517*. Bibliotheca Humanistica et Reformatoria, 11. Nieuwkoop: De Graaf, 1975.

2975 Guinsburg, Arlene Miller. "The Counterthrust to Sixteenth-Century Misogyny: The Work of Agrippa and Paracelsus." *Historical Reflections*, 8 (1981): 3-28.

2976 Heath, Terrence. "Logical Grammar, Grammatical Logic, and Humanism in Three German Universities." *Studies in the Renaissance*, 18 (1971): 9-64.

2977 Hildebrandt, Franz. *Melanchthon: Alien or Ally?* Cambridge: Cambridge University Press, 1946.

2978 Holborn, Hajo. *Ulrich von Hutten and the German Reformation*, trans. Roland H. Bainton. New Haven: Yale University Press, 1937.

2979 Hopkins, Jasper. *A Concise Introduction to the Philosophy of Nicholas of Cusa*. Minneapolis: University of Minnesota Press, 1978.

2980 Hughes, Barnabas B., O.F.M. "The Private Library of Johann Scheubel: Sixteenth-Century Mathematician." *Viator*, 3 (1972): 417-32.

2981 Kittelson, James M. "Humanism and the Reformation in Germany." *Central European History*, 9 (1976): 303-22.

2982 ————. *Wolfgang Capito. From Humanist to Reformer.* Leiden: Brill, 1975.

2983 Kleinhaus, Robert G. "Luther and Erasmus, Another Perspective." *Church History*, 39 (1970): 454-69.

2984   Kristeller, Paul Oskar. "A Latin Translation of Gemistos Plethon's *De fato* by Johannes Sophianos Dedicated to Nicholas of Cusa." *Niccolò Cusano agli Inizi del Mondo Moderno. Atti del Congresso internazionale in occasione del V centenario della morte di Niccolò Cusano, Bressanone, 6-10 settembre 1964*. Florence: Sansoni, 1970, pp.175-95.

2985   Kuspit, Donald B. "Melanchthon and Dürer: The Search for the Simple Style." *JMRS*, 3 (1973): 177-202.

2986   Lai, Tyrone. "Nicholas of Cusa and the Finite Universe." *Journal of the History of Philosophy*, 11 (1973): 161-68.

2987   Lawson, John. *Medieval Education and the Reformation*. New York: Humanities Press, 1967.

2988   McDonald, William C. "Maximilian I of Habsburg and the Veneration of Hercules: On the Revival of Myth and the German Renaissance." *JMRS*, 6 (1976): 139-54.

2989   McGarth, A.E. "Humanist Elements in the Early Reformed Doctrine of Justification." *ARG*, 73 (1982): 5-20.

2990   Manschreck, Clyde Leonard. *Melanchthon, the Quiet Reformer*. New York: Abingdon Press, 1958.

2991   Martinez-Gomez, Luis, S.J. "From the Names of God to the Name of God: Nicholas of Cusa." *International Philosophical Quarterly*, 5 (1960): 80-102.

2992   Meyer, Carl S. "Erasmus and Reuchlin." *Moreana*, 24 (1969): 65-80.

2993   Moeller, Bernd. "The German Humanists and the Beginnings of the Reformation." *Imperial Cities and the Reformation*, trans H.C. Erik Midelfort and Mark U. Edwards. Philadelphia: Fortress Press, 1972; repr. Durham, N.C.: The Labyrinth Press, 1982, pp.19-38.

2994   Nauert, Charles G., Jr. *Agrippa and the Crisis of Renaissance Thought*. Urbana: University of Illinois Press, 1965.

2995   ————. "Agrippa in Renaissance Italy: The Esoteric
        Tradition." *Studies in the Renaissance*, 6 (1959):
        195-222.

2996   ————. "The Clash of Humanists and Scholastics: An
        Approach to Pre-Reformation Controversies." *Six-
        teenth-Century Journal*, 4, no.2 (1973): 1-18.

2997   ————. "Peter of Ravenna and the 'Obscure Men' of
        Cologne: A Case of Pre-Reformation Controversy."
        Renaissance Studies in Honor of Hans Baron (item
        296), pp.607-40.

2998   Oberman, Heiko A. *Masters of the Reformation. The
        Emergence of a New Intellectual Climate in Europe*,
        trans. Dennis Martin. Cambridge: Cambridge Univer-
        sity Press, 1981.

2999   Overfield, James. "A New Look at the Reuchlin
        Affair." *SMRH*, 8 (1971): 167-207.

3000   ————. "Scholastic Opposition to Humanism in Pre-
        Reformation Germany." *Viator*, 7 (1976): 391-420.

3001   Ozment, S.E. "*Homo Viator*: Luther and Late Medieval
        Theology." *Harvard Theological Review*, 62 (1969):
        275-87.

3002   Pollet, J.V. "The Publication of the United Corres-
        pondence and Works of Julius Pflug (1499-1564)."
        Acta Conventus Neo-latini Amstelodamensis (item
        305), pp.867-74.

3003   Preus, James S. *From Shadow to Promise: Old Testa-
        ment Interpretation from Augustine to the Young
        Luther*. Cambridge, Mass.: Harvard University Press,
        1969.

3004   Rajewski, Mary A. *Sebastian Brant Studies.... with
        Special Reference to the Varia Carmina*. Washington,
        D.C.: The Catholic University of America Press,
        1944.

3005   Rice, Eugene F., Jr. "Nicholas of Cusa's Idea of
        Wisdom." *Traditio*, 12 (1956): 345-68.

3006   Ritter, Gerhard. "Lutheranism, Catholicism, and the
        Humanistic View of Life." *ARG*, 44 (1953): 145-60.

3007   ———. "Why the Reformation Occurred in Germany."
        Church History, 27 (1958): 99-106.

3008   Rowan, Steven, and Gerhild Scholz Williams. "Jacob
        Spiegel on Gianfrancesco Pico and Reuchlin: Poetry,
        Scholarship and Politics in Germany in 1512." *BHR*,
        44 (1982): 291-305.

3009   Rupprich, H. "Wilibald Pirckheimer: A Study of His
        Personality." *Pre-Reformation Germany*, ed. Gerald
        Strauss. New York: Harper and Row, 1972.

3010   Saunders, Jason Lewis. *Justus Lipsius. The Philos-
        ophy of Renaissance Stoicism*. New York: The Liberal
        Arts Press, 1955.

3011   Schnur, Harry C. "The Humanist Epigram and Its Influ-
        ence on the German Epigram." *Acta Conventus Neo-
        latini Lovaniensis* (item 288), pp.557-76.

3012   Schwarz, W. "Translation into German in the Fifteenth
        Century." *Modern Language Review*, 39 (1944): 368-73.

3013   Sigmund, Paul E. *Nicholas of Cusa and Medieval Poli-
        tical Thought*. Cambridge, Mass.: Harvard University
        Press, 1963.

3014   Skrine, Peter. "The Destination of the Ship of Fools:
        Religious Allegory in Brant's 'Narrenschiff.'"
        Modern Language Review, 64 (1969): 576-96.

3015   Spitz, Lewis W. "The Conflict of Ideas in Mutianus
        Rufus." *JWCI*, 16 (1953): 121-43.

3016   ———. *Conrad Celtis: The German Arch-Humanist*.
        Cambridge, Mass.: Harvard University Press, 1957.

3017   ———. "The Course of German Humanism." *Itinerarium
        Italicum* (item 298), pp.371-436.

3018   ———. "Headwaters of the Reformation: Studia Humani-
        tatis, Luther Senior, et Initia Reformationis."
        Luther and the Dawn of the Modern Era, ed. H.A.
        Oberman. Leiden: Brill, 1971, pp.89-116.

3019   ———. "Humanism in the Reformation." *Renaissance
        Studies in Honor of Hans Baron* (item 296), pp. 641-
        62.

3020   ———. "Ideas of Liberty in German Humanists."
        Church History, 31 (1962): 336-49.

3021   ———. "The Philosophy of Conrad Celtis." *Studies
        in the Renaissance*, 1 (1954): 22-37.

3022   ———. *The Religious Renaissance of the German Hu-
        manists*. Cambridge, Mass.: Harvard University Press,
        1963.

3023   ———. "The *Theologia Platonica* in the Religious
        Thought of the German Humanists." *Middle Ages-
        Reformation Volkskunde: Festschrift for John C.
        Kunstman*. Chapel Hill: University of North Carolina
        Press, 1959, pp.118-33.

3024   ———. "The Third Generation of German Renaissance
        Humanists." *Aspects of the Renaissance* (item 292),
        pp.105-21.

3025   Stayer, James M. "Zwingli before Zurich: Humanist
        Reformer and Papal Partisan." *ARG*, 72 (1981): 55-68.

3026   Strauss, Gerald. "The Course of German History: The
        Lutheran Interpretation." *Renaissance Studies in
        Honor of Hans Baron* (item 296), pp.663-86.

3027   ———. *Historian in an Age of Crisis: The Life and
        Work of Johannes Aventinus*. Cambridge, Mass.:
        Harvard University Press, 1963.

3028   ———. *Nuremberg in the Sixteenth Century*. New York:
        Wiley, 1966.

3029   ———. *Sixteenth-Century Germany: Its Topography and
        Topographers*. Madison: University of Wisconsin
        Press, 1959.

3030   ———. "Success and Failure in the German Reforma-
        tion." *Past and Present*, 67 (1975): 30-63.

3031   ———. "Topographical-Historical Method in Sixteenth-
        Century German Scholarship." *Studies in the Renais-
        sance*, 5 (1958): 87-101.

3032   ———, ed. *Pre-Reformation Germany*. New York:
        Harper and Row, 1972.

3033   Stupperich, Robert. *Melanchthon*, trans. Robert H.
       Fischer. Philadelphia: Westminster Press, 1965.

3034   Swanson, R. "The University of Cologne and the Great
       Schism." *Journal of Ecclesiastical History*, 28
       (1977): 1-15.

3035   Thomson, S. Harrison. "Learning at the Court of
       Charles IV." *Speculum*, 25 (1950): 1-20.

3036   Van Gelder, H.A. Enno. *The Two Reformations in the
       Sixteenth Century: A Study of the Religious Aspects
       and Consequences of Renaissance and Humanism*. The
       Hague: Mouton, 1961.

3037   Vocht, Henry de. "Andreas Masius (1514-1573)." *Mis-
       cellanea Giovanni Mercati* (item 295), pp.425-41.

3038   ————. *History of the Collegium Trilingue Lovani-
       ense*, 4 vols. Leuven: University Press, 1951-55.

3039   Watanabe, Morimichi. "Gregor Heimburg and Early Hu-
       manism in Germany." *Philosophy and Humanism* (item
       293), pp.406-22.

3040   ————. "Humanism in the Tyrol: Aeneas Sylvius, Duke
       Sigmund, Gregor Heimburg." *JMRS*, 4 (1974): 177-202.

3041   ————. *The Political Ideas of Nicholas of Cusa with
       Special Reference to His De concordantia catholica*.
       Geneva: Droz, 1963.

3042   Watts, Pauline Moffitt. *Nicolaus Cusanus, A Fifteenth-
       Century Vision of Man*. Leiden: Brill, 1982.

3043   Weiss, J.M. "The Six Lives of Rudolph Agricola. Forms
       and Functions of the Humanist Biography." *HL*, 30
       (1981): 19-39.

3044   Weiss, Roberto. "Jan Van Eyck and the Italians, II."
       Italian Studies, 12 (1957): 7-21.

3045   Wheelis, Samuel M. "Nicodemus Frischlin's 'Julius
       Redivivus' and Its Reflections on the Past." *Studies
       in the Renaissance*, 20 (1973): 106-17.

3046   ————. "Publish or Perish: On the Martyrdom of Phillip
       Nicodemus Frischlin." *Neophilologus*, 58 (1974): 41-51.

3047   Yule, George. "Medieval Piety, Humanism and the
        Theology of Luther. *Religion and Humanism* (item
        301), pp.167-79.

3048   Zambelli, Paola. "Magic and Radical Reformation in
        Agrippa of Nettesheim." *JWCI*, 39 (1976): 69-103.

3049   Zeydel, Edwin H. "Johannes a Lapide and Sebastian
        Brant." *Modern Language Quarterly*, 4 (1943): 209-12.

3050   ———. *Sebastian Brant*. New York: Twayne, 1967.

3051   Zida, Charles. "Reuchlin's *De Verbo Mirifico* and the
        Magic Debate of the Late Fifteenth Century." *JWCI*,
        39 (1976): 105-38.

See also items 561, 586, 1163, 1660, 1685-86, 1744, 1889,
        2052, 2084-85, 2109, 2114-15, 2132, 2135, 2169-70,
        2223, 2225, 2231.

XIX.   HUMANISM IN BYZANTIUM AND EASTERN EUROPE

Studies in English on the humanistic interests of late medieval Byzantine culture or thought and learning in eastern
Europe during the early modern period are comparatively rare.
Late Byzantine culture is well served by the studies of
Steven Runciman and N.G. Wilson, while Deno Geanakoplos has
documented the transmission of Greek literature to the West
in the fifteenth and early sixteenth centuries. Eastern
European humanism has attracted only a few studies in English,
mainly devoted to Latin learning in Dalmatia.

3052   Anastos, V.M.   "Pletho's Calendar and Liturgy."   *Dum-
       barton Oaks Papers*, 4 (1948): 183-205.

3053   Angyal, Andrew.   "Recent Hungarian Renaissance Scholar-
       ship."   *MH*, 8 (1954): 71-94.

3054   Birnbaum, Marianne D.   "An Unknown Latin Poem, Probably
       by Petrus Garazdi, Hungarian Humanist."   *Viator*, 4
       (1973): 303-10.

3055   Flynn, Vincent.   "The Intellectual Life of Fifteenth-
       Century Rhodes."   *Traditio*, 2 (1944): 239-55.

3056   Forster, Leonard.   "Some Examples of Petrarchism in
       Latin in Slavonic Lands."   *HL*, 27 (1978): 1-51.

3057   Gabriel, Astrik L.   "The Academic Career of Blasius de
       Várda.   Hungarian Humanist at the University of
       Paris."   *Manuscripta*, 20 (1976): 218-43.

3058   Geanakoplos, Deno J.   *Byzantine East and Latin West:
       Two Worlds of Christendom in Middle Ages and Renais-
       sance.   Studies in Ecclesiastical and Cultural His-
       tory.*   New York: Harper and Row, 1966.

3059   ————.   *Greek Scholars in Venice: Studies in the Dis-
       semination of Greek Learning from Byzantium to
       Western Europe.*   Cambridge, Mass.: Harvard University
       Press, 1962.

3060   ————.   *Interaction of the 'Sibling' Byzantine and
       Western Cultures in the Middle Ages and Italian
       Renaissance.*   New Haven: Yale University Press, 1976.

3061   Grant, W.L.   "The Italian in Poland."   *Manuscripta*,
       10 (1966): 28-38.

3062   Hall, B.   *John a Lasco: A Pole in Reformation England.*
       London: Dr. William's Trust, 1971.

3063   IJsewijn, J.   "Neo-Latin Satire in Eastern Europe."
        Ziva Antika, 25 (1975): 190-96.

3064   Kadić, Ante.   "The Croatian Renaissance." *The Slavic
        Review*, 21 (1962): 65-88.

3065   ———.   "Croatian Renaissance." *Studies in the
        Renaissance*, 6 (1959): 28-35.

3066   ———.   "Marini Drzic, Croatian Renaissance Play-
        wright." *Comparative Literature*, 11 (1959): 347-55.

3067   Kosztolnyik, Z.J.   "Pelbartus of Temesvar: A Franciscan
        Preacher and Writer of the Late Middle Ages in Hun-
        gary." *Vivarium*, 5 (1967): 100-10.

3068   Krekić, Bariša.   *Dubrovnik in the 14th and 15th Cen-
        turies: A City between East and West*. Norman:
        University of Oklahoma Press, 1972.

3069   Krešić, Stéphane.   "Croatian Neo-Latinists." *Acta
        Conventus Neo-latini Lovaniensis* (item 288), pp.347-
        57.

3070   Lewalski, Kenneth F.   "Sigismund I of Poland: Renais-
        sance King and Patron." *Studies in the Renaissance*,
        14 (1967): 49-72.

3071   Marcovich, Miroslav.   "On the Davidiad of Marko
        Marulić." *Acta Conventus Neo-latini Lovaniensis*
        (item 288), pp.371-80.

3072   ———.   "The Poems of Franciscus Natalis." *Acta
        Conventus Neo-latini Amstelodamensis* (item 305),
        pp.690-96.

3073   Novak, Viktor.   "The Slavonic Latin Symbiosis in
        Dalmatia during the Middle Ages." *Slavonic and East
        European Review*, 32 (1953): 1-18.

3074   Petrovich, Michael B.   "Dalmatian Historiography in
        the Age of Humanism." *MH*, 12 (1958): 84-103.

3075   ———.   "Croatian Humanists and the Writing of His-
        tory in the Fifteenth and Sixteenth Centuries."
        Slavic Review, 37 (1978): 624-39.

3076   Ross, D.J.A. "A Corvinus Manuscript Recovered."
        Scriptorium, 11 (1957): 104-08.

3077   Runciman, Steven. *Byzantine Civilisation*. London:
        Edward Arnold, 1933.

3078   ————. *The Last Byzantine Renaissance*. Cambridge:
        Cambridge University Press, 1970.

3079   Schaeffer, Peter. "The Emergence of the Concept
        'Medieval' in Central European Humanism." *The Six-
        teenth-Century Journal*, 7 (1976): 21-30.

3080   Schwoebel, Robert. *The Shadow of the Crescent: The
        Renaissance Image of the Turk*. Nieuwkoop: De Graaf,
        1967.

3081   Tezla, Albert. *Hungarian Authors: A Bibliographical
        Handbook*. Cambridge, Mass.: Belknap Press, 1970.

3082   Torbarina, Josip. *Italian Influence on the Poets of
        the Ragusan Republic*. London: Williams & Norgate,
        1931.

3083   ————. "The Slav Petrarchists of Renaissance Dal-
        matia." *Review of National Literatures*, 5 (1975):
        86-100.

3084   Webb, Diana M. "The Decline and Fall of Eastern Chris-
        tianity: A Fifteenth-Century View." *BIHR*, 49 (1967):
        198-216.

3085   Weltsch, Ruben E. *Archbishop John of Jenstein, 1348-
        1400: Papalism, Humanism and Reform in Pre-Hussite
        Prague*. The Hague: Mouton, 1968.

3086   Wieczynski, Joseph L. "Hermetism and Cabalism in the
        Heresy of the Judaizers." *RQ*, 28 (1975): 17-28.

3087   Wilson, Nigel G. "The Libraries of the Byzantine
        World." *Greek, Roman and Byzantine Studies*, 8 (1967):
        53-80.

3088   ————. *Scholars of Byzantium*. Baltimore: Johns Hop-
        kins University Press, 1983.

see also items 371, 839, 1063, 1074, 1354, 1423, 1443, 1452,
        1522, 1558, 1695, 2068, 2166, 2290, 2428, 2984.

INDEX OF AUTHORS, EDITORS, AND TRANSLATORS